## Lawyers Need This Book

*No lawyer wants to answer a client's question with "I have no idea." This book can help address a client's question while a lawyer develops a more detailed referral. I recommend this book to any lawyer whose practice serves boomers.*

—**Melinda Gustafson Gervasi**, Review in Wisconsin Bar Journal

## And So Do You

*We highly recommend it, a serious book about serious times and serious issues written in a reader-friendly format. A wonderful read.*

—**Jan Warner** and **Jan Collins**, syndicated columnists

*At last, help about the legal challenges of aging that seniors (and their friends) need, in language they can understand. Hegland and Fleming present the information that seniors and their families and friends need in a readable, helpful and, yes, even funny way.*

—**Professor Lawrence Frolik**, University of Pittsburgh,
author, *Elder Law in a Nutshell*

*Professor Hegland is simply one of the nation's best legal writers.*

—**Tom Sullivan**, Provost, University of Minnesota

*The book goes into many subjects, other than legal advice, related to getting older. I highly recommend this reasonably priced book. It is a great resource for baby boomers. Being one myself, I learned much and it gave me lots to think about.*

—**Dan England**, Blogger News Network

*The book offers simple and practical advice on living well and "being prepared" for life's transitions. Being prepared is more than an admonition for boys (the Boy Scout motto); it is critical. Here are sage and sound strategies for achieving the right path and plan—one that your family and you can live with!*

—**Robert P. Shannon**, M.D., Director, Palliative Care Fellowship,
Mayo Clinic, Jacksonville, Florida

*Studies tell us that learning new things is good exercise; this is one heck of a great workout.*

—**Joy Loverde**, author, *The Complete Eldercare Planner*

*Organized into sections, the book can be used separately if you are interested in a particular issue, but the entire book is well worth reading. A truly valuable resource.*

>—**Professor Rebecca Morgan**, Director, Center for Excellence in Elder Law, Stetson

*In an incredible short amount of space and with humor, intelligence and an obvious grasp of their subject matter, the authors have covered all the bases in an exceptionally readable style. From telemarketing scams to pension plans, from Medicare to "when should you stop driving?" they cover it all. Talk about "one stop shopping." I had already ordered a second copy for my brother before I'd finished reading it.*

>—**Stuart Zimring**, Past President, National Association of Elder Law Attorneys

*A valuable resource not only for seniors, but also for their families and advisors. The authors have done an excellent job in plain English (without use of legal jargon) of discussing complex issues and providing suggestions for solutions in a way that seniors can understand and appreciate. We highly recommend it to anyone who needs information about the issues facing all of us as we age.*

>—**Oast and Hook**, Elder Law firm, Virginia Beach, Virginia, client newsletter

# New Times, New Challenges

## Law and Advice for Savvy Seniors and Their Families

**Kenney F. Hegland**
James E. Rogers Professor of Law
University of Arizona

**Robert B. Fleming**
Attorney at Law
Elder Law Specialist

Carolina Academic Press
Durham, North Carolina

Library of Congress Cataloging-in-Publication Data

Hegland, Kenney F., 1940-
  New times, new challenges : law and advice for savvy seniors and their fami-
lies / Kenney F. Hegland & Robert B. Fleming.
     p. cm.
  ISBN 978-1-59460-737-0 (alk. paper)
  1. Older people--Legal status, laws, etc.--United States--Popular works. 2.
Estate planning--United States--Popular works. 3. Older people--Medical
care--Law and legislation--United States--Popular works. I. Fleming, Robert
B. II. Title.

  KF390.A4H443 2009
  362.60973--dc22

                                   2009028660

CAROLINA ACADEMIC PRESS
700 Kent Street
Durham, North Carolina 27701
Telephone (919) 489-7486
Fax (919) 493-5668
www.cap-press.com

*I have always known*
*That I would*
*Take this road, but yesterday*
*I did not know it would be today.*

—Nakihara, Ninth Century Japanese Poet

# Summary of Contents

# CONTENTS

# Prologue
## 64: Give or Take

*Will you still need me?*
*Will you still feed me?*

—The Beatles

Remember when?

When 64 was a myth, lurking at the outer edge of our imagination. We had better things to do: schools to finish, careers to start, mates to find. Etcetera. Sure, our grandparents were old, but they had *always* been old, *preferred* being old, *chose* to be old. Curious choice. Surely not ours.

A blur of momentous events. Viet Nam, civil rights, Berlin Wall, 9/11, a black man raising his right hand on January 20. Meanwhile, we finished school, started a career, found a mate, not to mention Etcetera. We didn't start the fire, but it has consumed us. Suddenly, quite suddenly, we just turned around, and, hey, it's us. Growing older or hoping to.

Growing old won't be as bad as we might fear. Most of us will stay in good health and find engaging things to do in retirement. But it's not eating a peach; it's not for sissies. There will be trouble and heartbreaks. This book will help you through hard times; it will help your family as well. Writing it, researching the law, I found so many critical things I didn't know and I'm a lawyer.

My problem is this. Some things you need to know now in order to *avoid* trouble. On the other hand, there are things you don't need to know unless you *get* into trouble. Think about living wills now, but don't worry about fighting age discrimination unless you're let go.

What's a poor boy to do?

Divide the book. Read the first part of the book, *New Times, New Challenges*. It's short! Consider it training for ill:

> *Since the world has still*
> *Much good, but much less good than ill,*
> *And while the sun and moon endure*

xix

*Luck's a chance, but trouble's sure,*
*I'd face it as a wise man would,*
*And train for ill and not for good.*

—A.E. Housman, *A Shropshire Lad (LXII)*

What can you expect as you age? How can you assure your last wishes are followed? How can you stay mentally active? How can you recognize one of the plagues of growing old: strokes? And, as retirement isn't always all that it is cracked up to be, how can you cope with existential angst? (Remember our college days, puzzling over the meaning of "angst" and then, convinced we were definitely victims, headed out to the lights and laughter of that night's party? Which was it: existence precedes essence or essence precedes existence?)

You might also want to read the chapter on how to protect your identity and recognize scams. (Chapter 22). I also, as mostly a loss-leader, explain the nature of evil.

You may think, "I can skip that part. I already know about living wills, hospice, and the virtues of exercise." But Samuel Johnson was right:

*"People more often need to be reminded than informed."*

Training for ill isn't pleasant. We would all prefer to go to the beach, to get around to it tomorrow. Training for ill today will allow us to avoid it tomorrow or, if we can't, to better cope with it. Resist your Little Voice shouting, "You don't have time for this now. Maybe tomorrow." Take a deep breath, sit down and read. On the bright side, not every bad thing I will discuss will happen to you.

Does training for ill work? It did for King Mithridates, the subject of Housman's poem. He knew his enemies were plotting to poison him. Training for ill, he prepared himself by taking small dosages of poisons to get used to them.

*They put arsenic in his meat*
*And stared aghast to watch him eat;*
*They poured strychnine in his cup*
*And shook to see him drink it up;*
*. . . .*
*—I tell the tale that I heard told.*
*Mithridates, he died old.*

—A.E. Housman, *A Shropshire Lad (LXII)*

Once you've completed your basic training, skim the rest of the book looking for chapters that address your immediate needs. Then put it aside for future reference. You never know when you might be the victim of age discrimination, find yourself raising your grandchildren, or to awake one morning turned into, not a gigantic bug, but a disgruntled heir.

The general topics:

*Retirement*: finances, housing and health insurance.

*Family matters*: divorce and remarriage, grandchildren, financial obligations.

*Trouble*: elder abuse, foreclosures, bill collectors, identity theft, scams, age bigots.

*Estate planning*: wills, living trusts, trusts for special needs, probate.

*Bad times*: disability and death in the family.

*Getting help*: dealing with doctors and lawyers and chatting with your family.

* * *

Finally, style.

I won't write down. Editors, mostly in their thirties, have advised:

> *"Your readers will be over 40, maybe over 60, or, egads, over 70. Kill the jokes, the poetry, the background stuff. Just tell 'em how to stretch their Social Security check."*

Despite what young folks might think (and probably what we thought when we were them), we don't shuffle over to the couch, sit blankly before a static TV, drooling oatmeal. We still have our humor, our curiosity, our intellectual excitement. We'll come and go, talking of Michelangelo, telling bad jokes, and reciting wonderful poetry.

If you're in it *just* for the information, you've picked up the wrong book.

Putting aside John Grisham, legal prose is pretty deadly. A law professor (from Yale!) once wrote:

> *There are two things wrong with almost all legal writing. One is style. The other is content. That, I think, covers the ground…. Readers like a dash of pepper or a dash of salt along with their information. They won't get any seasoning if lawyers can help it. Lawyers would rather be dignified and ignored.*

This book will help you and your family in difficult times. I won't let you ignore it; I'll put on a lampshade, paint my nose red, and do back flips.

OK. No back flips.

# PART 1

# NEW TIMES, NEW CHALLENGES

**Chapter 1 · What You'll Need to Know**

Anticipating, and hence avoiding, trouble; the virtues of pumping iron and doing crosswords; angst and retirement: recognizing strokes; thinking about death and talking to your family.

**Chapter 2 · Living Wills: Going Gently into that Good Night**

Often living wills don't work. If you really want to focus on issues that matter, write your own.

**Chapter 3 · Growing Older: What to Expect and How to Cope**

When waitresses start calling you "Dear" and your family thinks your only interest is Social Security.

# CHAPTER 1

# WHAT YOU'LL NEED TO KNOW

*Luck's a chance, but trouble's sure....*
—A.E. Housman

In the chapters that follow we'll deal with living wills (I recommend writing your own), and with the aging process (which, like it or not, happens—and, as they say, is better than the alternative). This chapter introduces the necessity of training for ill (trouble's sure) and covers a potpourri of ills which, while significant, do not warrant separate chapters: the existential anguish of retirement, the constant threat of stroke, the fear of disability and death, and, finally, the need to have an unpleasant (at first) talk with your family.

Training conjures grunts and sweats. And that's a nice transition into an optimistic aside. While death may be sure, disability isn't. In fact, the rate of disability, defined as the loss of one major life function (such as the ability to dress or feed oneself) has been falling among the elderly: among folks over 85, it is only one in five. Improved medical care has played a role, as has improved nutrition and, indeed, so have grunts and sweats.

## a. Pumping Iron and Working Crosswords

If you stop exercising, you get weaker; if you stop pushing yourself mentally, you get dumber. Studies show that learning new things is good exercise for the brain. Consider adult education, programs like Elder Hostel, not only for their intrinsic fun, but as a method of maintaining mental agility.

*Question* what you learn. "How could a study show that learning makes you smarter? Is he just making up studies?"

*What's the cube root of 27? Who said "Fee, fie, foe, fum, I smell the blood of an Englishman"? Explain chaos theory. Coherently.*

There are computer games for grown-ups designed to test and push their intellect. Ask your grandkids.

Travel helps. Going to new places is a mental challenge: making plans, reading maps, finding good restaurants, learning how to ask "Where's the bathroom?" in Greek. Even at home, varying your schedule can help. Following a routine, you do it without thought. Take the dog for a walk *before your* breakfast (not his—let's not live *too* dangerously); denounce the government *after* lunch. Variety, variety, something different.

As to physical exercise, yet another study showed that surprisingly little effort can produce much reward. One hundred men and women in their 80s and 90s, most so frail that they needed walkers, increased their strength 118% during a ten-week exercise program, walking faster and climbing stairs more easily. Some, so taken with their new persona, even began snarling: "Fee, fie, foe, fum ..."

Oddly (and disappointingly) when the trainers left nearly everyone stopped—even though the equipment was still there, even though the results had been phenomenal, even though the participants had all been trained on how to manage their own exercise regimen. So hire a trainer, join a club, start a group to work out together. That's the basic premise behind the "sport" of mall-walking: groups of mature adults meet every morning to walk in air-conditioned comfort, window-shop and gossip.

*Walk*! According to Blue Cross, Blue Shield, walking 10,000 steps a day will help you lose weight, lower cholesterol, and reduce your risk of heart attack. If everyone did it, it would reduce health care costs $77 billion a year. Blue Cross, Blue Shield, putting aside saving billions, are only thinking of you. And they have no idea what they are on to: consider the fabulous impact on your mental abilities, the concentration required to count all those steps, "Eight thousand, five hundred, fifty-one; eight thousand, five hundred, fifty-two; eight thousand, five hundred, fifty-three; eight thousand, five hundred, fifty ... fifty? Darn! One; two ..."(A cartoon shows aerobics in Hell with the Devil shouting, "OK, now 10,000 deep knee bends.")

Most of us can reach the magic figure of 10,000 steps by adding a *30-minute walk* to our daily routine.

# b. Existential Angst

You spent, what, eight, ten, twelve hours at work or caring for the family. There was no question as to your place in the universe: butcher, baker, candle-stick maker. How are you going to fill all of those hours? With the label gone, from whence your sense of self-worth? Of belonging?

Retirement can be rocky. Many wish they never retired and spend their golden years watching daytime TV (which is a fine choice, provided you really like it). After Dylan Thomas died, his widow wrote *Leftover Life to Kill*. Many turn to booze; some to violence. Some suffer physical and mental abuse at the hands of their spouse. Be aware of the dangers and, if they befall your lot, there are specific ways to deal with them. We will discuss them later in the book. But here, the root problem: *what will you do and how will you live?*

Sports agents advise their clients to keep a diary during their playing years noting what they like to do in their off time. Editors advise budding authors, "Don't write about what you know; write about what you *don't know* you know." Our advice is similar. Sit down and write out how you will spend your time and where you will get your sense of self-worth. You probably know, but you don't know that you know.

Don't just *think* about these questions. Write! We think too fast; writing slows the mind and allows ideas to bubble. And don't be too serious, not "I will serve mankind." Come on! Instead, "I'll run off and join the circus." Silly ideas lead to good ideas, "To join the circus, that means clown school. That's stupid. But, wait, how about *cooking* school? My pancakes have always been a hit!"

## c. Documents You'll Need

We'll spend a lot of time down stream discussing legal documents and all they can accomplish. Here, just a reminder that, if you don't have them, you will cause your family unnecessary anguish. And, if your parents are still living, you should make sure they have executed the documents or, down stream, you will suffer that anguish.

- *A Health Care Power of Attorney.* This allows someone to make your medical decisions if you are unable to do so.
- *A Financial Power of Attorney.* This allows someone to make your financial decisions if you are unable to do so (and, of course, can be somewhat risky).
- *A Living Will.* This allows you to direct the kind of medical treatment you wish or do not wish if you are unable to make those decisions. We devote a chapter to living wills; most are pretty worthless. The one we will suggest isn't.
- *A Will.* There are many ways to pass your assets at time of death, such as wills, trusts, joint ownership, life insurance, pre-death gifts. We

will give you the pros and cons of each but know this: it is important to discuss your options with a lawyer to get what is best for you and to get it right. Don't be cheap when it comes to your family. So get going. Stuff, often bad stuff, happens. Maybe tomorrow. Maybe later today.

# d. Strokes: STAT

This topic does not fit with our poetic forays nor our philosophic musings. But nothing ruins a good retirement like a stroke.

Strokes can lead to death or severe disability. The good news: if the victim receives medical attention within two or three hours, most of the damage can be avoided. The bad news: often the victim is unaware of the stroke and does not seek medical help. There may be no catastrophic event—perhaps only a stumble, a sudden dizziness.

Someone falls, gets up, and seems OK. Suspect stroke. Recite STAT.

"S"  Smile (if the person can't, trouble)
"T"  Talk (ask a question)
"A"  Arms (have them raise both)
"T"  Tongue (stick it out: if it goes off to one side, not straight out, not good)

If the stumbler flunks one test, call 911. Call 911 even if they pass all four if you still suspect a stroke.

How can you recognize that **you** have had a stroke?

- Sudden numbness of the face, arm, or leg, especially on one side of the body.
- Sudden confusion, trouble speaking, understanding.
- Sudden trouble seeing in one or both eyes, double vision.
- Sudden trouble walking, dizziness, loss of balance, or coordination.
- Sudden severe headache.
- Sudden drowsiness, nausea, vomiting.

In short, *sudden something*. Err on the side of caution. Call 911 immediately. With each passing minute, more cells die.

# e. Death

Overrated.

In a famously searing couplet, Dylan Thomas cries to his dying father:

> *Do not go gentle into that good night.*
> *Rage, rage, against the dying of the light.*

What a powerful phrase—the dying of the light. One almost chokes. But that's young Dylan's view of death; was it his dad's? What do those who have almost died tell us? They report feeling a sense of calm and acceptance; many report on seeing a bright light rushing toward them. A surgeon visits his patient in recovery.

> *"Lying on the operating table, I knew I was dying. You and the others were trying to save my life and that was O.K. But it was also O.K. if you didn't."*

When he was a young man, the 16th-century French essayist Michel de Montaigne was thrown from his horse, sustaining serious injuries. He was a bloody mess.

> *It seemed to me that my life was hanging only by the tip of my lips. I closed my eyes in order, it seemed to me, to help push it out. I took pleasure in growing languid and letting myself go. I was not only free from distress but felt that sweet feeling of sliding into sleep. I believe that is how people feel whom we see in the agony of death. We pity them without cause, thinking that they are troubled by grievous pains or have their souls full of distressing thoughts.*

So what of Dylan's father?

> *"That's O.K. Dylan. Everything will be fine. Now wipe away your tears and go back to bed. I want my rest."*

The fear of death, the denial of death, prevents us from living to the fullest. In *tuesdays with Morrie*, Mitch Albom writes of his Tuesday afternoon visits with his former professor. Morrie, dying of Lou Gehrig's disease, talks about denial:

> *"Everyone knows they're going to die, but nobody believes it. If we did, we would do things differently.... To know you're going to die, and to be prepared for it at any time. That's better. That way you can actually be*

*more involved in your life while you're living. Once you learn how to die, you learn how to live."*

Of course, learning how to die ain't easy. You're taking a little step reading this book, momentarily dropping your guard. Talking to your family will take you a little further. Ultimately you are pretty much on your own and will have to find your own way. But keep the goal in mind: acceptance, no blind fear.

# f. Talking to Your Family

Daunting stuff: the angst of retirement, the threat of disability, the certainty of death.

As you train for ill, there is more to come: your final illness, and the process of aging. Don't face all of this alone. Talk to your family. Down the road you and your family will face difficult times and difficult decisions. Training for ill means getting the team on the same page.

If you don't discuss these issues, they will not go away. One of our basic fears is dying alone. We tend to think of this in physical terms, focusing on the importance of having family around us. However, when the time comes, emotional isolation is just as frightening. Have your family emotionally around you as you face the future.

These conversations will bring your family together: they acknowledge the elephant in the room. They can even be fun, with recollections from the past, "Remember the motel and the big black bug in the shower and Dad going in?" The hardest part is starting the conversation. As we go along, we offer some opening lines.

Please, not a somber affair, with lists, and Mozart's Requiem playing in the background. Please, something more casual and more spontaneous, with the Beatles or The Mamas and The Papas. And, as long as we are quoting Housman, recall his famous couplet:

> *Malt does more than Milton can,*
> *To justify God's way to Man.*

# CHAPTER 2

# Living Wills: Going Gently into that Good Night

Preparing for ill is more than kicking back, reading. Here you'll to do some work, writing your Living Will.

"But I've already got one. Somewhere."

Nope, not good enough.

Of all the planning documents, such as Wills and Durable Health Care Powers of Attorney, Living Wills are the least important and, for that matter, the least effective. Why would we insist you write a new one?

Two reasons: first, to help overcome the fear of death and, second, to open a conversation with loved ones.

*"Everyone knows they're going to die, but nobody believes it. If we did, we would do things differently."* So said Morrie in *tuesdays with Morrie*. Fine, well and good. But he didn't tell us how. Writing your own living will, thinking long and hard about your last illness, might get you part way there. Morrie adds, *"Once you learn how to die, you learn how to live."*

Then there's the importance of having a conversation with your family on unpleasant topics. Getting it started can be difficult. Here an opening line: *"I just wrote my living will. I need your input, and you need to hear my views. Let's talk."*

Living Wills promise that, if we are unable to communicate our wishes at the time, we can decide what medical treatment we will receive during our last illness. Although one can insist that everything be done to prolong life, generally Living Wills are intended to curtail treatment—the guiding and terrifying image, the stuff of countless TV shows, being hooked to machines in ICU for weeks, dying a slow, painful, and expensive death.

Living Wills aren't very effective. Studies show that they have little impact on the medical treatment one actually receives. Partly it's because the wills aren't there when you need them and partly because the doctors who care for you in the hospital will be specialists who haven't seen you before and hence have no idea about your wishes. Further, even if your Living Will is bedside and insists on "no heroics," if your family insists upon them, most likely you will get them.

Is this a problem?

Not really. Most Living Wills are too casual, too vague, and too speculative to be taken too seriously. Many are of the "Check the Appropriate Box" variety and, in confusing medical/legalese, tend to boil down to two choices:

a. *"No, I don't want to be hooked up to a lot of machines,"* or

b. *"Yes, keep me alive as long as possible."*

Boxes are checked in crowded hospital waiting rooms, when you have more pressing matters, or in a lawyer's office, as part of your estate plan. With the meter running, there is no time to dally with stupid questions like, "Box 3(a) talks about 'a persistent vegetative state,' and just what is that, anyway?"

Life and death decisions should not be flip and this is a good reason families and doctors ignore many of them. But let's put the hurried and non-reflective Living Will aside. Let's say you brooded long and hard and, with appropriate angst, finally checked "No heroics." When the time comes, if your family and physicians decide that heroics would be best, what then?

The root problem, the unsolvable problem, is that Living Wills are written long before they come into play: We are asked to decide *now* what we want *then,* and usually we don't have a clue. The stuff of Greek tragedy, especially since we *think* we have a clue—we are clueless about our cluelessness.

Putting aside the inherent problem of changes between now and then, such as advances in medical treatment and pain control, if you found yourself dying and *you were able to communicate,* would you automatically reject (or automatically insist upon) all heroic medical interventions? Of course not. You would talk it over—with family, religious counselors, doctors. Are you 63, 73 or 93? How certain the diagnosis, and how great the pain? How costly the stay, how rich your family? How sharp your mind? Do you need more time for final goodbyes? And, finally, of course, how many of your loved ones and family are left?

We misjudge the future. When I was a teen, I firmly believed that sitting in an office all day, writing stuff, would be a fate worse than death. I no longer *firmly* believe this.

Healthy, visualizing our ourselves lying in a hospital bed, hooked to machines, we think, "I would rather be dead." But would we rather be dead? Doctors tell us that most of their patients who *can* communicate show an overwhelming preference for life.

That you cannot predict the future does not mean you shouldn't have a Living Will. However, consider one less dogmatic, less demanding, less legalistic. Consider something more humble, more folksy, a letter sharing your thoughts with family. Assume that you do not want heroic interventions, as breathing machines and feeding tubes, rather you want to go gently into that good night. One way to achieve our goals is to ask: What might get in the way?

- Family members thinking love means keeping you alive.
- Family members fighting as to the best course, with the default choice almost always being heroic measures.
- Doctors fearing legal liability if they give you too much pain medication or quit treatment too early.
- Doctors and family members failing to acknowledge just how dire your situation is and hence continuing fruitless, yet painful and expensive, treatment.

You can use your Living Will to deal with these problems. Here's one possibility:

*A Letter to My Family, My Friends and My Health Care
Providers Concerning End-of-Life Matters*

*This letter addresses medical issues that may arise near the end of my life. As no one can predict specific circumstances, I do not wish to dictate medical decisions but ask that they be made in light of my preferences, in light of my best interests, and in light of the best interests of my family, including the cost of any treatments. I have no desire to bankrupt my family.*

*I hope that those involved carefully listen to each other. If they cannot agree, I appoint _____ as the final arbiter and as my health care power of attorney. If _____ cannot serve, then I appoint _____ .*

*I know that your decisions may hasten my death. No one should feel guilty in making such decisions or feel that the only way to show love for me is to prolong my life as long as possible. The opposite may be true.*

*Candor. Death is a reluctant topic, even for doctors. I ask that my family insist that my doctors tell them the truth about my situation, even if it is grim.*

*Pain. Health care providers may fail to give me enough pain medication in fear that it might addict or kill. I want medication adequate to relieve my pain even if that runs the risk of creating addiction or hastening my death. I further request that none of my family or friends institute any action against any of my doctors claiming I received too much pain medication.*

*End-of-Life Medical Treatment. I do not want my life extended by medical interventions if my prognosis is grim in terms of my ultimate recovery and the quality of life. I realize that some health care providers, fearful of malpractice claims, may pursue aggressive treatment even if that is unwarranted. I request that none of my family institute any malpractice action premised on the notion that the treatment I received was not aggressive enough.*

*As a general matter, I disfavor cardiopulmonary resuscitation in any form and artificially administered food and fluids. I expressly authorize my family to reject any form of resuscitation and to decline or later remove any forms of artificial administration of food or fluid which can keep one alive almost indefinitely.*

*Furthermore, I would prefer not to be taken to the hospital. I would much prefer to die at home or in a hospice. I do not want to die alone or among strangers. I do not want to die in an intensive care unit or in a nursing home.*

*I consent to organ donations and to an autopsy realizing that much can be learned from it to understand the cause of my death and to help others. Though I want to help my fellow humans, I am somewhat leery of experimental treatments and research studies.*

*Burial. I prefer cremation and an Irish Wake.*

*I intend that this letter, which I shall sign before witnesses, shall be as legally binding and as enforceable as my Living Will and Appointment of Health Care Agent as is provided in any state in which I reside at the time that this letter would be effective. Furthermore, I intend that my wishes be binding on my estate.*

*Signed: _____*
*Dated: _____*
*Witnessed by: _____*

*We, the author's family members, have read and discussed this letter with the author. We understand it and agree to follow it.*

*Signed: _____*

"Yikes!" my wife shouted after reading the letter. "You promised something humble and folksy and this reads like, well, the Internal Revenue Code. You don't really expect your readers to sit down and write something like this!"

"Legal training," I sheepishly shrug.

Okay, here is something more folksy (but don't show it to my overly-precise and overly-verbose colleagues).

*A Letter to My Family*

*If there comes a time I am quite sick and unable to make my own decisions, I want my family to make them for me. If they can't agree, then it is up to _____ and, if not _____, then _____.*

*I realize your decision might be to "pull the plug" and remove me on all life support—breathing machines, feeding tubes. At some point that is absolutely the right decision. Keeping me alive beyond that is not an act of love but probably one of cowardice, hopefully not of revenge. One thing to consider is money. I would rather help my grandchildren with college or their first house than live another two weeks, half dead and drugged.*

*Don't keep me alive simply because no one wants to face the bad news. Insist that my doctors tell you my chances of recovery, how long it would take, and what would be my condition afterwards. I can live without walking but really don't want to live if I can no longer appreciate my family and friends and can no longer understand the world around me.*

*As you know, I am a wimp when it comes to pain. Tell my doctors to give me enough pain meds even if it means they might kill me, that that's my choice and my family supports it.*

*I want to die at home or in hospice. Short stays in ICU are okay to stabilize my condition and figure out what to do. Donate what you can of me.*

*As to burial, cremation and Irish Wake. But don't let cousin Joe speak.*

_____

*We family members have read this and we agree to follow it.*

_____

That's better. Now you can write your own. Not to put too fine a point on it, you owe your dying self, and you owe your distressed family, an hour of serious thought.

You may be tempted to give more specific directions in order to protect your family from the anguish of decision. On the Internet you can find forms that detail, in painful detail, every possible horrible situation you might find yourself in and allow you to direct exactly what should be done.

Will such a document get your family off the hook? Well, maybe. However lawyers will tell you that the more language you use and the more specific you are often the more ambiguous a document becomes—e.g. the Internal Revenue Code.

And, as a philosophical matter, ultimately no one can avoid the anguish of decision. As Sartre once said, even if God showed up and told you what to do, you would still have to decide whether it was God or the Devil. In this context, "Yes, Dad made it quite clear that he wanted to die under those circumstances, but a good daughter would have challenged the doctors more— maybe he wasn't in a persistent vegetative state."

Leaving the tough decision to your family seems right, not only pragmatically (they will probably have to decide anyway), but philosophically. We are not islands, not in our lives and not in our deaths. Our families are part of us; they need time say goodbye, to comfort us, and to be with us.

Of course, if you want your family to follow your wishes, rather than drop a legal document on them at the last minute, *talk* with them now. Now the *key* to this entire chapter. Have *family members sign off* on the letter. This is not required for Living Wills and, indeed, is rather novel. It is a wonderful idea.

We are sure that you have been advised to discuss your specific wishes with your family and we are sure you knew that this was good advice and that you nodded in agreement. Probably it never made the "To Do" list. Our approach *requires* this discussion. And it is simply easier to start with "I need you to do something for me" rather than "Do you have 30 minutes for a dismal discussion about my death?"

Make no mistake about it: your death is the elephant in the room. Ignoring it is stressful for everyone. Talk.

The value of the letter is *now*, not *then*. The value is the simple message, "I love you, I trust you, and it's time to spend a few minutes talking about my final illness. It's really nothing to dread. Pass the wine."

Tell your family this *now*. As to *then*, as to the tough choice, it probably won't ever come up; you'll probably be run over by a bus.

# CHAPTER 3

# GROWING OLDER: WHAT TO EXPECT AND HOW TO COPE

*Three tough things about growing old. First, you're not as spry. Second, you forget things.*

You're probably not there yet but maybe you're hearing "Times winged chariot hurrying near."

The good news is that people are living longer and living in much better health. "Happiness" surveys put seniors as the most contented. But we have not come to praise old age. Some of the news is not good: physically, we will lose prowess; mentally, we will lose some memory and will have more difficulty learning new things; socially, things might not go as well, with some even accusing us of crankiness. Add to all of this: getting used to seeing one of our parents in the bathroom mirror.

Why do we cut so easily? Why do our faces wrinkle? Fewer cells. Babies are so cute, so plump, so lovable, because they are bundles of cells. Cut them and they heal instantly. Over time, cells die. This does not mean that we can't be buff—a friend, a ninety-pound weakling his entire life, started lifting weights when he turned 70. Now he wears muscle T-shirts and, decades after that rather unfortunate incident at the beach, he got his gal back (or at least we like to think he did). With exercise, the cells we have can be made larger, but those we have lost cannot be replaced.

Along with cell loss comes a general decline in physical prowess—our hearts and our lung capacity shrink, we become less sure on our feet, we tire quickly. As we slowly make our way to the supermarket check-out line, middle-aged folks wearing nifty sun visors and dressed in fashionable exercise garb, pretending to be looking the other way, cut in front us. Our solace: the process of physical decline begins around age thirty—their smugness is illusion, and the clock, not us, will exact the revenge we only dream about in a civilized society.

Evolutionists tell us that this makes sense—by thirty we have had our children and raised them to the point where they can bring on the next generation. From an evolutionary point of view, after thirty, we aren't needed. An interesting question: if we are obsolete at age thirty, why do we go on living well beyond that age? Probably the answer is "excess capacity": when we send a rocket ship into space, we install two computers just in case the one goes bad—to make thirty, we are equipped to go much further.

Of course, gray hair. For most it is about half gray at the age of 50. In a terribly misguided apology, Mother Nature tries to make this up for this by sprouting vast amounts of hair on our ears.

*You'll gain weight.* As we age, our metabolism slows. Looking at the generation before us, we might get it wrong and conclude that one loses weight as one ages—"Those folks are skinny." What we fail to realize is that that generation was always skinny (unlike, alas, us). To use cross-generation comparisons to make predictions is dangerous: doing so in Miami, for example, one would conclude that most folks are born Cuban and die Jewish.

Expect a *loss of hearing and vision.* There are things to be done, but vanity may get in the way. 'Fess up and get a hearing aid.

Viagra and scores of "Dirty Old Man" jokes attest that *sex* is well and thriving. In nursing homes this presents something of a problem (or not). And, of course, the odds have shifted substantially: there are usually four or five widows for each "eligible" man.

*Mental powers* will decline. As you age, you will do less well on IQ tests and have a harder time learning new tasks. But, then again, you have much less need to do well on IQ tests and much less need to learn new tasks: experience and knowledge trumps mental agility—take that, whipper-snapper!

*Short-term memory loss*—"Senior moments"—are to be expected. We can wish we had that excuse for all of the stupid gaffes committed by our younger selves. (One thing about aging, though: gaffes, falls, and lost keys are no longer shrugged off as they were before; they now seem to signal ominous things.) You can combat memory loss by writing lists and being a tad more conscious of the need to remember things. Rather than just parking your car at the mall, confident that you will remember where you parked, recite to yourself "I am leaving the car in the third row about halfway down." (Don't try "I'm parked next to the red van.")

Don't panic, the mere fact you can't remember where you left your keys does not mean that soon you will not know where you live. While advanced dementia is terrible, it is not inevitable—many people are mentally active and agile in advanced old age despite occasional lapses.

Exercise helps the mind as well as the body: "Use it or lose it." Forcing yourself to learn new things, to do crossword puzzles, to read up on geezer law, will help. If you insist on sitting in front of the TV, drinking beer and smoking Camels, make it the Discovery Channel. Unfortunately, the History Channel becomes less challenging when you've already been through the subject material once—yes, that was *us*, and yes, we did wear tie-dye Ts. And, yes, we can't believe it either!

*Personality changes* are possible. Not all of us, but some of us, turn grumpy. One reason, discomfort trumps charm; it's hard making small talk if it hurts to sit or if you're concerned about your next doctor's appointment. Some economists have a less forgiving explanation: there is less need for charm as you age. As you no longer need to impress employers and friends, all those smiley faces are no longer worth the effort. It seems you aren't *getting* grumpy; you were *always* grumpy but hid it. I refuse to believe this (except in the case of my co-author).

How people treat you will be, frankly, quite unnerving. Waitresses will call you "dear"and almost pat you on the head, cheerful young men will hold open the door, and family members will think all you are interested in are Social Security, your current illnesses, and your grandkids—never mind politics, books, movies and, yes, sex. (Have you ever told a dirty joke to either your child or your parent?) Suddenly, quite suddenly, you are no longer a "player."

Being old used to be special. The old were valued. They looked dignified, told wonderful stories, taught younger generations how to make things work and, in times of trouble, provided wise counsel. What happened?

Dignified? Millions and millions of dollars went to convince us that gray hair and wrinkles are ugly, to be avoided at all costs and with every new scientific (man in the white coat) breakthrough. *Does she? Or doesn't she?* And, thanks to terrific advances in public health and medicine, older folks are no longer rare, they're everywhere, crowding the malls, taking their sweet time turning left, and bankrupting Social Security. As for their stories, they don't come close to MTV and HBO. As to their knowledge and wisdom, they made a *grievous* mistake: they published. Books and the Internet have made them unnecessary.

Perhaps the most visually compelling illustration of how our society discounts older folks, and how wrong it is to do so, occurred when Susan Boyle of Blackburn Scotland (where?) appeared on amateur talent show, "Britain Got Talent." Pudgy, 47, and definitely not glamorous, she announced she was to sing "I Dreamed a Dream" and was met with sniggers, rolling eyes, and raised eyebrows. This was going to be embarrassing but no doubt a good laugh.

Then she sang! Once you finish this chapter, which is something of a downer, go to www.youtube.com and search "Susan Boyle."

Growing older we have to deal with the unpleasant truth that we too are ageists, that we too would have sniggered. As with most biases the best cure is first to acknowledge them and then to take steps to overcome them by getting to know individuals. There is no doubt, for example, that folks become much more accepting of homosexuality if they know gays and lesbians. Law students who spent five hours a week delivering Meals on Wheels or volunteering at Senior Centers ended their semester thinking of those they served, not as old people, but as folks with names, unique stories and varied, and often quite pleasing, personalities.

Before it becomes your turn, it might be a good idea to do some of this yourself or, if you have more time, volunteering at Hospice. Getting beyond the stereotypes of old age is important, Otherwise the negative image may become a self-fulfilling prophecy and you will never get up to sing.

\* \* \*

Cheer up. Old age will likely be much better than you fear. We generally over estimate how bad the things we fear will be.

"Maybe," you think, "that might be true of trips to the dentist but what about crippling falls? AIDS? Cancer? Surely they are as horrible as advertized."

Christopher Reeve, of Superman fame, believed that he was better off after he was crippled; Anthony Perkins, of Psycho fame, believed himself blessed with AIDS; and cancer patients tend to be more optimistic than healthy folks.

Nancy Mairs is paralyzed from the waist down and has lost total control over one arm, partial over the other. She has fallen from her wheelchair and has been unable to get up, lying there until someone happened by. She cannot feed herself, and someone must dress her.

A fate worse than death? It seemed like that to us, but we were wrong. In *Waist-High in the World* she writes:

> There are readers who need, for a tangle of reasons, to be told that a life commonly held to be insufferable can be full and funny. I am living that life. I can tell them.

Growing old, commonly held to be insufferable, can be full and funny. Millions are living that life. They can tell you.

So don't lament. *Studies have repeatedly shown that older folks are generally happier than younger ones; the odds are you will be, too.* Reread that!

Why not? You are free from the restraints of adulthood. You are no longer the teacher on the playground, you are yet again the kid. Free to sleep in, free to wear your trousers rolled, free to eat a peach, and free to disturb the universe (or perhaps, less grandly, your neighbors).

But despite the fish oil, the water aerobics, and the new friends, there will come a time when you and I slow down. Those who already have tell us that that's not so bad either. Sure, their physical infirmities prevent much running around, but somehow that is now OK. It's as if their mind and body are in sync: they no longer *want* to run around, be busy, get things done. While they never expected it, they tell us that it's fine just to sit, and that Time's winged chariot no longer bothers them.

In *The Brothers Karamazov*, an old man sits, and reflects:

> *The old grief, by a great mystery of human life, gradually passes into quiet, tender joy; instead of young, ebullient blood comes a mild, serene old age; I bless the sun's rising each day and my heart sings as before, but now I love the setting even more, its long slanting rays, and with them, mild, tender memories, dear images for the whole of a long and blessed life.*

# PART 2

# LET THE GOOD TIMES ROLL: RETIREMENT

---

# MONEY, HOUSING, MEDICAL CARE

## Introduction

*We have only two questions: How should we live? What should we do?*

—Tolstoy

While the "How should we live?" question has been with us all of our lives as we dealt with life's ethical and moral issues, for many of us the "What should we do?" question hasn't been forefront. Parents, teachers, bosses, jobs, pretty much told us what to do. Now, at retirement, the question shrieks for an answer. Deciding, rather than following instructions, is scary, yet exhilarating. Lucky you!

**Chapter 4 • Retirement: An Overview**

Good news in terms of health, housing, working, and volunteering.

**Chapter 5 • Social Security**

There may be benefits you are unaware of.

**Chapter 6 • Veterans' Benefits and Safety Nets**

If you have ever been in the military, even if you never saw combat and no matter how long ago, you are probably entitled to VA benefits.

**Chapter 7 • Private Pension Plans**

Types and what to do with the money at retirement.

### Chapter 8 · Retirement Finances

You'll have less income and new expenses, mostly in the area of medical care and insurance. Should you keep your life insurance? What about withdrawals from IRAs?

### Chapter 9 · House Rich, Cash Poor

Many of us have paid for our house but find we need money. How can you get cash out of your house without selling it? There are several methods, including *reverse mortgages* where the *bank pays you* a monthly payment. We'll also look at the options of renting or selling your house. We have some great news in terms of capital gains taxes.

### Chapter 10 · Retirement Housing

Should you join us in the Southwest? The issue may be getting help in your own home or moving to an *assisted-housing* facility. We look at the options and consider pros and cons. Nursing homes are discussed in Chapter 34.

### Chapter 11 · Medicare and Health Insurance

What are your insurance needs before the magical year of Medicare Eligibility (65)? After 65, there is *Medicare*. What does it cover? More importantly, from a planning perspective, what *doesn't* it cover? Should you get additional insurance or join a new Medicare HMO? What about drug coverage? We close with some tips on buying insurance.

### Chapter 12 · Long-Term Care

Long-term custodial care can trigger major financial problems. We will discuss a relatively new form of insurance: long-term care insurance. We will also look at the federal *Medicaid* Program—which does pay for long-term care—and how you might make yourself eligible without first bankrupting your family. This is sometimes referred to as *Medicaid Planning*.

### Chapter 13 · Tax Breaks for Seniors

You (and your children) may be missing some benefits. Discover just one and you have more than paid for this book.

# CHAPTER 4

# RETIREMENT: AN OVERVIEW

*"How's retirement?"*
*"Love it."*
*"Busy?"*
*"Busier than ever."*
*"What do you do?"*
*"Well, let's see. I get up, have coffee. Read the paper. Go for a walk."*

We have spent a lifetime accomplishing things.

*"What did you do today?"*
*"Took the kids to soccer. Got them into college. Engineered a hostile takeover of NBC."*

Retirement will require a major shift in our thinking, a major shift in how we see ourselves in the world. Before retirement we knew our goals, at work, do a good job, get promoted, make money, and, at home, get the kids into Princeton or, perhaps more realistically, get the kids off drugs. After retirement we must not only figure out what to do but also rethink what it is that is valuable to do. Before retirement, having a cup of coffee, reading the paper, going for a walk, would be a nice time out from our *real* lives. After retirement the trick is to realize that having that coffee, reading that paper, and taking that walk is just as meaningful, just as satisfying, just as legitimate as engineering hostile take-overs (or, in my case, writing books).

During retirement, existential angst might actually be real. (Remember the salad days of Philosophy 101 and the wondrous times lamenting the essential tragedy of life with friends, music and etcetera?)

To cope with retirement angst sit right down and write yourself a letter: "These are some of the things I can do during my retirement. These are some of my fears. These are some of my hopes." (Put a lotta kisses on the bottom; you'll be glad you got 'em.)

Before looking at your basic choices (work, go into business, volunteer, or simply smell the flowers), some common questions and fears about retirement.

# a. Questions about Retirement

## When can I retire?

You can begin drawing Social Security at 62 and under many pension plans, you can retire well before then. On the other hand, if you go on working after 62—or simply delay drawing on your Social Security, even though you may be "retired"—every year you work (until the age of 70) will increase your Social Security benefits and your benefits under most pension plans. *Mandatory retirement is illegal* in most occupations. See Chapter 21.

## How much income will I need?

To maintain your pre-retirement life-style, as a rule of thumb, many advise that you'll need pretax retirement income equaling about *70 to 80 percent* of your pretax working income.

Expenses go down: no more saving, no more college tuition, and no more work expenses (work clothes, business lunches and Mylanta). One expense that will go *up* is medical insurance even after you are eligible for Medicare at age 65.

We'll spend a lot of time in chapters that follow discussing the financial side of retirement: Social Security, pension plans, getting money out of your house, and financial planning and budgeting.

## How about medical insurance?

*Medicare* is a marvelous program providing for hospital care and doctor's visits, plus some of the costs of drugs and medical supplies. However, *you will not be eligible for Medicare* until you are 65 and thus medical insurance may be a major expense if you retire before then (and lose your employment-based medical coverage). As we will indicate later, you will probably be able to keep up your insurance from work to cover you before you turn 65 but only by paying a premium—possibly a hefty one.

*Medicare*, the basic Medicare, known as Part A, does *not cover* many routine medical expenses such as doctors' visits and prescriptions. You'll have to buy additional insurance or enroll in an HMO. There are many choices and we describe them in Chapter 11.

## What about housing?

Many move to more forgiving climates—here or abroad—and may buy into Retirement Communities. There are both legal and emotional ramifications of such moves as well as substantial risks which we will discuss in Chapter 10.

As we get older, health and medical concerns must be considered in relation to housing. How will you get to the store if you can no longer drive? Does a two story house, with stairs, make sense if you have trouble walking? We'll look at making your own house safer or moving into a Continuing Care Retirement Community.

## Is death on the doorstep?

Most people will spend *15 to 19 years in retirement.* That's a lot of time; consider that in your *first* 15 to 19 years: you learned to walk, to talk, to blame your parents, and if you were lucky, to get a date.

**Current Life Expectancies**

| Age | Men | Women |
|-----|-----|-------|
| 50 | 26.0 more years | 31.0 more years |
| 55 | 21.9 | 26.7 |
| 60 | 18.2 | 22.5 |
| 65 | 14.8 | 18.7 |

## I will get sick?

A recent study: 37% of retirees showed no change in their health; *40% got better.*

And you haven't been reading the daily newspaper if you are unaware of the numerous studies showing the remarkable benefits of physical exercise programs. These programs can be started anytime—except tomorrow.

## I will get senile?

*Senility* is not a disease. It is a symptom of different medical conditions, many of which are treatable. We discuss this in Chapter 30.

Retirement will create a void. Working keeps us on our mental toes. Science shows that our *minds,* as well as our biceps, *need exercise.*

Take classes at community colleges. Learn a new language. Work crosswords. There are now "adult" computer games which tax the intellect (not to be confused with those "adult" games that tax other parts of the anatomy).

For couch potatoes all of this means both bad news and good news: the bad news is that they'll get fat; the good news is that they won't realize it!

## If I work, what are the tax implications?

If you retire before your "full retirement age" (65 to 67, it's going up), the amounts you earn over a certain minimum (around $14,000 in 2009) will be subject to a rather stiff tax: a reduction in your Social Security check of $1 for every $2 you earn until you reach your full retirement age. Because there is much talk about the need to change Social Security to save it, this may change. (Of course everything changes, save vending machines.)

# b. Working, Opening a Bookstore, Volunteering

- Folks working part-time are often healthier than those who don't.
- Mental abilities tend to remain strong if used; by continuing to learn new things, memory is improved. (We have said this before. True or False?)
- Retirement jobs can be *more fun* because they are *less filling* (who cares if you don't get promoted).

*Dare to eat a peach*! No need to do the same old stuff. Raise chickens. Teach children. Rob trains. That last one is a joke—trains no longer carry the mine's payroll, so rob espresso bars, where the real money is.

## Getting a job

Small companies are best. They are more flexible in terms of working conditions and in recognizing and using your talents and experiences. However, some large companies go out of their way to hire seniors (they tend to show up).

Some jobs take *advance planning*. Learn the computer. Many consider "going into teaching." Teaching certificates are required for public school teaching. Community colleges, elder hostels and other community education programs may welcome you with open arms. Teach a class on contract bridge; teach kids to weld.

If you have a hard time finding work, then maybe you have been discriminated against because of your age. Age discrimination in employment is generally illegal. See Chapter 21.

## Starting your own business

Look before you leap. Opening a business is *risky*. You can lose your life's savings. Unless you are a corporation, or flee to Brazil, you will be personally liable for the debts your business runs up. And, despite what you may think, opening a restaurant is risky, even if you went to cooking school.

Be leery of retirement work *scams*. Folks selling *franchises* and *home work opportunities* make their money selling to *you*. Sharks circle, offering exciting, *can't miss*, big buck opportunities. Work at home! Open your own franchise!

Ask for references—people who have already invested. In retirement you cannot afford the risk of losing your shirt.

*Never, ever* cash in your retirement or your savings to invest in a business unless you are very, very sure. Run opportunities past your most cynical and pessimistic friends or past a professional well trained in both attributes, i.e. your lawyer. Even if everyone tells you to take the chance, wonder why they are not putting *their* money into the sure thing.

*Get disinterested advice.* The person offering you the opportunity is *never* disinterested. That person is a salesman. If they have a secret way of always making money in real estate, don't you think that they would be doing it?

SCORE, the Service Corps of Retired Executives can put you in touch with people who have "been there" and "done that."

## Volunteering

George Bernard Shaw wasn't one to sit on the sidelines:

> I am of the opinion that my life belongs to the whole community and as long as I live, it is my privilege to do for it what I can. I want to be thoroughly **used up** when I die, for the harder I work, the more I will live. I rejoice in life for its own sake. Life is no brief candle for me. It is sort of a splendid torch which I have got hold of for a moment and I want to make it burn as brightly as possible before handing it on to future generations.

Wow! That's why he's George Bernard Shaw. (At the opening of one of his plays, answering the call "Author! Author!" Shaw came out to take a bow. Thunderous applause. After several minutes, it began to die down. A guy in the front row was then heard booing. Shaw acknowledged him, "Sir, I quite agree with you. But who are we two against all the others?")

There is a lot to be said for Shaw's approach. Helping others, being of service, is deeply human. Many tell us that their volunteer work is the most rewarding of their lifetime. And it needn't be full-time!

You have a lifetime of experience. Many in your community could use it. Most locales have *Volunteer Clearing Houses.* In addition there is the RSVP (Retired Senior Volunteer Program) in nearly every community. You really can make an important difference in the lives of children, seniors, shut-ins and others in all sorts of programs in your area.

And we're not talking about your specialized knowledge. Sure, even if the good folks of McCallsburg, Iowa, have no need of a hostile take-over specialist, if you can drive a car you may find opportunities to transport seniors who can't. Contact *beverlyfoundation.org.* Or you can help kids learn how to read. Contact *experiencecorps.org.* We hope you get the idea: there are lots of folks who need your help regardless of what your training and experience might have suited you for, or failed to suit you for, prior to retirement.

Check out the new bipartisan Edward M. Kennedy Serve America Act which was signed into law by President Obama in 2009. It provides for "encore fellowships" for folks over 55 to volunteer to accredited community organizations and earn "education awards" which can be used to further their own education or be transferred for their children or grandchildren to use. A year working with AmeriCorps can result in an education award of $5,000 while 350 hours of service to any accredited organization will earn a Silver Scholarship of $1,000.

*Ask what you can do for your country.* What unique talents, interests, skills, can you contribute to make a difference in your community? Write your *own* service plan, find a sponsoring agency, and you may be off to the races. A unique aspect of Serve America allows you to come up with your own service plan. Get thinking!

Volunteering need not be full time. Often there are one-day opportunities. *Area Agencies on Aging* often have coordinators: "I have Tuesdays free. What have your got?" There are over 650 Area Agencies throughout the United States; every community is served by one because it is required under the Older Americans Act. In fact, there are all sorts of good things going on at your Area Agency on Aging, and throughout this book we will refer you again and again to this wonderful agency.

Gail Sheehy, in *New Passages,* calls the years between 45 and 85 a "Second Adulthood" and details many of the exciting possibilities once the responsibilities and worries of one's "First Adulthood" are gone. As she points out, many do their best work after the age of 60, including Winston Churchill, Earl Warren and Ronald Reagan. Grandma Moses gave up embroidery in her 70s because of arthritis, and took up painting. You may have heard of the favorable results.

A great gag:

> *During retirement, don't get your car lubed and a haircut on the same day!*

Your retirement can be much, much more. But don't expect contentment to drop in your lap! Retirement is hard work. Confront and overcome your fears about aging. Many give up and what they feared became a self-fulfilling prophecy. Alcoholism and depression are common (and often confused by relatives as senility).

> *The world is so full of a number of things, I'm sure we should all be as happy as kings.*
>
> —Robert Louis Stevenson

If you're *not* happy as a King, get out a pen and start writing about how to have a terrific retirement. You may get a novel out of it and, yes, more tax consequences.

# CHAPTER 5

# SOCIAL SECURITY

## a. What Most of Us Don't Know: Benefits and Recipients

Social Security is not only a retirement plan, it also provides disability and life insurance benefits.

- If you are working and become permanently disabled, you may receive disability payments for the rest of your life.
- If you die, even before you retire, your family may be entitled to monthly payments. Spouses, children and, in some cases, even parents, may qualify.

Family members (spouses, minor children, and sometimes grandchildren) may be entitled to monthly payments when you retire. These benefits can increase your family's monthly benefit by as much as 150% to 180%.

Divorcees may sometimes qualify based on their ex-spouse's work history.

You need 40 calendar quarters of work history to qualify for retirement benefits (fewer for disability, depending on how old you are when you become disabled). If you are close, try to get the 40 quarters; while you may not get a big retirement check, you will be eligible for Medicare (otherwise it will cost you a bundle).

All of this, and much, much more, will be explained, in painful detail.

## b. Social Security: Contents and Discontents

Social Security, child of the Great Depression, folks selling apples, losing farms, praying that things wouldn't get worse. Franklin Roosevelt is elected President and reassures the nation *"The only thing we have to fear is Fear itself."*

Social Security has done wonderful things.

- The poverty rate among folks over 65 is no longer 70% as it was before Social Security; it is now 12% (about the same rate for people under 65).
- 90% of retirees draw benefits. Of those drawing benefits, 65% receive more than half of their income from Social Security.
- In addition to retirement benefits, Social Security protects young folks by providing both life and disability insurance.
- Its administrative costs are about *1%* (compared to around 15% for private pension plans).

*The bad news: monthly benefits are low.* As of 2009, the average monthly payment for an individual was $1,153 and, for a couple both receiving benefits, $1,876.

Social Security was *never intended* to be a full retirement plan. At the time it was passed, most folks died before reaching retirement age of 65. Financial planners talk about the "three-legged stool" of retirement—with private wealth and individual pensions intended to provide the two strongest legs of the stool.

Benefits are calculated so that lower income workers receive a higher percentage return than do higher earners. Workers who have earned only half the national average will receive about 56% of their average salary, average workers about 42%, while folks at the high end typically get about 28%.

For a comfortable retirement you should arrange to earn about 70% or 80% of your pre-retirement income, not 56%, 42%, or 28%. It is a *serious mistake* to think that Social Security will maintain your standard of living.

If you aren't making ends meet, *Supplemental Security Income (SSI)* pays additional benefits to people who are 65 or older (or blind or disabled), *and* have very limited income and property. See Chapter 6.

And we all know that Social Security is *going broke*. Well, it isn't. And not for a long time. Currently Social Security is *making* money—collecting more from workers than it pays to retirees. It is financed by a payroll tax on the first $106,800 of earnings. Currently it is 15.30% (split between worker and employer). (Medicare payroll tax is an additional 1.45% with no wage cap.) These figures are likely to change as Congress tries to assure long-term solvency.

In *2017*, give or take, Social Security will begin to *lose* money, paying out more than it collects. However, it will still have an initial surplus of $3.3 trillion.

> *Big numbers like $3.3 billion are essentially meaningless. We have no idea what they mean, only that they are a lot. Why not, after say 100,000, just one number: "lotsa"—"The moon is lotsa miles from the earth." "McDonald's has sold lotsa hamburgers."*

If the lotsa surplus is actually *there* at the breakeven year, Social Security will remain solvent for another decade or so. (We will see why the money might not be there in a moment.)

Why will Social Security begin to lose money? The number of workers paying into Social Security, compared to the number of retirees taking from Social Security, is falling—from 5 to 1 in 1960, to 3.3 to 1 in 2006, to 2.1 to 1 in 2031. This is because folks are living longer *and* because the birth rate is falling. Note that the worker/dependent ratio is not as stark as it may first appear—with falling birth rates, current workers, while supporting more retirees, support fewer kids.

Where is the lotsa surplus? Not under the President's pillow. It's in government bonds (government IOUs). Currently Social Security can *only* put its surplus in government bonds. The government uses this money for other programs; the fear is that when the time comes, in 2017 perhaps, the federal government will not be able to pay back the money it has borrowed from Social Security, or will have to raise other taxes, or cut other programs to do so.

Bottom line: today there are 48 million recipients; in 2030, an anticipated 83 million. Solutions to the crisis are the stuff of daily newspaper editorials and Presidential Commissions: raise social security taxes, reduce benefits, raise the retirement age, allow for *privatization,* either by allowing individuals to invest some of their Social Security dollars in the stock market *or* by allowing the Social Security Trust Fund to play the market. One objection to privatization is that politics, rather than financial judgments, may dictate investment decisions. And, of course, the market itself is another objection.

Currently there is a general political attack on "entitlements." Some attempt to foment generational hostility by convincing younger workers that Social Security will not be there for them and that, while they toil, retirees play golf in Florida. That image, besides being unfair and inaccurate, misses several other points.

The cost of caring for the elderly will not go away. Shift it from Social Security and it falls on sons and daughters, or the elderly will return to poverty and government welfare benefits.

Besides, Social Security is not just retirement benefits. Of the more than 48 million currently receiving benefits, one-fourth are the families of workers who have died or become disabled.

However, we have come to praise Social Security, not to solve it. Solutions are, as we academics (who haven't a clue) like to say, "beyond our scope." The nitty-gritty isn't.

# c. Eligibility and Computation of Benefits

You must have paid into the system for *40 calendar quarters* (generally a *ten-year* work history). These quarters need not be continuous. Some government work is not covered by Social Security, nor are some forms of private capitalistic endeavor, such as drug dealing (reason enough to go straight).

Every year, about three months before your birthday, you will be sent a statement estimating your monthly retirement amount, and indicating what you have contributed in prior years and what benefits your relatives may be entitled to. And you can get one by calling 1-800-537-7005 or requesting one on the Internet: http://www.ssa.gov.

Check that your wages have been reported correctly. This is important as benefits are calculated on your earnings. Generally you have *3 years* to make corrections—but if you find that an employer simply didn't report any income, you can have this corrected at any time.

How does Social Security compute your benefits? Pretty much this way:

> *A train leaves New York going West at 60 mph. Two hours and 13 minutes later, another train leaves Los Angeles, going East at 62 mph. What is the capital of Nova Scotia?*

The basic idea is to figure out how much your *average monthly salary* was while you were working and then give you a *percentage of that figure*. It is assumed that you worked *35 years*: your total earning will be spread out over this period. Some really good news: the calculation of your earnings history is adjusted for current average earning levels, so that your thirty-year-old income may be multiplied by somewhere between 5 and 7 in determining your work history. Even though you will be *eligible* for Social Security after 40 quarters, *the longer you work and the more you earn, the greater will be your benefit.*

The key figure is *Primary Insurance Amount (PIA)*, the monthly amount you will receive at *full* retirement. If you retire early, you'll get less; if you retire late, you'll do better.

# d. Early, Late, and Full Retirement

When you reach your "full retirement age" you will receive your full PIA. What is your full retirement age? It is going up.

| Year of Birth | Full Retirement Age |
|---|---|
| Before 1938 | 65 yrs |
| 1938 | 65 yrs and two months |
| 1939 | 65 yrs and four months |
| 1940 (Year of the Dragon) | 65 yrs and six months |
| 1941 | 65 yrs and eight months |
| 1942 | 65 yrs and ten months |
| 1943–1954 | 66 yrs |

After 1954, it goes up two months every year until, if you were born after 1959, your full retirement age will be 67.

You can begin drawing benefits at 62 (that age is not going up) and get a monthly check. Should you? There are a host of individual factors such as your health, your other sources of income, and, ultimately, how pessimistic you are (think you'll get to 65?). Here are some general things to consider: *First, the prices to be paid for early retirement.*

*You still won't be eligible for Medicare.* You have to wait until 65, so your health insurance will still be a concern. Under a program called *COBRA* you will be able to continue your employer's health insurance but you must pay the premium. See Chapter 11 for more details.

*Your monthly check will be a little lighter.* If you retire at 62 (the earliest age you can begin receiving benefits), there will be a *permanent* reduction of *25% to 30%* in your monthly benefits. This may sound like a lousy deal, but remember: you will be getting those checks, albeit smaller ones, for a longer period. The closer you retire to your retirement age, the less will be the reduction.

*Your earnings from outside work will incur a penalty.* There will be a rather stiff tax on amounts you earn over (currently) $14,160 or $1,180 monthly. Your Social Security check will be reduced $1 for every $2 you earn over that amount until your full retirement age (the benefit reduction ends when you reach that magical age of full retirement).

Before taking early retirement from Social Security, check its impact on your private pension plan. Some private pension plans have what is known as an *integration of benefits* clause which operates to *reduce your pension payments* in light of what you receive from Social Security. Depending on the rate of reduction, it might be well to delay taking Social Security as long as possible.

On the other hand, there may be *financial incentives to retire early*. If you have a *child under 18* or *a spouse over 62*, when you retire *they can begin* drawing benefits from your Social Security. This may increase your family take by as much as 150% to 180% of your monthly benefit.

Even if you do not begin drawing a Social Security check at age 65, *you are still eligible* for Medicare at that age. If you go on working after age 65, you can increase your monthly check at the time of your eventual retirement. If you wait until 70 to begin drawing your benefits, your checks may be between 24% and 27.5% higher. After the age of 70, there will be no further increase in benefits—virtue finally then becoming its own reward.

# e. Taxes and Your Benefits

*A portion of social security payments may be taxed as regular income.* If you have no income other than Social Security, *none* of it is taxed. If you have substantial income (from all sources, including, alas, royalties—and also including nontaxable earnings like interest on municipal bonds), then up to 50% of your Social Security Benefits may be counted as income. You can request Social Security to withhold federal taxes for you. It cannot withhold state taxes, however.

And, as we have just seen, if you retire early, the amounts you earn over a certain limit can result in a substantial reduction in your benefits.

# f. Family Benefits: Spouses, Kids, and Grandkids

When you retire your income will go down. If you have a family to support, you will need more money. The following people can begin drawing benefits *when* you do:

*Spouses.* Your spouse, if 62 (or younger, if caring for one of your children under 16) can draw a benefit of up to half the amount of your monthly check. Of course, many spouses age 62 will qualify for Social Security in *their own right*. Social Security will automatically pay the higher of the two amounts.

*Kids and Grandkids.* Your unmarried and dependent kids (adopted, out-of-wedlock, whatever) under 18 (or 19 if still in high school) are entitled to draw up to one-half your monthly benefit. So too older *disabled* children, if they were disabled before they turned 22. *Grandchildren*, if they are "dependent" upon you, may also draw benefits.

Payments to these folks *will not* reduce your check. There is, however, a *family maximum*: the *combined* payments to your spouse/kids will *not be allowed to exceed 150% to 180% of your monthly payment.*

Finally, if you defer your retirement beyond 65, these folks *cannot* receive benefits until you do. This is a good reason for early retirement.

# g. A Note to Divorcees

At the time of a divorce, the family's assets are divided. Pensions create problems. How do you divide something that has yet to mature? (We aren't talking about your ex-spouse; we're talking about his—or her—pension.) Divorce lawyers get rich figuring this one out.

Social Security has an automatic solution. As an ex-spouse, if you were married *at least ten years and have not remarried,* you are entitled to a benefit equal to one-half of his or her full retirement amount. You must be 62, or younger if you are providing care for a dependent minor.

Your take *doesn't* reduce your ex-spouse's check—Social Security ain't perfect.

# CHAPTER 6

# VETERANS' BENEFITS AND SAFETY NETS

## a. Veterans' Benefits

Surprisingly many "vets" don't think they are. Many women who were in the military do not think of themselves as "vets" nor do many others who think that to be a vet one must have seen battle or at least been in a battle zone. Even among those who know they are vets many believe that they are not entitled to Veterans' Benefits unless they applied for them immediately after they left service or if they had something other than an "Honorable Discharge." Not so.

*If you ever served this country in the military,* even long ago, it is *very* worthwhile to check to see if you are eligible for benefits. They are extensive and often better than what is offered by Social Security. They include monthly compensation, pensions, medical and nursing home care, and support services in the home. Benefits are available if you have a service-connected disability or are low-income with a non-service-related disability. Spouses, dependent children and survivors may also draw benefits.

A national tragedy is the number of vets living on the streets, often the victims of drug or alcohol addiction, caused by war trauma. Veterans' hospitals have programs to help these individuals and have turned countless lives around. If you have a relative or know someone on the streets who is a vet, urge them to make contact or, if they refuse, contact the VA hospital for advice. (To recognize what they have given to us, a charitable contribution would be appropriate.)

The Department of Veterans Affairs publishes a yearly edition of *Federal Benefits for Veterans and Dependents*. Local offices have copies, or you can obtain it online at http://www.va.gov.

# b. SSDI (Social Security Disability)

If you are working and contributing to Social Security and become disabled, you may be entitled to a monthly benefit. The disability must be serious:

1. It must prevent you from doing the job you did before and,
2. It must be one that will last for a year or until your death.

Get a lawyer to help you present your case. The cases are hard to present as they involve tricky medical issues. Social Security will pay the lawyer, not you. The average payment for a disabled married worker, with children, was, in 2009, $1,793 per month.

# c. SSI (Supplemental Security Income)

This is a welfare program run by Social Security. It pays monthly checks to the elderly, the blind, and to people with disabilities who don't have much income or property. If you are entitled to SSI, you usually get food stamps and Medicaid which helps pay hospital and doctor bills.

To qualify you must be 65 *or* blind *or* disabled (if blind or disabled, you are eligible at any age). Disability means a physical or mental problem that is expected to last at least a year or result in death, and that makes you unable to perform any "substantial gainful employment."

As of this writing, the base monthly payments are $603 for one individual and $904 for a couple if both are eligible. These amounts may be higher in some states or lower if you or your family has other income coming in.

Even if you are over 65 (or blind or disabled), to be eligible you cannot own much and cannot have too much income.

*Property.* Generally, personal items and the value of your home or car are not counted. Cash, bank accounts, stocks and bonds are counted. At this writing, for a single person, they cannot add up to over $2000; for a couple, $3000.

*Income.* Basically everything coming in is counted: Social Security, pensions, earnings, and even the value of other welfare payments you receive in the form of food, clothing, and shelter. The amount of income you can have and still be eligible depends on the state where you live.

Call Social Security at

1-800-772-1213
Hearing impaired: 1-800-325-0778

You should also ask these people about Medicaid and those programs that help low-income folks pay premiums for additional Medicare coverage, like payment of Medicare Part B (doctor visits) or Part D (prescription drug) premiums.

# d. Medicaid

Not to be confused with *Medicare* (the program for folks over 65), *Medicaid* is a federal program for low income folks administered by the states. There are income and property limitations but no age limitations. It provides a full range of medical services, including long term care.

More on this program at Chapter 12.

# CHAPTER 7

# PRIVATE PENSION PLANS

*The powers not delegated to the United States by the Constitution, nor prohibited by it to the states, are reserved to the states respectively, or to the people.*

10th Amendment, United States Constitution

The federal government has the power to build post offices, make war, and, as we all know, grant letters of marque and reprisal. But the Constitution doesn't delegate pensions to the United States. So how come most pension plans are governed by Federal law?

What the federal government cannot do directly, it can do by way of Big Carrots and the Internal Revenue Code. If a business wants to deduct its contributions to pension plans, those plans must conform to Federal requirements. If the plans do, employee contributions are deductible from current income.

A rule of thumb about retirement accounts: *"Deduct now, pay later."* If money going into your pension fund was deductible from your income tax, when you draw it out, it will be taxed. This usually works well. When you are working, your income (and tax rate) is higher. "Deduct now, pay later" tends to even things out.

Compare this tax treatment to money you set aside in a savings account. As these were *post tax* dollars, when you take them out, they do *not* constitute income. Visualize yourself as an apple; the IRS cannot take two bites.

## a. Pension Plans: Defined Benefit, Defined Contribution, 401(k) Plans

Pension plans vary a great deal. In general:

1. They favor, unlike Social Security, higher paid employees.
2. They favor long-term workers; the longer you work, the more you will get.

43

3. The normal retirement age is 65.
4. Your employer is obligated to give you a yearly statement of where you stand.

There are two kinds of basic pension plans.

## Defined Benefit Plans

Under these plans, your retirement payments are based on a percentage of your earnings (usually the average of your last three to five years of work). The percentage goes up the longer you have worked, say 2% per year. If you have worked 30 years, you might get 60% of your average earnings over the last few years.

## Defined Contribution Plans

Under these plans, retirement contributions are put in a retirement account. This amount is invested. If the investments do well, your retirement benefits will be high; if the investments do badly, you are in trouble.

In a defined *contribution* plan, the employee takes the risk of market variations; in a defined *benefit* plan, the employer takes the risk. It is also worth noting that contribution plans are not insured while benefit plans usually are.

## 401(k) Plans

These plans are like defined contribution plans, but give the employee somewhat more flexibility as there are no fixed contributions. The employer may match an employee's contributions up to a certain amount. 401(k) Plans can be risky. First, they depend on how well the investments do, and second, they are not insured. On the other hand, depending on the market, they can do much better than defined benefit plans.

Before the collapse of Enron, companies could insist that all of one's 401(k) contributions went to buy stock in the parent company. Now more flexibility is allowed. In a word, *diversify.*

What type of plan should you have? You generally don't have much of a choice in the matter; you take the kind of plan your employer offers.

Assuming you are locked into your pension plan, what do you need to know?

1. *Before you retire,* you need to know if you are *vested.*
2. *When you retire,* you need to know your options on taking your money.
3. If there is *trouble,* you need to know where to look for help.

# b. Vesting

If you have made contributions to your retirement account, you are entitled to get them back, no matter what, whether you were laid off, fired or quit. However, you will *not* be entitled to your *employer's* contribution until your rights *vest.* (This amount may be substantial.) Most plans vest after *five* years, but this varies widely: some vest in a month, some in seven years (the maximum length allowed under federal tax law).

Before you quit a job (or retire), make sure your rights have vested. Check your *Individual Benefit Statement* (a document your employer will give you). If you only have a year or so to go before vesting, stay. For older employees, rights vest at the normal retirement age, even if they haven't put in the traditional number of years. Get a job at 62. If the normal retirement age is 65, you can retire at 65, and be entitled to your pension even though it usually takes longer for it to vest. (But the pension won't pay very much.)

Some employers, to get their money off the table, fire folks shortly before their retirement rights vest or, in the alternative, make their jobs so miserable that they quit. This is known as a "constructive discharge." If you think this is happening to you, a legal consult is in order.

# c. Choices at Retirement: Cashing Out or Buying an Annuity

Many retirement plans allow you to *cash out* when you retire, as it were, taking it with you. However, this can be *very dangerous,* even if you don't take the Red Eye to Vegas. Unless you do it right, you will have to treat the entire amount as *current* income and your tax bill will be *staggering.*

Best to roll the money over into an IRA and perhaps into an annuity, and perhaps the best of all, a little of each. The problem with putting all of your money into an annuity, while it will pay top dollar, is that you won't be able to get at it in the case of emergencies or that long considered trip to the Galapagos. Place some of your money into an IRA where you can get at it.

In an *annuity* you give all (or some) of your accumulated retirement benefits to a bank or other financial institution and it agrees to pay you a certain monthly amount for a certain number of years, perhaps until you die. There are several variations.

## Fixed Term Annuities

These pay monthly payments over a fixed period of years. The risk is that you will outlive the fixed period and then you will be in a fine kettle of fish (although the alternative is even worse). However, if you have assets to cover this possibility, a fixed term annuity may be the way to go; monthly payments will be higher than with a *life annuity.*

## Life Annuities

Payments continue until death.

## Joint and Survivor's Annuities

Here monthly payments are made to you and, after you die, to your designated survivor, usually, but not always, a spouse. Because the annuity is now betting against two lives (so to speak), the monthly payments will be less. Another alternative is the *joint and 50% survivor's annuity,* which pays half the monthly amount to the designated survivor.

Under federal law, *if you are married,* you must elect a joint and survivor's annuity, with the survivor getting at least 50%. A single life annuity (one paying only you, leaving nothing for your spouse at your death), is possible *only* if your spouse agrees in writing.

A *single life annuity,* which will pay the highest monthly payments, may make sense *if* your spouse has adequate retirement income *or* is in such bad health that it is unlikely he or she will outlive you.

If you are in the fortunate position *of not needing all of your pension,* consider making your *children* the surviving beneficiaries. This will probably take a big bite out of your monthly check, but it will provide your children with monthly payments long after you have gone. Who knows? They might actually thank you.

# d. Pension Troubles

The newspapers are full of stories about pension plans reducing benefits, cutting out health care, and even going broke. The legal principles are quite complex and beyond the scope of this book. Here are some basics to get you started.

## Your plan goes broke.

*Defined benefits* are usually insured by the Pension Benefit Guaranty Corporation (1-800-400-PBGC). *Defined contribution plans* are not. Even in those plans which are covered, some of the plan's benefits may not be, such as disability and early retirement.

## Your employer changes the plan.

If your employer changes the plan to your detriment, first make sure that the plan allowed him to do so. Get a copy of the plan. This is a tricky, fact-specific area. If changes in benefits are substantial, consult a lawyer who specializes in employment or pension law.

## Your individual claim for benefits is turned down.

Plans will tell you how to appeal. Again, some lawyers specialize in pension law.

## You get divorced.

You will probably have to divide the worth of the pension—and this gets complicated. See Chapter 20.

## You forget where you worked.

Remember after the War? You spent four or five years with that little company outside of town. What was its name? Did it have a pension plan that you just forgot? Old tax forms will give the employer's tax number and perhaps the number of the retirement plan. If you haven't kept old tax forms, for a fee the IRS will provide a copy. Once you have these numbers, perhaps the Pension Benefit Guaranty Corporation can help you (1-800-400-PBGC). www.pbgc.gov.

Remember Monopoly? You may be looking at Bank Error in Your Favor! Don't tip over backwards.

## CHAPTER 8

# RETIREMENT FINANCES

*Wives make the little decisions, like what to have for dinner, when to go on vacation, where to live, and where the kids go to college. Husbands make the big decisions, like whether Red China should be admitted to the U.N.*

This is a pre-Nixon gag but a good one. Much has changed but many husbands still handle the money. Wives need to get involved. Be subtle, not "Dear, you're not looking good today; tell me about our investments." Community colleges might offer courses, and one good website is WIFE (Women's Institute for Financial Education). www.wife.org.

This chapter covers rethinking money, budgeting, investment options, the danger of flat investments and cookie jars. It might even help the men folk (it's *not* the same as asking directions).

## a. Rethinking Money

Retirement requires a *major* shift in thinking about money.

Working, you could count on occasional raises and could ride out new roofs and old cars on borrowed money. No more. Credit recedes and "fixed income" becomes a stark reality.

1. How much income will you need?
2. If you have some left over, how should you invest it?

Your income should exceed your expenses, some advise by 150% to 200%. You'll have a cushion against all those things you didn't anticipate. (As Ben Franklin said, unless you want a dismal vacation, figure out how much it will cost and then double it.)

As to investments, *inflation happens*. Even at an historically low inflation rate of 3%, your money is worth half in 23 years. *Moral*: invest something with an eye to growth.

# b. Budgeting: Big Ticket Items, Life and Medical Insurance

Probably a good idea to make a budget. Work expenses will be gone: professional dues, fancy clothes, business lunches and, if you were a lobbyist, legislative bribes. Some expenses will go up—you may have to purchase services, yard work, home repair. There are no doubt computer programs and scores of budget books, with blanks to be filled in, long depressing lists of expenses we don't even know we have.

The problem with most budgets is that they focus on current expenses. You need to think ahead. Will you need a new car in a few years? A new roof? A new furnace? Include a "future expenses" item on your budget and put something aside each month. You will find it more difficult to borrow money *even though* you may have good security. Lenders look not only at security but also at income stream.

Include in your budget some travel … you've earned it. The bad news, include an inflation factor; things will be more expensive next year.

Life insurance, should you keep it? Medical insurance, how much?

## Life insurance

> *A crowded kitchen, an elderly couple, and their unshaven, tattooed, middle-aged son: "Larry, your mom and I would like a little time by ourselves before we die."*

When our children were young, we purchased life insurance in case "something might happen." Many cancel their life insurance when their children are grown, have jobs, and, in some cases, have actually moved out.

Canceling life insurance will help you meet current expenses and may allow you to move money into something producing income or into *long-term care insurance*. See Chapter 12. On the other hand, life insurance is a good way to pass on money to loved ones. They will receive it immediately and need not await probate. Further, if you have whole life policy with a strong company, your money might be safer there than elsewhere. See Bernie Madoff.

## Health insurance and medical costs

Medical costs will be a *major* hit.

*A 65-year-old couple retiring with Medicare will need nearly a quarter of a million dollars ($240,000) to cover medical expenses. This according to a 2009 study which assumed no other insurance and life expectancies of 17 years for the husband, 20 for the wife. This is a 50% increase from a similar study seven years ago.*

If you retire before age 65, you will need to *purchase* health insurance to cover what you lost when you retired. This costs a pretty penny.

At 65, likely you will have Medicare, a great program but one covering mostly just hospital stays. It is estimated that the basic Medicare plan (hospitalization) will cover only about half of your medical expenses and, with budgetary pressures on the system, perhaps less in the future.

Most everyone will get some additional coverage by joining a Medicare HMO or staying with the basic Medicare plan by purchasing Medicare Part B (doctor visits) and Part D (some drugs). These additions can run several hundred a month. We discuss medical insurance in Chapter 11.

As to your retirement income it is, to use a rather silly metaphor, a three-legged stool: Social Security, pensions, and our topic, the third leg, investments. (Social Security is also known as the "third rail" but you know what they say about consistency.)

# c. Investment Options

*In high school I worked as an usher at the Del Mar race track. I felt the lure of the "hot tip"—"I overheard a guy who overheard a woman who knows the cousin of one of the jockeys say...." I learned why, in spite of all the contrary evidence, most of us believe we are good at picking winners—"Sure, my horse, Blue Bird, came in last but I almost bet on the winner, My Fast Rocket." The truth of the matter is that, before the bet, not only were Blue Bird and My Fast Rocket considered, but probably every other horse in the race: no matter who wins, we came 'that close.' Theories abound: bet the jockey, bet the trainer, bet the hot horse, bet the one who is due. Most painfully and personally, I also learned that most people lose.*

Are stocks more predictable?

Are "hot tips," even those touted on CNBC, better than those of the stylish woman standing in the betting line? (It is amazing that we believe people *simply* because they are on TV. Well, I've been on TV.)

Is the most recent "beat the market" book better than "bet the horse with the longest name"? (If the theory *would* make you a millionaire, would the author still be doing book tours?)

*Get investment advice* if a lots at stake. You have a choice.

> *Professional financial planners* work on a *set or hourly fee* and not on a commission which might skew their advice. But they might lack the needed expertise when it comes to stocks, annuities, and other investments.
>
> Insurance agents, stock brokers, bank advisors *have both the expertise (good) and a dog in the fight (bad).*

It is extremely difficult to outsmart the market. New Yorkers who play the market went to business school to learn how and they have devoted their allotted time on earth to the ridiculous pursuit of money. Give them their due—they will outsmart you—they even get up earlier. And they lose their fair share as well.

Investing concerns not only our income and security but also that of our family; investing merges with estate planning. For example, while continuing our life insurance may not make immediate sense, it may be a good way to leave your family cash. More on this in the chapter on estate planning.

## IRAs, Annuities, CDs, Stocks and Bonds

If you are still working, put as much as you can into your retirement account or IRA. Your contributions are *deductible* from current income. When you take it out you will pay taxes but you will probably be in a lower tax bracket. Assume you put $1,000 in an IRA. If your tax rate is 30% the $1,000 deduction will result in a tax savings of $300. Now when you take the money out, at your retirement, assuming you are now at a 20% tax rate, your tax will be $200. Thus you have saved $100. And not only that: the money your IRA earns is not taxed until you take it out. Earnings on saving accounts, bonds, and stock dividends are taxed as earned. If you want to play the market you can do so with the money in your IRA—it can be thought of as a shell.

The downside to IRAs is that you can't reach the money until you reach the age of 59 1/2 (without paying a substantial penalty). If you anticipate needing money in the short haul, keep it out of IRAs.

*Annuities.* There are *immediate* and *deferred* annuities. With an *immediate annuity,* you give an insurance company a bundle of money and it guarantees you monthly payments, for a set number of years or for your life. You can have a secondary beneficiary, your spouse or child, who will receive payments when you die. The longer you are projected to live, or the longer your beneficiary is, the smaller the monthly payments.

Annuities are only as secure as the insurance company that issued them. Go for big, established ones, preferably *mutual insurance companies.* These companies do not have stock holders so there is no pressure on management to turn a profit. They are owed by the policy holders.

There are a wide variety of options. One variable to consider: if you need some of the money back, can you get it? Another: if you die before the principal amount has been paid to you, does it go to your heirs or does the company keep it? (Smoke, smoke, smoke that cigarette.)

Alas, there is a new "annuity" *scam.* Older seniors, in their 80s or 90s, are sold lifetime annuities. They promise large monthly payments. How can they? Some provide that payments won't *start* for several years. In any event, the company, knowing the individual's life expectancy, is counting on keeping most of the bundle for itself. Again, there will be nothing left over.

*Deferred annuities.* They are pushed by your local banker as a way to earn higher interest. You put your money in an insurance company affiliated with the bank, and agree not to withdraw it for some number of years—typically seven. If you do need your money back before that date, you will have to pay a penalty—typically beginning at 7% and shrinking by 1% each year—for the early withdrawal. In return, the insurance company promises you extraordinary rates of return, and no income taxes until the annuity matures.

*CDs.* Certificates of Deposit, pay less than annuities as they do not consume the principal. They allow for more flexibility as you invade capital when they mature. Many retirees split their "nest egg" into various CDs, at different banks, so that all of their money is insured.

*F.D.I.C. insured accounts.* The Federal Deposit Insurance Corporation (now you know) insures bank deposits, including CD's held by them, to $100,000 per account. (To reassure depositors Congress raised this to $200,000 to expire at the end of 2009. That increase may be made permanent.) Although it is important to be careful not to exceed the $100,000 per account, there is no advantage to having dozens of $10,000 accounts scattered all over the country. We frequently see estates where the decedent shopped carefully for the highest interest rate available on the internet every time he scraped a couple thousand dollars together, and the result is that the cost of figuring it all out, closing all the small accounts and calculating the taxes and estate division dwarfs any small increase in return during their life.

# d. The Danger of Flat Investments

*If, in 1975, you decided you would need two postage stamps per year, you would need 20 cents. Six years later, you could buy only one stamp and, today, not even half a stamp.*

The problem with CDs and safe market investments is that, while they guard the principle investment, they do not account for inflation: after a period of time, the purchasing power of the original investment will be less than it was originally; rather than two letters, you will be only able to send one postcard.

Add to this the problem of invading principal. Say you have $600,000 (a nice nest egg) and to play it safe, divide it in insured savings accounts paying 5%. This will generate $30,000 a year. Not bad. But what if you need $70,000 to live? You invade your principal for the extra $40,000. Next year you have $560,000 in savings. That amount will pay you $28,000 and hence, to get to $70,000 you will have to invade principal by $42,000, leaving you with only $518,000 which will pay, the following year, $25,900 interest. You get the drift: *downwards.* (This is not to assert that you should never invade principal. You worked hard for it; take a trip, buy art, tip big—better you than your ne'er-do-well kids.)

How to protect yourself from inflation and downward drift? Invest some of your money in growth opportunities, perhaps real estate, most likely stock. We all know the dangers of such investments, just like we all know the dangers of the race track.

Steven Thel, a professor of securities at Fordham advises:

> *"The overwhelming evidence is that most people make serious investment mistakes, which is why they should put their money into index funds and bond funds with low costs and not spend too much of their time trying to become financially literate."*

This brings us back to the track.

> *The only person I saw who won day after day would bet only one or two races, putting his money on the overwhelming favorite to "Show"—he would win, but not much, if the horse came in first, second, or third.*

No doubt he invested his winnings in index and bond funds, made a modest but fairly constant return, stayed a tad ahead of inflation, and spent his free time reading great novels, not boring financials (which are, unfortunately, not entirely free of fiction).

# e. Cookie Jars: Savings Accounts, IRAs, Roth IRAs

If you are lucky you have salted away money in savings accounts, CDs, stocks and bonds, and IRAs. The basic rule is to make IRAs your last cookie jar. It has to do with taxes.

The money you have in savings accounts or CDs is your money in the sense that you can take it out without tax consequences. You already paid taxes on the money. The money you put in probably came from your job earnings (and you paid income tax on it) and the money you earned on the interest was taxed as regular income as it was paid).

As to stocks and bonds, whether they are a good cookie jar to raid depends mostly on their current price. As to the tax consequences, however, the amount you paid for them (your basis) is your money in that you used post-tax dollars to pay for them. However, if you are lucky enough to sell them at more than you paid, this is a tax event but a favorable one: you will pay a generally much lower capital gains tax.

This leads us to IRAs. They were a marvelous investment and, if you are still working, invest as much as you can. The amount you invest can be deducted from your current income (thus lowering your tax bill) and the money you earn as interest, unlike savings accounts, is tax free until you withdraw it. (The only disadvantage to an IRA is that, unlike a savings account, there is a big penalty if you need to get the money out before you turn 59 and a half.)

*When was the last time you added "and a half" to your age? Sure, "Five and a half" makes sense but not so "Sixty-five and a half." Thus the Internal Revenue Code doth make children of us all.*

Now the bad news: when you take money out of your IRA you have to pay taxes on it. It is regular income. This is why it should be your last cookie jar. I think the Beatles said as much in Tax Man.

So, if you can otherwise afford it, why not never draw down your IRA account and leave it all to your heirs? Because the IRS won't let you. You must start drawing down, by a complicated formula, when you turn 70 and a half.

What about a Roth IRA? They are better than a regular IRA when it comes time to get money out. First, there is no 70 and a half rule: you need not take any money out of it. Second, all the money you take out of it, including the amount it earned in interest, is tax free. What's the catch? The money you put into the Roth IRA is not deductible at the time. So, if you are still working and don't need a current deduction, look into a Roth IRA. Even if you are not, it is possible to convert a regular IRA into a Roth IRA but not on our dime. See your accountant.

Finally, if you do everything I say, things will come out perfectly. To quote the most famous economist of all, John Kenneth Galbraith:

> *The only function of economic forecasting*
> *is to make astrology look good.*

# CHAPTER 9

# House Rich, Cash Poor

If you are having a difficult time making ends meet, you may wish to get the money out of your house and into your pocket, assuming your house is still worth something. You should probably make this the last place to look for money. The money you have in your house is the most important and secure money you have. Not only does it put a roof over your head but, under the laws of most states, the only creditor that can go after that money is the creditor holding a mortgage on the house. General creditors, such as hospitals and credit cards, cannot. Once you take that money out of the house, and put it in the bank or buy stock, your general creditors can go after it.

Go slow.

There are three ways to get money out of the house: borrow against it, sell it, or rent it. Consider too a *reverse mortgage*. First some warnings.

Crooks target your home. They come offering free roof inspections only to find that you need major repairs (that they, of course, will provide). Others come offering you terrific loans which simply require your putting a mortgage on your house or perhaps giving them title to your house "for the short term." *Never, ever,* sign any paper giving someone a security interest in your home unless it is a bank.

The new scam on the block is the "Mortgage Rescue Scam" which promises help for those facing foreclosure. See Chapter 23 on "Recession Blues."

One piece of good news. Some locales give property tax breaks to seniors. Check.

## a. Traditional Borrowing

The great advantage of borrowing money, rather than selling or renting, is that it allows what most of us want: to stay put. The problem is that it puts your home at risk, if you don't pay you lose the house. (On a foreclosure, your house would be sold and your creditor would take off the top what you owed; if there is any remaining, you would get the balance. For more on foreclosures, see Chapter 23.)

Make your home your very last nest egg. Don't borrow against it to pay off credit cards or to go on a cruise. *Don't* mortgage your home without first seeing if you are eligible for *SSI, Medicaid* or another welfare type program. See Chapter 6. Generally these programs do not put your home at risk.

One advantage of *traditional mortgages* and the newer *Home Equity Accounts* (essentially a line of credit secured by a mortgage on your home) is that the amount you pay in interest is tax deductible. There is talk in Congress of axing this deduction. The amounts you pay in interest on credit cards, car loans and other consumer purchases are *not* deductible. (Note: under current law, you cannot deduct interest payments on home equity loans over $100,000 unless the money was for home improvement.)

# b. Reverse Mortgages

*Reverse mortgages* offer a great opportunity, if you are over 62, to get some of the equity out of your home without requiring you to move. The lender pays you a monthly amount—hence the "reverse" moniker. The loan does not have to be repaid until you move or die. The money you receive is not taxed and will not impact either Social Security, Medicare or Medicaid. There are no out-of-pocket costs, with closing costs being picked up in the loan. Title stays in your name.

The federal government's Home Equity Conversion Mortgage Program, the principal, and most principled, of the reverse mortgage offerings, is regulated by the Department of Housing and Urban Development-HUD. There are no income limits on who can apply. The owners must all be 62 or older. Basically any kind of house can qualify, from mansion to house trailer, with the exceptions being cooperative apartments and newly-built (less than a year) dwellings. One of the best elements of the federal program: every borrower must first complete a free reverse mortgage counseling program. In our experience, the counseling program shows many, perhaps most, of the interested prospects how to better arrange their finances without going through the reverse mortgage—and that's a sign that the program is more interested in good results than in closings. Beware, however—there are reverse mortgage scams in the world, and not all lenders are scrupulously honest and careful about your best interests.

Eventually the money borrowed in a reverse mortgage must be repaid, with interest. The interest rates will vary and are usually adjustable rather than fixed. You can terminate the loan when you wish and repay it at that time. When you die, if your spouse is on the deed, the loan payments will continue.

If not, your house goes to your heirs with the mortgage lien upon it. Your heirs can either pay off the loan and keep the house, or allow it to be sold. If the selling price exceeds the amount due under the loan, that money goes to the heirs.

You must continue to live in the house at least half time and reverse mortgages, due to the paperwork and costs, aren't a good idea if you plan to move. Talk to a specialist in the area. To find one, contact your Area Agency. On the AARP website you can find a wealth of information on reverse mortgages, from eligibility, basics, and lenders, to options and loan calculations.

# c. Selling Your Home

If you sell it for more than you paid, there is good tax news. Since 1998, there are no federal capital gains taxes on the first $250,000 of profit ($500,000 for married couples). *However,* you must have lived in the home for two of the previous five years. This, incidentally, is the major danger of renting—if you rent your home out for more than three years, you will no longer be able to meet the two-of-the-last-five requirement, and suddenly all the appreciation in your home's value will be taxable if you sell it.

A major legal drawback to selling is that your home is generally an *exempt* asset; the money you receive from it isn't. In most states, a homestead can be filed (or may exist automatically, without even needing to be "filed") to protect your home from creditors (they cannot seize it and sell it); on the other hand, once you have sold it and put the money into bank accounts or stocks, creditors can get it by obtaining appropriate court orders. (The folks who hold the *mortgage* on your house can go after it even if it is homesteaded.)

Similarly, most welfare programs (*Medicaid, SSI* and the like) allow you to *keep* your home but not much of your cash. *Go slow in selling your house if it looks like you will have to go on welfare.*

# d. Renting or Leasing Your Home

This might be a good choice if you are moving to smaller digs, particularly if it looks like there will be no need to sell the house in the near future. Moving from the house for more than three years (assuming you have lived there for at least two years already) will mean that you will not be entitled to the exemption from capital gains taxes which was described in the last section.

As to the hassles of renting, thankfully there are management companies that will do the heavy-lifting—collecting, making repairs, etc.

With a little creativity, you will be able to avoid *income* taxes on most or all of the rents you receive (there may be local *sales* taxes on rentals; those will be hard to avoid and you should set the rental rates accordingly). Rental income is taxable income. Management fees and costs of repairs (and *rental insurance*, a must) are *deductible*. As you actually pay out these amounts, there is no real savings. However, now that your house is income-producing, you can *depreciate* it. A depreciation allowance allows you to reduce the income tax you pay on the rent you receive without actually paying out money.

A *depreciation allowance* is given to income producing assets (such as factories and buildings) in the recognition that, in 20 or 30 years, they are likely to wear out and must be replaced at that time. It is assumed that the owner is spreading the replacement cost across the life of the asset by putting money aside. *However*, there is no requirement that you actually put money aside or pay out anything.

The way the government gets its money back is to reduce your *basis* by the amount you took in depreciation. Say what? Assume you purchased your home for $100,000 and that you subsequently sold it for the same amount, $100,000. There would be no capital gain. However, if you rented the house and took a total of $40,000 in depreciation to offset your rental income, your basis would be $60,000 and thus, when sold at $100,000 there would be a capital gain of $40,000. One nice thing, however, is that if you leave the house to your kids, they will get a *stepped-up basis*—the amount the house is worth at the time of your death. So they won't have to worry about capital gains; regrettably, you won't either.

Complicated stuff. Talk to an accountant. The IRS has pamphlets that can help as well.

527—Residential Property

946—How to Depreciate Property

Finally a bottom line. At your age it is finally safe to talk to strangers, but not about security interests in your house.

# CHAPTER 10

# RETIREMENT HOUSING

Move or stay in our current house?

At some point we all face that question. Is our current place too big? Will we be able to do the upkeep? Will it be safe when we have a harder time with stairs, showers, and sidewalks? Is it convenient to carless shopping? On the other hand, if we move to a new location, what will it be like to make new friends? Find new restaurants? Create new routines? One draw of moving to a retirement community, however, is that everyone is in the same boat; you no longer have to put up with younger folks cutting in front of you at the supermarket.

We'll look at staying put (getting help and making things safer) and then at the plethora of new housing options created for seniors, including CCRCs: continuing care retirement communities.

## a. Staying Put (with a little help from our friends)

Some move because they think they cannot afford not to. Take a look at our discussion of reverse mortgages in the last chapter. Others move because they fear that they won't be able to manage. Here we consider your options in getting help in your home when and if you need it.

You can have a relative stay with you, perhaps promising to leave the house to them. Or you can hire help. Before the potential problems with each, an important warning about having *anyone*, adult children included, live in your house: *abuse*, either physical, financial, or both. Abuse is the subject of Chapter 14. Always maintain and insist upon contacts *outside* the home: the favorite ploy of abusers is isolation. Have a weekly bridge game, hair appointment, or other regular weekly activity. If you can't get out of the house, make sure you are visited weekly by friends or relatives and insist on talking with them *privately*.

Sometimes children or other *relatives move in* to help out. There may be an understanding that, when you die, they will get the house. This might make a great deal of sense. But *don't put the title in their names now!* If the house is in their names, their creditors might be able to reach it. And there are tax consequences. It is generally a *bad* idea to make a lifetime gift of your home to your children (they will *not* get a stepped-up basis, and you may incur a gift tax). It is better to give it to them at the time of your death under your Will. They will get a stepped up basis which means, when they sell it, any capital gains will be based on the value of the house when you died, not when you bought it.

Another big problem, and as a lawyer I am trained to see nothing but problems, is that there may be a fight and your relative will force you to move.

Rather than giving them the house now, you can make a formal contract to do so. In return for described services, you promise to give them the property by your Will. To be enforceable, the contract must be in writing and signed by all parties. Best to see a lawyer and best to make sure all of your relatives know of the arrangement. Otherwise there might be fights about who should get the house.

*Hiring help* is another option. As these people will have the run of your house, best to seek advice as to hiring trustworthy and competent people. Want ads aren't a good idea nor is it a good idea to pay bottom dollar; likely you won't get quality and likely you will get someone who will *supplement* their meager wage with your nicknacks, change, piggy banks, stocks, and, ultimately your identity. Keep things on a formal basis and resist giving your caregiver extra money or the loan of your car.

Finally, in terms of getting help, don't overlook all the services, such as *Meals on Wheels*, provided by your Area Council on Aging.

If you're planning to stay put, it is never too early to make your house safer. Add several years to your age and walk around the house. What are the dangers for your older self? Killer bees. (A cartoon shows a small beehive with the sign, "Lawyers." "Those are the lawyer bees," someone is explaining, "They represent the killer bees.")

*Seniors fall.* Are your rugs secure? Does the shower have slip-proof mats? Are there grab bars? Are the tables solid so they won't flip? *Seniors lose night vision.* Are there enough night lights to get them from bed to bath? *Seniors lose strength.* Do the chairs have arms that they can use getting up? *Seniors have slower reaction times.* Is the hot water heater set so that it will not produce scalding water? *Seniors have emergencies.* Do you have smoke detectors? Do you change the batteries? Are phones accessible? Cordless phones are best.

It may be necessary to make structural changes to your house (wheelchair ramps, widened hallways, modified bathroom facilities). If you are renting, your landlord *must* allow you to make these changes as long as you agree to take them out when you leave.

An occupational therapist can be quite helpful in making specific suggestions. For example, if the elder is a gardener but has knee or hip problems, raised plant beds can work wonders. Someone with bad arthritis will find lever handles more friendly than door knobs.

Two web sites that can help: mysafehome.net and aarp.org (home safety). To pay for any home modifications, check your long term care contract, if you have one, or consider a home equity loan or a reverse mortgage, discussed elsewhere. Your area council on aging might have additional ideas.

# b. Moving to Warmer Climes

Golf, sunshine, and bridge. Not a bad combination, that. The salespeople are marvelous—ever sign up for a free vacation trip with the only obligation being to sit through a short presentation (which you knew you would easily resist)? *Go slow.* Many buy into a retirement community only to find:

- that it is on shaky financial ground and that many of the promised benefits are in jeopardy;
- that they miss their friends and family and even the shrieks and laughter of the neighborhood kids; and
- that their golf slice is incurable and, as they always suspected, their spouse compulsively overbids.

Trying to resell, they find the bottom has fallen out.

One way to avoid trouble is to *rent* in the new location before you buy. If you do, you may want to rent out your own house back home. In the previous chapter, we discussed some issues surrounding renting your house. Check with your insurance company to see if your home is covered for renters.

So, where to go?

*Lake Woebegone* and *Margaritaville* will immediately come to mind, although not to the same mind. Alas, neither exist. And, if that weren't bad enough, winters and hangovers both get worse. (Trust us.)

David Savageau's *Retirement Places Rated* can provide you with good information about different locales. Many move to such places as Mexico, Costa Rica, Canada, and Ireland where the cost of living is less. Check the quality of medical care, whether your insurance will pay (Medicare won't), and the cost of airfare back to the States.

If you are going to buy a new home, even if you are extremely active now, you may not be later. If looking for a new home, make sure it will accommodate possible disabilities. Are the hallways wide enough for a wheelchair? Is the house located near shopping? Medical facilities?

Finally, *transportation*. There will come a time when you will be unable to drive. If you are buying a new house, how will you get around when that time comes? We cannot stress this enough. Unless there is public transport or things are within walking distance, the inability to drive will mean staying at home and, isolated, life becomes quite burdensome.

Whether you stay put or move to a new home, at some point you may decide that maintaining your own home is too much work. You might want to move to a facility where you don't have to do all the cooking and cleaning, and where there are new people to meet and new opportunities to explore.

# c. Assisted-Living Facilities

The housing options for older persons are quite numerous, not only in size and location, but also in the level of support they offer. The questions, however, are the same:

- What are the costs?
- What are the conditions?
- What programs and services are offered?
- How much independence will you have?
- How about complaints? What have they been and how have they been answered?

Shop around, visit at least two, visit at different times of day, and talk to residents as well as officials. Many states license these facilities, usually the Department of Public Health or similarly-named agency. On their websites there will be a list of facilities and a searchable database of past enforcement actions.

Your options run from essentially *boarding homes* and *assisted-living facilities* (apartments with various levels of support services), through the newer *continuing care retirement communities* (CCRCs). CCRCs claim to provide extensive care, support, and nursing facilities on site. Many purport to guarantee care for life, first in an independent unit, then, if necessary, in the nursing or intermediate wing.

# d. Continuing Care Retirement Communities (CCRCs)

Most assisted-living facilities charge by the month; others insist on a *buy-in*. Be careful buying in.

- Some have bought in with their life savings ($300,000 to $500,000) only to have the facility go broke.
- Others have bought in and died in the first year, with the facility keeping all of their money.
- Others have bought in while healthy only to find, when they need it, that the types of care they need are not covered in the contract.
- Others have found after ten or so years that they want to move, but all of their money is tied up.

There are about 1,200 CCRCs nationally and there are *no* federal regulations. Some states regulate them. To get into such a facility, one must be in relatively good health, and often pay a hefty up-front payment (from $300,000 to over $500,000 per person). There are set monthly fees and perhaps additional charges for nursing care.

Some points to consider:

- Treat the move as you would a major investment. Ask for an audited financial statement. Have your accountant review it. A guarantee of life-care is only good as long as the facility does not go bankrupt and as long as it maintains adequate beds in various levels of care.
- Once you buy in, it may be difficult to get your money back if you don't like it. Before buying in, *hang out*. Ask other residents about the facility.
- Are the medical facilities and services up to what is advertised?
- Are there enough physicians? Are there long waits? Are specialists covered or must you pay for them yourself?
- What is the policy about moving residents into the nursing wing? There have been complaints that some facilities do so quickly, so that they can then sell the individual's apartment to someone else. Along these lines, what are the policies about the institution seeking guardianship over residents?
- If a spouse dies, must the survivor move into a separate single's unit? A forced move at this time can be traumatic.
- Will the facility take Medicare payments? Some will not.

- What is the refund policy? If you die relatively soon, do your heirs get any of the money back?

# e. Section 8 Housing for Low-Income Folks

If you are age 62 or older and have an income below the median in your area, you may be entitled to "*Section 8*" *rent subsidy* for certain independent facilities. Under it, you will pay only a certain percentage of your income as rent with the federal government picking up the difference. Although many Americans hold onto images of government housing being clustered into substandard buildings in dangerous neighborhoods, Section 8 subsidies today may be available for rental units pretty much anywhere in town.

# f. More Info

The American Bar Association *Guide for Older Americans* has a nice checklist of questions concerning assisted living and continuing care facilities. It is published by Time Books, a division of Random House.

The American Association of Homes and Services for the Aging publishes *The Consumer's Directory of Continuing Care Retirement Communities.* 800-508-9442; *www.aahsa.org.*

The *AARP* has several publications:

Staying at Home Selecting Retirement Housing
Housing Options for Older Americans
1-800-424-3410
*http://www.aarp.org*

And your local Area Agency on Aging can help too.

# CHAPTER 11

# MEDICARE AND
# HEALTH INSURANCE

*I can't get sick and end up in the hospital, I'll lose everything I've worked for and bankrupt my family.*

Our parents were haunted by that fear. No more. Thanks to Medicare, passed in 1965 under Lyndon Johnson, hospitalization, now with even short stays running up bills in excess of $70,000, no longer bankrupts families. A wonderful achievement.

Now all we have to do is wade through a confusing list of choices: Medicare, Parts A, B, C, and D; Medigap policies; long-term care insurance; dread disease insurance; disability insurance, and, oh yes, COBRA. This will give you a basic overview, beginning with what insurance you might need before you turn 65—the magical year.

## a. Insurance Needs before 65

### Disability Insurance

A bad back at age 58 can prevent you from reaching retirement in good financial shape.

Don't rely on Disability under Social Security. Under Social Security, your disability must be severe and the payments will be small. Social Security pays only if you are unable to perform any substantial gainful employment—even as cashier at a self-service gas station, or a crossing guard.

### COBRA

*"COBRA," like life itself, is full of sound and fury, signifying nothing. (Actually it signifies "Comprehensive Omnibus Budget Reconciliation Act"—which, in turn, signifies nothing.)*

If you retire (or are laid off) before 65, most likely you will lose your health insurance, COBRA helps.

If your employer has 20 or more covered workers, COBRA is the federal law that allows you to continue your employer's health plan if you lose coverage because of early retirement or layoff. You can continue the policy for up to *18 months*, but must pay the premium (usually the same rate charged the employer plus a 2% administrative charge). This is known as Continuation Coverage.

If the first 18 months doesn't get you to the magical year of Medicare coverage (age 65), you have a right to convert the policy but at a higher premium and with more restrictions. This is known as Conversion Coverage. Professional organizations, service clubs, and the AARP offer group policies that will likely save you money.

If you had to retire because of disability, it may be possible to obtain COBRA coverage for longer than 18 months.

A related program protects you if you change jobs. The Health Insurance Portability and Accountability Act of 1996 (HIPAA) allows you to take your health insurance eligibility with you if you change employers. That means you cannot be denied coverage under your new employer's health plan. However, your coverage may not be with the same insurer or under terms as favorable as your former employer's health coverage.

## Long-Term Care Insurance

Medicare does *not* cover most nursing home expenses and they are quite high. There is insurance; the sooner you buy it, the lower the premium. More on this in the next chapter.

# b. Turning 65: Medicare

A quick overview of the morass.

1. When you turn 65, sign up for Medicare *Part A* even if you are not going to start taking your monthly checks. Part A is free (you paid for it while you worked through wage deductions) and covers hospital stays.

2. Unless you have other insurance, sign up for Medicare *Part B* which covers doctor visits. You will pay for this but it is a very good deal; you pay only about 25% of what the coverage is worth.

3. You might also want to pick up a *Medigap* policy which covers things that A and B don't, such as eye glasses, hearing aids and so forth.

4. You might also want to enroll in Medicare *Part D* which covers prescriptions.

## Or an HMO

An HMO will pick up much or all of the coverage provided by 2, 3, and 4. While an HMO might be a terrific choice for you, there have been reports of heavy pressure brought to bear by folks trying to enroll you, some even claiming that they work for Medicare. Before you sign up have a good idea of what you want and how much it would cost if you went traditional medicare. More anon.

You still aren't home because most of us have fairly substantial over-the-counter medical purchases. The good news is there is one kind of medical insurance that is problematic: *Dread Disease Insurance.* It is usually pitched on late night TV by aging actors and what it covers is probably covered by your other plans. Few, if any, need to buy it.

Now, if you are still with me, some details.

## Medicare Part A

To be eligible for Medicare, you must be 65 (or disabled or blind). In addition to being 65:

- You must be eligible for Social Security (that does not mean you have to be *receiving* Social Security—just that you must be eligible); or, if you aren't,
- You must be a spouse, widow, or widower of an eligible member. Ex-spouses, if married for more than ten years and not remarried, can also qualify.

If you don't fit into one of these categories, and are 65 or older, you can still purchase coverage. It is costly, over $450 per month. (It will be less if you have at least 30 Social Security quarters.)

While you may want to put off taking your cash benefits from Social Security at age 65 (to get larger cash payments later), and while you may want to delay signing up for other Medicare Programs (because you are otherwise covered), there is *no* reason not to sign up for Part A when you turn 65. Apply for Medicare through your Social Security Office three months before you turn 65.

Medicare Part A basically covers most hospital costs, many skilled nursing facility care costs, some home care costs, and hospice. All of this gets quite technical and you will receive a booklet explaining the ins and outs—*Medicare and You*. But, for now, you don't need to know the details of what Part A covers; what you need to know is what it *doesn't* cover:

> *Doctor Visits*
> *Prescriptions*
> *Dental, Hearing, and Eye Care*
> *Long-term Custodian Care*

To get coverage for routine doctor visits, prescriptions and dental, eye care and hearing, you have two basic choices, staying with Medicare and adding to its coverage, or opting for a Medicare HMO. Two points before we begin.

It will cost you, no matter which way you go. You already paid for hospital coverage (Part A) through your payroll taxes, but you must purchase additional coverage.

Second, you should make your decision as soon as possible. If you wait too long after you become eligible (usually three months after you turn 65), you will have to pay more for the same coverage. The higher premium protects Medicare from "adverse selection" (not buying insurance until you are sick, not placing your bet until the ball has stopped bouncing). The *only time you should delay* is where you are covered by a better health plan after you turn 65, through either your or your spouse's insurance.

## Medicare Part B: Doctor Visits

Medicare Part B covers doctor visits and helps with outpatient hospital services (including emergency room visits), ambulances, diagnostic tests, laboratory services, some preventive care such as mammography and Pap smear, outpatient therapy services, durable medical equipment and supplies, and a variety of other services. It also picks up some home health care services.

You pay a $135 deductible per year and 20% of the other charges. You may have to pay more if your doctor does not agree to accept Medicare approved limits on charges.

When you sign up for Medicare, unless you opt out, you will be automatically enrolled in Part B. You will pay a monthly premium, at this writing, of about $100 per month. (If you have a large income, your premium will be higher—a single person earning over $200,000 is looking at about a $300 premium). The premium will be taken from your Social Security check. It is a great value. In fact, the federal government is required to peg the premium at 25% of the cost of the care provided to all participants—so you can expect that comparable coverage in the private market (if you could buy it) would cost about four times as much.

Part B does not cover prescriptions, dental, hearing, or vision services. What's your next move?

## Medicare Part D: Prescriptions

Part D of Medicare provides for a voluntary outpatient drug benefit. Private insurers provide these benefits and the premiums and extent of coverage vary with each. There will be yearly deductibles and co-pays.

There is also what is known as the "donut hole." You will be covered until your out-of-pocket expenses have reached $2,250. After that you will have no insurance coverage until your out-of-pocket has reached $3,600. Some policies, at an additional cost, will cover the "donut hole."

Medicare recommends that you sign up for Part D as soon as you turn 65, even if you are currently healthy. Prescriptions can help keep you that way. The longer you delay in signing up, the higher your premiums will be.

There are many insurance companies offering these plans with many options. Choice becomes something of a nightmare. (Recall the good old days when there were only Chocolate, Vanilla, and Strawberry, and, of course, only black or white coffee.) Go to www.medicare.gov and access its Prescription Drug Plan Finder. You can enter your specific needs and it will calculate your "Estimated Annual Cost," and then give you two or three plans to choose from and tell you how to contact them. Some good questions to ask:

- Can I buy the drug I want or must I try another drug first?
- Does the plan have to approve the drug before I buy it?
- Can I buy drugs through the mail? Can I use drug stores not in the network?
- What if I travel a lot?

In choosing a plan, think in terms of overall costs. Don't focus exclusively on premiums: the plan with the lowest premiums may be more costly when you consider out-of-pocket expenses.

Even with Part D, you're not home yet.

## Medigap Policies: Dental, Glasses, Hearing Aids

Neither Parts A nor B covers services not related to treatment of illness or injury, such as dental care or dentures, cosmetic surgery, routine foot care, hearing aids, eye exams, or glasses. Except for certain limited cases in Canada and Mexico, Medicare does not pay for treatment outside of the United States.

You can purchase Medigap policies, which cover some of these gaps and provide coverage for some of the co-payments and deductibles in the Medicare programs. Some even cover prescription drugs. In order to simplify purchasing and make it possible to make meaningful comparisons, the federal government restricts Medigap insurance plans to one of 13 basic policy benefit lists—your first step should probably be to figure out which plan type you want and need, and then to comparison shop among companies offering that plan.

## The HMO Alternative

Again, your two basic options:

1. Staying in Medicare program: Part A and B, a drug policy under Part D, and a possible Medigap policy.
2. Joining a Medicare HMO.

Health Maintenance Organizations are run by various insurance companies. The idea was to get private industry involved to drive down Medicare costs. This is currently controversial, the allegation being that HMOs take the healthy seniors while leaving the sick, and more expensive, to the traditional program. You can expect changes as Congress looks at the entire Medicare program.

Basically you assign your Part A and Part B benefits to the HMO. One big advantage of staying with the basic Medicare program is that you are free to choose your own physicians and other health care providers. Many HMOs, though not all, restrict your choices.

First talk to your current health care providers. If you go with an HMO, will you still be able to see them? If you go on straight Medicare, same question. Some physicians, due to the fact that Medicare is notorious in paying late, are refusing to see Medicare patients.

Next, figure out what coverage is important in terms of the drug benefit and the incidental benefits under a Medigap policy. How much will they cost? Armed with this information, you can approach the numerous HMOs . Ask their representatives to compare their drug coverage to what you could get under Part D and then ask for the same comparison of dental, hearing and vision coverage that you could get in a Medigap policy.

You will get a whole lot smarter.

# c. Help!

Most of us will need help, our eyes too tired to read scores of websites, our time too valuable to spend it figuring out, while reading long lists of what is covered, what is not.

There are insurance counseling programs, public presentations, and other resources available to those about to turn 65, older beneficiaries, and family members who are forced to make the choice for a Medicare recipient. There are great websites explaining much of this information—among the best of government websites is the one laid out by the Medicare program at www.medicare.gov. But for our money, the absolute best resource for your inquiry is your Area Agency on Aging. Every region of the country has one, and you can find yours by looking in your local telephone book or visiting the Administration on Aging's website at www.aoa.gov.

Unfortunately, you're still not covered for long-term care. But this chapter has been too long, too boring, as it is. But read on, no time to say "enough."

> .... *lay on, Macduff;*
> *And damn'd be him that first cries, "Hold, enough."*
>
> —Macbeth

# CHAPTER 12

# LONG-TERM CARE

Nursing homes have something of a bad rap, with images of folks zonked out in front of static TVs, drooling oatmeal. Not necessarily so, though the stereotypes do exist. There can be new friends to meet, games to play and, yes, even sex (we are, after all, talking about humans). Chapter 34 is devoted to nursing homes; here, paying for the freight.

Long-term care can bankrupt. Yearly costs can easily exceed $100,000 and stays of five years or more are possible. *Medicare* and *Medigap* policies will cover only a *small* portion of these costs. This is a particular problem for women, since men are more often cared for at home (by their women) and women live longer.

What to do?

Long-term care insurance is now available. And once a family has exhausted its own resources, *Medicaid* is available.

Note: If your family is currently paying large nursing home bills, they may be deductible from Federal Income Tax.

## a. Long-Term Care Insurance

This is a new and tricky area. Get advice. Do you need it? How much should you pay? What is the best policy for you? States regulate long-term insurance and have free or low-cost insurance counseling programs. To run down the one in your area, contact your Area Agency on Aging or call *Eldercare Locator* 1-800-677-1116

There is also *A Shopper's Guide to Long-Term Care Insurance* put out by the National Association of Insurance Commissions. It even has a worksheet and may be available at local libraries or at your Area Agency.

Long-term insurance may not be for you. Like all forms of insurance, it is a gamble. Maybe you will never go into a nursing home—most people never do. Estimates vary. A study in the *New England Journal of Medicine* projected that of those who turn 65 in 1990, 67% of men and 48% of women will never enter a nursing home. Of those who enter a nursing home, many will stay less than a year (45%) but a large number will have extended stays, more than five years (21%). Obviously these are simply educated guesses and your odds will depend on current health, family history, and luck.

You may be rich enough to be self-insured or poor enough not to care. The latter sounds a tad cruel, but the truth is that insurance in essence protects your estate from being devoured by nursing home costs before you turn to Medicaid. If you don't have a lot to protect, then insurance may not be needed. Put another way, the classic candidate for purchasing long-term care insurance is a middle-class individual (or couple).

Assuming you are in the market, the earlier you start, the lower the premium and the better the coverage. Also, if you wait until your 60s or 70s, a medical condition may lead the company to deny your application—they have that right.

On the other hand, any policy will be canceled if the premiums are not kept current. If you are buying a policy early, be sure you can afford it later. If not, you will forfeit your coverage. To give you some idea of costs, a policy today at age 55 is around $1600 per year—though even suggesting this figure is dangerously simplistic, since the extent of benefits, your health condition, the area of the country where you live, and the benefit restrictions you choose will all have a huge impact on the actual cost of your policy.

Other desirable features in such policies include:

- Protection against inflation—if the benefits remain constant and the cost of care doubles before you need it, you are in trouble.
- Coverage of all levels of nursing care (skilled, intermediate, custodial).
- Home and assisted care coverage—you don't want the policy to cover only your last choice. Most policies today will pay as much for home care as for care in the nursing home, though the actual costs of care in the home will probably be higher. Look for restrictions on who can provide the care in the home, or the effect of using the home care option on the remaining term of your coverage.
- Low deductibles and not too difficult prerequisites—such as hospitalization.
- At least one year maximum benefit period, preferably at least 3 years—and 5 years is better, particularly if you are expecting the policy to cover your care while your family waits out the Medicaid ineligibility period occasioned by transferring your assets (more on that later).
- Coverage of dementia, like Alzheimer's disease.
- A forgiving pre-existing conditions limit—no longer than six months.

# b. Safety Net of Medicaid; Medicaid Planning

Our worst nightmare: we wake up sick and alone, on a dirty city back street. *Medicaid* guards against that: you will not be thrown out of your home to wander the streets just because you are broke and need medical care.

In 1965, Congress passed Medicaid (known in California, in an apparent effort by state law makers to steal the credit, as *MediCal)*. This program is a safety net for the poor, providing a full range of benefits, from doctors' bills to hospitalization. It *will* pay for custodial (nursing home) care in some situations. (It is also driving most states broke; but that's another book.)

Live long enough, paying several thousand a month for nursing home care, and you may qualify. It is only available if you have insufficient resources to pay for your own care—though the government's definition of "insufficient" may not match your own. There is some state variation, but the general rules are federal: some assets will not be counted—usually your home, your car and most personal items. Your *spouse* may be obligated to pay for some of your care but he or she will not be left destitute: there are property and income exemptions. Your children are *not obligated* to pay. In most states, *children have no duty to support their parents*—talk about a one way street! (In other countries, and in earlier times in this country, children did have that obligation, and some state laws still address the concept, but are not generally enforced or enforceable.)

Rather than spending their life savings on nursing home care and hoping to leave their children a little something, some middle-class folks take steps to get themselves eligible for Medicaid if the need arises. This is known as *Medicaid Planning* and, as with triple bypass operations, should not be attempted at your kitchen table.

It entails shedding yourself of the assets and income which would make you ineligible; in other words, making yourself poor. The downside, of course, is that you will be poor.

You'll have to give most of your life savings away. They won't be there for an emergency, or, more hopefully, for a totally irresponsible fling. Most people give their assets to their kids, counting on them to bail them out if need be. But even if your kids are more grateful than two of Lear's daughters and drink less than Falstaff, *their* creditors can get what were *your* assets. How's the kids' driving?

To guard against all of this, you may decide to play it cagey: keep your savings until the very last minute. Alas, the Feds have seen you coming. Transfers you make within five years of seeking Medicaid assistance will delay your eligibility. Further, and it's our job to remind you of unpleasant possibilities, when the very last minute comes you may have lost your shrewdness … if you then lack legal capacity, you can no longer give away your stuff. To deal with this possibility, I recommend a durable power of attorney (Chapter 24). Add a provision, not included in most, that your financial agent can make gifts—otherwise your agent might not have the legal power to do so.

One step you can take without running the risks inherent in giving your savings away is to convert them into exempt assets. In lay terms, sell your stocks and buy a fancy house. (Of course this move has its own dangers: lack of liquidity, income stream, and possible growth.) The Feds have seen you coming here, as well—Medicaid rules now restrict the value of your home as an exempt asset, though the $500,000 limit can still buy a pretty fancy crib in most states. Warning: although having a home may not keep you off Medicaid, it may be that the state has a claim against your estate—including that house—when you die after receiving Medicaid benefits. The rules are complicated and getting more complicated, so you can begin to see why we strongly suggest you get professional help in this area.

Medicaid planning is tricky and is getting more so every year as Congress tries to close loopholes. Mistakes can be quite costly. Find a lawyer who specializes in the area. For a referral, contact the National Academy of Elder Law Attorneys. 1-520-881-4005 or www.naela.org.

One final concern: Will you get worse care if you are a Medicaid patient? Often Medicaid will choose the home and the doctor. In most cases (and in most states) Medicaid patients are cared for side-by-side with private-pay patients. Some even believe that you might get better care as a Medicaid patient as you will be assigned a case manager to oversee your care. One problem: as Medicaid costs increase and states find themselves more financially strapped by their share of the program's cost, their largesse may continue to shrink, and the quality of care may suffer in the future.

# CHAPTER 13

# TAX BREAKS FOR SENIORS

Taxes are certain ... and *certainly complicated*. Here we flag some tax benefits you may be overlooking. For specific questions:

Call the IRS. 1-800-829-1040 (Ed. note: Cute, "1040," very cute!)
http://www.irs.ustreas.gov

See an accountant. Fees paid for tax advice and help are *deductible*.

## a. If Your Children Are Supporting You

If your children are supplying more than one-half of your support, they may be entitled to significant tax breaks. They may be able to claim you as a dependent (and thus get an additional *dependency exemption),* and may also be able to claim head of household status (and thus increase their *standard deduction* as well as taking advantage of the *head-of-household* tax rate). Finally, if you have substantial medical expenses, they might be able to deduct some of them.

## b. Federal Tax Benefits

Let's define some terms and show their impact on your tax bill. *Deductions* reduce your taxable income. They reduce your tax bill, but not by the full amount: only by the amount that would have been taxed had the deduction been included. Assume you are paying taxes at the 28% level: a $700 deduction will translate into a tax savings of $196 (28% of $700).

*Exemptions* work the same way. If some of your income is exempt, it need not be reported and hence will not be taxed.

*Tax credits* are better (and rarer). They reduce taxes dollar for dollar: a tax credit of $500 would reduce your tax bill by $500.

What federal tax rules might be of most interest?

## Standard Deduction

Turning 65 entitles you to an additional amount if you are taking a standard deduction and *not itemizing* deductions. Additional amounts can be taken if the taxpayer is blind.

## Personal Exemptions

Regardless of age, every taxpayer is entitled to a personal exemption. In 2006, it was $3,300. This exemption is not increased at 65 nor for blindness. You can take this exemption whether you itemize or not.

## Medical Expense Deduction

If you have *significant* medical expenses for yourself, your spouse, or a dependent, some may be deductible. *You must itemize to take them.* Medical expenses not compensated by insurance are deductible *in excess of 7.5%* of adjusted gross income. This is the major limitation; most people never get up that high. When they do, only the amount over the 7.5% threshold is deductible.

And what counts toward that 7.5%?

- The costs of medical care including "diagnosis, care, mitigation, treatment, or prevention of diseases … affecting any structure or function of the body." This includes medicine, prescription drugs, medical transport, glasses, seeing-eye dogs, artificial teeth, and artificial limbs.
- The costs of *medically required home improvements,* prescribed by a physician, to the extent their cost exceeds the increased value they give the house. For example, if a $1,500 elevator or therapy pool increases the value of the home $600, then $900 would be counted as a medical expense. (The $600 would be added to the basis of your house and thus, when it is sold, would not represent a capital gain.)
- The costs of nursing homes can be included, but only if the primary reason was medical care, as opposed to custodial care. This is generally not a difficult deduction to make since medical care is arguably a major component of any nursing home stay.
- A portion of long-term care insurance premiums.

## Tax Credits Concerning Disability

A tax credit is available to folks 65 and older or those under 65 who are retired on permanent and total disability. The amount is 15% of the taxpayer's "section 22 amount" and its calculation defies easy description. Just be aware of it, discuss it with your accountant, or look for it on your 1040.

## Interest Deductions

Interest you pay on your home mortgage (and home equity loan) is deductible. Other kinds of interest payments, such as on credit cards or store accounts, are generally not deductible.

## Home Taxes

Many states give taxpayers over 65 a break on property taxes. In terms of federal taxes, if you are still paying for your house, that portion of your payment that represents interest payments continues to be deductible. The cost of home improvements is not deductible unless they were medically required (see the discussion of "medical expense deduction" above). However, keep records as to home improvements as their cost can be added to the amount you paid for your house to figure its basis. What this means is that if you sell your house for more than you paid for it, you can deduct from your gain the cost of home improvements. This is less important than it used to be in light of the next point.

## Capital Gain Taxes from the Sale of Your Residence

Since 1998, you can sell your home and pay no federal taxes on the first $250,000 of profit ($500,000 for married couples). This exemption requires that you have lived in the home for at least two of the prior five years.

## Reverse Mortgage Payments

In Chapter 9, we discussed how you might get cash out of your home's equity without selling it. The most popular way is the reverse mortgage. The monthly payments are not taxable as they are really loans to you.

## Exempt Income

Money you receive from certain sources or for certain reasons need not be included in your gross income. Here we list some of the most common:

*Inheritance and gifts.* This means that if you make a gift to your children, they do not declare it as income (and you do not get any income tax deduction). Income earned on the gift after it is made is taxed to the recipient.

*Compensation for physical injury or illness* through insurance, judgments, or Worker's Compensation.

*Public assistance benefits.*

*Interest on some government bonds.*

*Veterans' benefits.*

*Social Security.* Generally about 50% of your Social Security payments may be subject to taxation. The exact percentage will turn on the amount of other income you have.

Earnings on criminal activity are *not* exempt from income taxes. Al Capone learned this the hard way. This puts criminals in something of a bind. Report your income, the IRS turns you in and you get arrested. Don't report your income, the government need not show that you committed any specific crime, only that you had a lot of income and didn't report it. The IRS allows individuals to file returns, not with their names, but with a number. If they then get caught with large amounts of cash, they can point out that they were at least paying taxes on it.

# c. State and Local Taxes

Almost all states offer older citizens tax breaks in one or more areas: sales tax, income tax, or property tax. States may adopt the federal approach to some deductions, but not others. Because of the wide range of state approaches, we advise you to contact your accountant or the agency in your state that is responsible for collecting taxes.

# d. Taxes on Pensions, Annuities, and IRAs

*"Dollars will be taxed just once. But once for sure!"*

If the money you put into your retirement plan was tax deductible at the time of contribution, your retirement benefits will be treated as regular income when you receive it. Money going into most pension plans is deductible, as is money going into traditional IRAs. When the money comes out, it is taxed.

However, if the money that goes into the retirement plan was not tax deductible at the time, then when *that* money is returned to you, it is not taxed. This is because you already paid taxes on those dollars before they went into the retirement account. When you get the interest earned on those dollars, though, it is taxed as regular income.

To illustrate this, let's take the example of an annuity. Say you have $100,000 and don't want the trouble of investing it. You can buy an annuity. For your $100,000, a bank will promise to pay you a certain monthly amount over the next several years. Because it will have the use of your $100,000 from Day One, it will pay you interest. Assume that at the end of the annuity, it will have paid you $150,000. (Don't go to sleep!)

As to each payment, two-thirds will be return of capital (and not taxed), and one-third will be the interest earned (and taxable).

The new Roth IRA is a bright and shining exception to the rule "dollars will be taxed at least once." Money coming out of Roth IRAs that represents earnings on contributions is *not* taxed. See Chapter 8.

# PART 3

# TROUBLE: GETTING IN AND GETTING OUT

## THE LIMITS OF LAW: A CAUTIONARY TALE

Many of these chapters deal with family problems—raising grandchildren, financial dealings between family members, divorce and remarriage, and abuse and neglect.

Of course, there will be laws; there will always be laws. But lawyers may not be your best bet. Mediation and counseling may be.

Lawyers work best in a world of strangers, where they can snarl questions, point fingers, and stamp feet. When the dust settles, strangers pay up and walk away. Scars mend or are forgotten.

Kin *never* walk away; kin are for the long haul.

Lawyers are good in that small portion of the universe where people "start it"—where they run red lights, deliver defective widgets, and pull hair triggers. No one ever "starts it" in the family. Sure, Sis did hit us first, but in our hearts of hearts, we know we pushed her to it with our cruel taunts (which, of course, she richly deserved for what she said last week).

We are a society of *rights*. Individual rights are critical; without them, others would push us around and we would never be safe from bullies. *But a society based solely on rights is likely to fly apart.*

Long ago there was a great legal reform movement in China: the laws should be written down so people could know them.

Who could argue with that? The followers of Confucius. If people know their rights, they argued, they will *insist upon them*. They will no longer compromise nor consider the interests and needs of others. The center will not hold. Happy societies, and happy families, need compromise and compassion.

In fights with family members, and indeed with neighbors, the question is not who is right according to the law. The question is how the fight can be resolved so as to restore peace. Counselors and mediators, trained in conflict resolution, can help you redirect focus from what happened in the past to what will happen in the future, from casting blame to sharing credit.

On the other hand, many law schools now offer courses in mediation and many lawyers are quite good at it. Nothing wrong with getting a lawyer, but get a conciliator, not a snarler. Lawyers specializing in elder law are a good bet.

# Overview to Part 3

*"Baby isn't talking. I'm worried. It's been months. Not a single word. Not even 'Mama.' Something must be wrong! I'm calling Dr. Scott."*

*"But Dear, it's two in the morning"*

When our children were small, we turned to Dr. Spock. With *Baby and Child Care* on the night stand, we slept better. It got us through the tough times. We looked into the future—"The First 12 Weeks," "Teething," "The Terrible Twos"—and took comfort knowing that others had gone before. We learned when to phone the doctor, and when to go back to sleep.

This part gives you a heads up on trouble you or your family might face.

Chapter 14 deals with the *abuse* and *financial exploitation* of elders, how to recognize it and how to deal with it. We even have some advice for where abusers can get help. Abuse and exploitation are very serious matters—you must realize that your family is not immune.

Chapter 15 deals with a different kind of abuse, *self-abuse*, running off to Vegas or, depressed, committing suicide. In regard to that, we discuss the controversial issue of guns in the home.

The next two chapters discuss matters near and dear to us all, *sex* and *driving*. These are discussed separately because they should always *be* separate.

*Grandkids*, Chapter 18.

*Family loans* and *support obligations*, Chapter 19.

*Divorce* and *Remarriage* (in that order) Chapter 20.

Finally bad guys. First bigots who *discriminate* against you in employment and housing because of your age, disability, or cat. That's Chapter 21. Next, common *scams* and ways to protect your *identity*. The last chapter deals with recession blues: *foreclosures* and *bill collectors*.

Read the chapters that seem to apply to you now and be aware that they are there should the need arise at a later date. Like Spock. Once you learn that babies learn to talk at different times, you can skip *Talking, late* and go to *Parental Rejection, early.*

# CHAPTER 14

# ABUSE, NEGLECT, AND FINANCIAL EXPLOITATION

*Abuse gets <u>worse</u>, not better, more frequent, more severe. It does <u>not</u> self-correct—intervention is imperative.*

Most think of abuse as being *inflicted* on the victim and this is the topic of this chapter. However, much abuse is self-inflicted: mom flies off to Vegas with her life savings or dad buys a gun and seems depressed. We will look at self-inflicted abuse in the next chapter.

We approach inflicted abuse from three perspectives: from that of a concerned relative, from that of the victim, and from that of the abuser. How can relatives recognize and deal with abuse? How can victims protect themselves? How can abusers stop their destructive and criminal ways?

## a. Recognizing Abuse and Getting Victims Talking

Abuse comes in many forms: *physical abuse* (slapping, bruising, sexually molesting, restraining); *psychological abuse* (threatening, humiliating, ridiculing); *neglect* (abandonment, denial of food or health services); and *financial exploitation*.

Just because an elderly relative seems okay doesn't mean all is well. The signs of abuse are often hidden and those that do appear often go unnoticed. We're busy with our own lives. It is easy to accept cuts and bruises as being the result of falls; and it is easy to dismiss complaints as evidence of senility or the "natural grumpiness of old folks."

Abuse happens in the best families, abuse happens in the worst families; it happens on Boardwalk, and it happens on Baltic Avenue. Don't think your family is immune.

Most of the physical violence suffered by the elderly is inflicted by spouses, with husbands being the more frequent victims but wives the more severely injured. Frequently, the abuse is of *recent* origin. Retirement requires couples to work out whole new ways of living. Conflicts happen and old scores settled. Alcohol abuse becomes more common and frequently leads to physical abuse. If one spouse is disabled and the other becomes the care-giver, this adds extra strains. Caring for another is tough — see our suggestions in Chapter 33.

Given the prevalence of elder abuse, if you have a fragile relative, unless you *know* all is well, *suspect abuse.*

Look for *isolation* and *changes.*

*"Mildred's a little too tired to come to the phone just now."* Abusers keep victims isolated so no one knows what is happening, and so the victim becomes more dependent on the abuser. There are always excuses why Mildred can't be seen or heard. Abusers then turn victims against their relatives. *"Mildred, isn't it a shame your son never calls?"* Now Mildred feels more isolated and, if her son ever gets through, she will be less likely to confide in him.

Akin to isolation is the tactic of always speaking for the victim. *"Oh yes, Mildred has been doing much better on her new meds."*

Insist on visiting. Look for *changes.*

Unexpected or unexplained deterioration of health, bruises, burns, welts, cuts, punctures, sprains and broken bones; dehydration and weight loss; missing eyeglasses, hearing aids, or dentures. Abusers will explain these away as the results of falls or illnesses. Insist on details by asking them to explain exactly how and when things happened.

Insomnia, excessive sleep, and change in appetite may indicate depression and hopelessness due to *psychological abuse.* So too can tearfulness, paranoia, low self-esteem, excessive fears, ambivalence, confusion, resignation, or agitation.

As to financial exploitation, the sudden inability to pay bills, withdrawals of large amounts of cash, and living well below one's means, spell trouble. Children steal ("Well, I'll get the money later, anyway."); home-care workers steal. Others exploit the elderly in less criminal ways, often targeting those who live alone: home shopping channels offering companionship and political action committees offering protection from "gathering political storms."

Insist on looking at the checkbook. And even the checkbook is probably not enough — we have seen many, many cases of financial exploitation fueled by debit cards and cash withdrawal machines. If the senior doesn't know what an ATM is or where her card has gone, count it as a likely sign that something might be awry.

Other signs of abuse come, not from the victim, but from the care-giver. Is the care-giver drinking? Depressed? Resentful? Overworked? Or, alas, driving a new car? All of these may point to something amiss.

Why all this Sherlock Holmes stuff? Why not simply ask? Victims aren't likely to talk because they are scared or because they believe nothing can be done. Most often, the abuser has convinced the victim that they will be institutionalized if anyone acts to end the relationship, or that they will be physically injured by the abuser. To get the victim talking, first address those fears.

- *"I'm concerned that someone may be mistreating you. I know this is very hard for you to talk about. Before we get started, let me tell you a few things that might address some of your fears."*
- *"People who are abused often blame themselves, think it is somehow their fault, that they deserve it, or that it shows that they can no longer run their lives, that they are getting senile. Abuse is found in all kinds of families and it's not your fault. I won't think less of you no matter what you tell me."*
- *"Maybe you think I'll call the police and you don't want the person to go to jail. I promise not to call the police if you don't want me to."*

Usually you can keep this promise—though whether you really want to may be another matter altogether. There is generally no obligation to report crime. Some folks, however, are required to report: for example, the person's legal guardian, medical provider, or social worker. In many states, medical, legal, and mental health professionals must report physical abuse, not to police, but to a designated agency, most likely Adult Protective Services. Even if you report, unless the victim presses charges, police will not arrest the abuser, except in the case of extreme physical abuse. But you should feel a general obligation to the human community to not only punish abusers, but also to prevent them from acting again.

*"Another fear is that the person abusing you is your care-giver. If you tell, what will happen to you?"*

This is the tough one. But there are solutions. Perhaps the abuser is just overworked and help can be found. Alternative living arrangements are possible.

*"If you tell me, you might be afraid of getting beat up. There are ways to protect you."*

Short-term shelters are available, as well as the option of hospitalization. Many jurisdictions allow for easy-to-obtain domestic court orders of protection which will prohibit the abuser from coming to the victim's home. Locks can be changed.

Once you have addressed the victim's fear of talking, you still must convince the victim that it is in his or her interest to talk.

> *"Abuse gets worse, not better. Even if the person has promised never to do it again. There is help available for you and the person mistreating you. I want to help you. I can't, unless you tell me what's going on."*

There is one matter that is very difficult to raise, not only for you, but for us—we don't want you to throw this book across the room. Abuse is not always a one-way street, not always a black and white affair. Some victims trigger abuse by being too demanding, too sarcastic, too unappreciative. How can this be so? Because there may be payoffs for the victim, a sense of vindication when the abuser stumbles, falls, strikes out, and then, on bended knee and with flowers, seeks forgiveness. Such are humans.

As you work towards a possible solution with the victim, consider:

> *"Is there anything you might be doing that triggers the abuse? Sometimes victims stay in bad situations because they get something from them, like flowers and apologies. Anything like that going on with you?"*

Once the victim opens up and starts talking, you can begin working out a solution.

Often it will involve helping the person take steps themselves and we make some suggestions in the section "Self-help for Victims." But what if the person can't act for themselves due to mental impairment?

## b. Helping Helpless Victims

If the victim is mentally impaired and hence unable to protect themselves, emergency *guardianships* can be sought to remove the victim from an abusive situation. Emergency *conservatorships* can be sought to freeze assets to protect against financial exploitation. The mechanics of these are discussed in Chapter 30.

If the individual is in a *nursing* home, the best way to prevent abuse is simply to stay involved. Visit often and at different times of day. Ask questions of nurses and doctors. Periodically ask to review the person's chart. Under the

Nursing Home Bill of Rights, as the patient's representative, you have the right to examine current clinical records (within 24 hours after request) and to make copies of them. Discuss concerns with the staff and try to find solutions together. You are all working toward the same goal.

If problems continue or get worse, report them to the administration, and to any federal or state agency that oversees the home. Signs should be posted in the nursing home as to how to file a complaint and how to contact these agencies. See Chapter 34 for more on nursing homes.

There is a soft form of financial exploitation worth mentioning. A good friend works for the Public Fiduciary's office and part of her job is to visit the homes of seniors living alone. She often notices two things, piles of unopened merchandise from *home shopping TV channels* and piles of letters from *political action committees,* all predicting the certain fall of Western Civilization unless a contribution is made *immediately.*

Lonely folks want to talk. Home shopping channels not only *seem* to talk to you but they *do* talk to you—if you simply phone in and buy. If you find that a vulnerable relative has fallen into this pattern, call the station, point out that the person doesn't have contractual capacity (probably true) and will pay for no further orders.

As to political action committees, and others seeking "what you can afford" for a host of good causes, the best you can do is to point out that Chicken Little was wrong.

# c. Self-Help for Victims

If you are a victim of abuse and are like most other victims, you just take it. You are isolated, feel guilty, and do nothing. You feel both helpless and hopeless.

The abuser wants to keep you isolated, wants to keep you quiet. Your friends and relatives will be discouraged from visiting and you will be told that they don't visit because they don't care. Trips out become less frequent and those that occur are always with the abuser in attendance.

You'll need an ally. Someone outside. You need a plan.

But guilt may stay the effort. "Being abused is my fault. It shows how weak and senile I am. I deserve it." Fear of the future stays the effort. "If I say anything, things will go worse. Where will I live? Who will care for me?"

There are no easy answers and perhaps no happy endings, only improvements. Doing nothing means that the abuse will get worse, not better. That is the clinical history of abuse.

- Taking action to protect yourself does not mean that the person will be arrested. *Unless you file a criminal complaint,* only in extreme cases of abuse will the police arrest the person.
- The abuser may get help. Abuse may stem from overwork or lack of knowledge about community services that are available. These can be remedied. Counseling may address other problems.
- If you have no place to go, there are emergency shelters at secret locations. Friends and relatives can also offer shelter. To get help, call police, your Area Agency on Aging, or the Information and Referral Agency.

Where to find an ally? In emergencies, use 911. Talk to your doctor or lawyer. Call a relative. Information and Referral will have other sources of help. Most locales have Adult Protective Services which specializes in protecting the elderly. Again, the national clearing house: 1-800-677-1116.

## Coping with Spouse Abuse: Protective Orders

The law has been moving quickly to deal with spouse abuse. Local police are being trained to be more sensitive and are less likely to treat abuse lightly. In most jurisdictions, it is possible for a battered spouse (not always the wife) to go to court, fill out a simple form, and get a court order which will require the aggressor to stay away. There is no need to get a lawyer. You can get a protective order even if the person lives in the same house; he or she will have to move out. If the abuser shows up, they can be arrested for *violating* the order; they need not do anything more in terms of threats or abuse.

## Abuse by Adult Children

It is very difficult to admit that your children are abusing you. Yet it happens. Physical is easier to recognize than financial. Most mental health hospitals have closed, and now many mentally ill live with their parents. Their continuing dependent relationship may fire violence and abuse.

It is easier *not* to let children move back in than it is getting them out. If they have moved in, you have the legal right to have them removed. Call police and change the locks. Protective orders, like those against spouses, are likely to be available.

Financial abuse is common as well. Children may seek a guardianship over you, not to protect you, but to protect their inheritance. Even if they don't have a formal guardianship, if they manage your finances, they may do so at your expense. It may be, for example, best for you to move into an assisted living facility, but your child will discourage that in order to save money. Again, the main block to doing something about this is making the painful realization that your child, the child you raised, is stealing from you.

## Financial Exploitation

Dishonest children, friends, or nurses may simply forge your name to checks or, on their way to the bank to deposit your checks in your account, suddenly see a better alternative.

*Get hold of your monthly bank statement.* Check to see if all deposits were made and whether any of the returned checks have been forged. If you report a forgery within 30 days of receiving your statement, the bank *must* make it good; otherwise, probably not.

If your bank statement is missing, bells should go off. Dishonest relatives may have stolen it. If you suddenly stop getting your bank statement, check with the bank as to when it was sent. Duplicates can usually be sent, although it takes time.

If you are under guardianship, you have the right to demand an accounting of your financial affairs. Contact an attorney.

## Nursing Home Abuse

Nursing homes that receive Medicare or Medicaid funds (and most do) must comply with the Nursing Home Bill of Rights. Your most important rights include:

- The right to be free of physical or drug restraints unless needed to protect you or other residents and only then upon the written order of a physician.
- The right to receive and send unopened and uncensored mail.
- The right to reasonable access to a phone and to make calls in private.

Area Councils on Aging maintain an office of Ombudsman to take and investigate nursing home complaints.

# d. Help for Abusers

Abusers, like everyone, including Darth Vader, like to think highly of themselves and hence construct a world view that makes whatever they do, if not noble, at least justified; if not innocent, at most "guilty with an explanation."

If you are a caregiver, ask yourself, "If I were the patient, would I like being treated the way I am treating them?"

If you are an abuser, the first step is to 'fess up. You're a criminal.

The following are *not* defenses to a criminal charge:

- the victim was hard to deal with;
- the victim abused you in the past; or
- the money, down the road, would have been yours, anyway.

Abuse is hard to self-correct; the natural course of abuse is downward, toward greater frequency and severity.

*Confront* the fact that you are abusing someone. It is easy to lie to yourself. Ask the cause and *seek help* dealing with it.

Read our discussion on caring for others (Chapter 33). It offers tips on how to cope with caring for the elderly. It is a very tough job. Frustrations and lack of sleep can lead to abuse. But there are several sources of help.

## Alcoholism and Drug Abuse

> *A police officer friend, who has responded to over 300 cases of domestic violence, reports that all but one involved alcohol. All but one.*

Alcohol gets more toxic as we age. Our bodies lose the ability to process it. We may slip into alcoholism or drug abuse and these conditions may trigger us to abuse others. Programs are available, such as Alcoholics Anonymous (AA). Many AA chapters are exclusively for seniors.

## Psychological Resentments

Abusers are often financially dependent upon their victims and, resenting that dependency, resort to abuse. Sometimes spouses, over the years, begin to resent each other. Counseling may help. Separation, and even divorce, are possible solutions.

# CHAPTER 15

# Self-Abuse: Vegas, Booze, and the Question of Guns

Some of us don't age gracefully, burning their candles at both ends, running through life savings, buying extravagant items, taking weird trips, falling victim to various charlatans. Others fall to abuse alcohol and still others contemplate suicide. The presence of handguns in the home no doubt contributes to the high suicide rate among seniors. We close this chapter discussing that issue.

We know you are alive, kicking, and aging gracefully. Reading this book is a sure sign. However, you may know someone who isn't: this chapter suggests what you might do to help.

## a. Flying to Vegas

If a loved one suddenly begins to waste money, a conservatorship (in some states, "guardianship of the estate" or even, as in Louisiana, a "curatorship") can be sought on an emergency basis. The appointed conservator will take charge of the person's finances—bank accounts, property, stocks. See Chapter 31. Before that, banks, credit card companies, and financial institutions can be notified.

The rub: what looks like reckless to you may not look that way to the "victim." It may look like sowing one's oats. Say your aunt is giving the gardener money and is taking him on weekend trips to Las Vegas. Unless she no longer has legal capacity or unless he is putting undue pressure on her, she is free to spend her money any way she wants—even if it means *you* won't be getting any.

> *My candle burns at both ends;*
> *It will not last the night;*
> *But ah, my foes, and oh, my friends—*
> *It gives a lovely light!*
>
> —Edna St. Vincent Millay, *A Few Figs from Thistles*

Read the chapter on deciding for others, which gives some ideas on how to filter out self-interest and allow for lovely light. (Chapter 32)

## b. Booze, Depression, and Suicide

Alcoholism is a serious problem, especially drinking of recent origin. Interventions are possible. A group of friends and relatives show up to confront the individual, not only with the harm drinking causes the person, but how it harms *them*. "You know, your grandchildren used to love coming over here; now I can't bring them." Interventions are intense and often effective. Local AA programs can help.

Suicide. The elderly lead all age categories in suicides; white males lead the pack. In our discussion of Oregon's Death with Dignity Act (Chapter 36, allowing physicians to prescribe lethal medicine), we indicated that sometimes suicide might be a rational choice. Our concern here is with the hasty choice, fired by depression and perhaps alcohol. Another concern is with self-neglect: not caring for one's basic needs.

Depression fuels both. Dealing with depression is very difficult. Begin by discussing the situation with your physician. In extreme cases, consider *civil commitment*. Under most state laws, mentally ill individuals who present a danger to themselves (not eating, threatening suicide) or to others (not careful with fire), can be taken into emergency custody and, after a hearing, committed to a mental hospital for treatment. The length of the commitment and the procedures vary according to state statute. Contact Adult Protective Services.

## c. Guns

Handguns, not rifles, are the weapon of choice in elderly suicides. Guns don't require much planning: they are quick, easy, and the stuff of momentary despair. Further, guns in the house, at the time of a heated argument, often prove lethal. Murder/suicides are the stuff of daily newspapers. Much of physical violence committed on the elderly is committed by spouses; often that violence is of recent origin. The fact that a couple is quite happy today does not mean that there will not be violence tomorrow. The lurking threat of domestic violence suggests that the presence of weapons is a very bad idea.

But what about self-defense? The presence of guns, rather than affording protection, may make things worse. With guns drawn, stakes are definitely raised and home invaders may simply disarm, and then shoot, their victim.

Gun critics, however, overlook the peace of mind having a gun may bring. An elderly couple with a gun in their home may not be safer but they *feel* safer and live less fearful lives. As home invasions and suicides are rare, the psychic benefits of gun ownership may outweigh the risks.

If you are going to have a gun, first don't advertise that you do with signs like "These Premises Protected by Smith and Wesson." This will just draw gun thieves. Second, realize the dangers guns present: suicide and family violence. These may not seem like possibilities now, not in your family, but they never do. Make it hard to use the gun in moments of blind rage or deep depression. Keeping the gun unloaded, keeping it locked up, and having trigger locks are possibilities.

If you have grandkids, keep the gun locked and know the state law on gun ownership. If the law permits you to carry a gun in your car, if you are stopped by police, with your hands on the wheel, immediately tell the officer that you have a gun in the car.

Learn how to use your gun. Take shooting lessons, to learn gun safety and to realize their lethal power. Some make shooting clubs a social focus.

Finally, consider a rifle, not a handgun. Rifles are less likely to be used in suicide or in domestic violence and they offer good protection. Possibly even better: shotguns. You don't have to be a good aim with a shotgun (as a Vice President once discovered). The buckshot spreads after leaving the barrel. And, we are told, nothing is quite as unnerving to a burglar as the sharp sound of a shotgun being cocked.

# CHAPTER 16

# SEX

*"George is hot stuff here in the nursing home. The ladies love him, fight over him. He can dance ... and he has his teeth."*

This is not a product placement, paid for by the dental floss industry (unfortunately). Nor is it a ploy to increase book sales by appealing to prurient interests. Sex is serious.

When we first learned about "it," it was inconceivable that our parents did "it," at least more than once. As for our grandparents, not thinkable. But they did, probably frequently.

We report, you decide.

While looks and stamina fade, sex hangs in there. A study of healthy people, aged from 80 to 102, found that 88% of men and 72% of women have sexual fantasies. Furthermore, 72% of men and 40% of women engage in self-stimulation and 66% of men and 38% of women continue to have sexual intercourse. This last stat may puzzle the careful reader. It seems to suggest that many more men are having sexual intercourse than women. How can that be? Perhaps strange things happen as we age, women become floozies, men become gay. Probably not. Recall that at this age there are many more women than men; if the same number engage in intercourse, it would result in a lower percentage of women than of men. Do the math.

Sex is always more than sex. For the elderly it is a statement of continued involvement with life, a source of emotional support, and a validation of self-worth. It may not even result in orgasms. It can be simply caresses and gentle touching. Self-help manuals abound, and many describe techniques and approaches to sex that are more elder-friendly.

The law of sex is pretty straightforward. Competent adults, in privacy, can do what they want. Recently the Supreme Court underscored that right by striking down a Texas statute that criminalized gay sex, holding that it violated the Due Process Right of privacy.

On the other hand, forced sex is criminal. (We don't call it "rape" anymore; we call it "sexual assault.") "No" means "no" and sometimes "yes" means "no" as well. Consent obtained by threats, tricks, or force, is not consent. Nor is the "consent" given by someone legally unable to consent, children under the age of 16 or 18, and mentally impaired adults. "Impaired" means something like "unable to understand the nature or consequence of the sexual act," rather than what their prudish adult children might prefer.

Forced sex, in addition to being a crime, is a tort. This means that the perpetrator can be sued for money damages. Not only can the perpetrator be sued, but so too anyone who had a duty to protect the victim but didn't.

All of this straightforward law pretty much means a headache for the administrators of George's nursing home. He and the ladies who fight over him have a right to do what they wish and a nursing home that attempts to prevent that is demeaning their personhood. (It would *not* be acting unconstitutionally as the Constitution limits only governmental actors, not private.) However, the picture changes if George is forcing himself on the ladies or if he is having sex with women who, due to dementia, do not have the legal capacity to consent, no matter what they say or do. In these two cases, George is guilty of sexual assault and the nursing home, under a duty to protect its residents, may be sued.

How nursing homes handle the situation varies a great deal. Many have no formal policies, handling the matters case-by-case. All will attempt to prevent non-consensual sex and some will tell family members if a resident is engaging in consensual sex. Some nursing homes, recognizing therapeutic goods flowing from relationships, openly discuss geriatric sex. If you are considering a nursing home, for you or your parents, you might want to inquire.

Sex is not just a concern of nursing homes. Fragile elders can be sexually abused by home-care providers and, as we discuss in our chapter on Elder Abuse, one should be sensitive to this possibility. Like its counterparts—teen sex, young adult sex, middle-age sex—elder sex can lead us into doing foolish and destructive things. In our chapter on Self Abuse, we discuss the "Vegas Fling Problem."

What about STD (sexually transmitted disease)?

Yep.

Same advice one gives to everyone. Know your partner. Engage in safe sex. Use protection. And, if things go south (that metaphor probably is ill advised here), fess up to your doctor and get a shot.

Finally, knowing of our continued interest in sex, crooks will attempt to exploit it. One scam involves sending false bills to grieving widows, claiming that pornographic material was sent to their husbands. If you are male and frequent the internet, no doubt you get scads of daily emails offering Viagra and other sex aids. Best to talk to your doctor. Many of these medications will interact badly with your current meds; others will kill you outright. (These email scammers should realize that men our age will not spring for penis enhancement, having made our peace long ago.)

Have you ever told your parents a dirty joke? Despite the bravado of the Sixties, sex remains taboo. Get over it. Just as your parents once told you of the birds and bees, tell them now that *you* know that they continue to sing and buzz.

Buzz.

# CHAPTER 17

# DRIVING

*"You might as well shoot me," said a nurse when told she could no longer drive. "It's like telling a patient they have terminal cancer."*

Well, not quite. But still, having to stop driving is a horrible passage. Driving was the mark of adulthood; when we first got behind the wheel, we became the master of our own fate. Giving up driving signals a loss of independence, vitality, and control.

But it's not just symbolic. There are very practical issues at stake. Many of us live far from shopping and far from the center of our social lives: churches, movies, restaurants, friends' homes, social clubs. Public transport is often infrequent, scary, and difficult to access if you are in any way disabled. Even where local authorities offer special vans for the elderly, the picture is not bright. Often this transportation is only for the necessities (shopping and medical) and not for visiting, not for concerts. Even if your community has an efficient and adequately-funded public transportation system (and few do), the wait for a ride can seem interminable, the equipment shabby and even threatening, and the availability sporadic.

Loss of transportation has more than a purely psychic effect. For the senior without wheels, life can become afternoon TV and a quick decline into depression and illness.

Driving entails danger to the driver and others. Drivers over 75 have more fatal accidents than any other age group save teenagers. Even younger senior drivers may be more dangerous—though they have fewer accidents than their younger peers, that statistic is skewed by the fact that they drive far fewer miles. Add a little dementia and elderly drivers are 7.5 times more likely to crash, exceeding the rate of even drunk drivers.

Why are the elderly bad drivers? First, a higher incident of sudden illness, strokes and heart attacks. Second, impaired vision, particularly night vision. Third, slower reaction time. Dementia adds two additional problems: forgetting one has those impairments and suddenly getting confused about where one is.

First, the legal issues: who is liable? If you negligently cause property damage, personal injury or death, you're stuck, perhaps for very big bucks. It is no defense that you never had a ticket before. It is no defense that you have bad night vision or slow reaction time due to a disability. (Driving with these conditions simply makes you more negligent; however a sudden and unexpected medical emergency, such as a stroke, might be a defense.)

If a judgment against you exceeds your insurance coverage, the person you injured can come after your life savings. It is no defense that you need them to support yourself in your retirement: you're to go on welfare, not the person you injured.

You may be putting others at legal risk as well. For example, if you convince your daughter to loan you her car, a plaintiff might sue her on the theory that, knowing your condition, she was negligent in doing so. If you are under guardianship, your guardian may be liable for not taking preventive steps.

But, no matter our relationship, we don't want the driver to be killed or to kill others. What to do? A family conversation, before the issue becomes pressing, helps. An agreement can be made and signed: "I agree that I will accept the decision of Dr. Kildare, my attending physician, or my younger sister, when either of them writes to me that they think I am no longer a safe driver."

Once bad driving becomes an issue, check for correctable causes. The AARP offers a refresher course ("55 Alive"). It stresses defensive driving. Commercial driving instruction companies do as well. While these courses certainly cannot hurt, and may help individual drivers, there is (sadly) little evidence that the functional driving abilities lost with normal aging can be compensated for by training, even specialized training.

Special equipment is also available, such as rear mirrors that provide a wider view of the road. Cars and vans can be outfitted to cope with many disabilities.

Certain medications can affect driving ability. Check with the doctor or pharmacist. Trip planning helps. Avoid rush hour, left turns, and frequent trips. Co-pilots help. If the driving doesn't improve:

> *"Mom, I'm worried about your driving. You don't want to get in an accident. I know you think you are fine. You are probably right. But I want you to take a driving test."*

Most State Departments of Motor Vehicles will conduct field driving tests to confirm or reject your fears. Private evaluators are also available, and the screening may even be covered by Medicare.

Talk to Mom's physician. If necessary, the physician can play the heavy (not you) and pull the plug on driving. Remember, though, that simply suspending the driver's license will not stop every driver.

If Mom is Irish—or for some other reason strong-headed—take off the plates, hide the keys, or disable the car by disconnecting the spark plugs. If your Mom's 100% Irish, she will call a mechanic to fix the disabling condition. Leave an explanation where the mechanic (but not Mom) will find it. Most often, redirection is the best approach—when Mom heads for the car you interrupt her train of thought, interpose a new and different task, and deflect both the threat of driving and the frustration and anger that will come from a failed attempt.

The good news about all of this is that there are a growing number of programs that provide stranded seniors transport. In some locales, there are programs where the family car is donated to the agency which in turn provides taxi services. There is a national movement fostering what is known as Supplemental Transportation Programs (STPs). They are run by local governments, churches and non-profits. The Area Agency should have information on them. A prime mover in the movement is the Beverly Foundation and information can be found at www.beverlyfoundation.org.

If you are retired, still a good driver, and still love it as much as you did as a teenager, these programs can always use volunteers. But no peeling out!

# CHAPTER 18

# GRANDCHILDREN

*After all the years, the work, the bruises, the alarm clocks, after all our successes and failures, it has finally become our turn, our turn to be that quiet old lady, sitting with our grandchildren, whispering "Hush."*

Well, maybe not.

Some grandparents not only put their grandkids to bed, they wake them in the morning, feed them, get them off to school, and help them with their homework. Usually this is because of divorce, unwed or too-young motherhood, parental incarceration or illness, and/or drug abuse. At the other end of the spectrum, some families are so fractured that grandparents are not allowed to visit. Tolstoy was right: every unhappy family is unhappy in its own way.

This chapter will look at the legal steps you can take in both situations, if you are raising your grandkids or if you are denied visitation rights. We also cover the situation where you are simply caring for the kids during the summer.

## a. Raising Grandchildren: Legal Issues

You have joined a growing number. The AARP is on it! Its "Grandparent Information Center" (GIC) offers information on raising grandkids and step-grandparenting, message boards, and referrals. There is even a free newsletter, available in English and Spanish. Email: gic@aarp.org or phone 1-888-OUR-ARRP. Another source of help: *Generations United*: www.gu.org.

The legal issues usually revolve around custody, financial support, inheritance, and, sometimes, housing.

## Custody

Physical custody does not equal legal custody. Not having legal custody can lead to problems—doctors may insist on a parent's consent to a medical treatment, and school and welfare officials might also require it. If the child's stay with you is to be temporary, say over the summer or until the parents can relocate, then a *Parental Power of Attorney* should suffice in most states. Signed by the child's parent, it will give you power to act in the parent's stead in relation to medical and educational decisions. Even a letter, signed by one parent, is better than nothing:

> *To whom it may concern:*
> *I am the parent of* _____ *who will be staying with her grand-*
> *parents,* _____, *this summer. I give them the right to consent to*
> *any and all medical treatment for my child, and to exercise parental con-*
> *trol on my behalf.*
> *Signed (and better still, notarized)*

Things become much more complicated if your grandchildren are living with you more or less permanently.

> *Sally, 22 and unwed, leaves her six-month-old baby with her parents*
> *"until she can work things out." She has an irregular work history, a*
> *minor drug problem, and a scuzzy boyfriend. Two weeks ago she went*
> *out for a pack of cigarettes; other than one collect phone call from Okla-*
> *homa, she hasn't been heard from since.*

What to do? *Consider adopting.*

Unless you have legal custody, Sally can suddenly reappear and pick up the child, insisting "This time I will make a go of it." Often, revolving doors. Young children need love and *permanence.* A general Power of Attorney does not guarantee permanence. It can always be revoked by the parent—or even by the *other* parent. Without legal custody, both you and the children will be hostage to the whims of the parents, and you already know how dysfunctional they are.

If you adopt and the parent gets her act together, you can return physical custody to her. Without adoption, however, it is her choice; with adoption, it is *yours.*

Parents can agree to adoption. The father will have to be notified. If he is unknown, publication in the local newspapers will probably be required. The father, married or not, responsible or not, probably has a stronger legal claim to his child than do grandparents. A good adoption lawyer can tell you what your state laws require to show abandonment by either parent; expect that it will be a higher standard than what you personally think constitutes abandonment.

If the parents do not consent, you have some options. Some states allow for *permanent guardianships.* They do not sever parental rights but would protect you and the children.

Another route is a *dependency* action. These are usually instituted by the state, but some states allow for private actions. Briefly, child welfare officials seek a court order declaring the children to be *dependent.* If a court determines a child to be neglected or abused by his parents, the legal custody of the child will be transferred to child protective services. The child will then be placed in a home and, as grandparents, you're probably first in line. Meanwhile, the parents will have parenting and, most likely, drug counseling. If they eventually get their act together they can regain custody. If they do not, the court can sever parental rights and put the child up for adoption.

If you adopt, you have all the rights and obligations of a parent, including the legal duty to *support* the child until he or she reaches the age of 18 or is emancipated. In some states, for low income individuals and/or special-needs children, an adoption subsidy is available to help offset some of the expenses of raising your newly-adopted child.

## Financial Help

Adopted children are entitled to your Social Security benefits just like other children. That may mean that your under-18 adopted child receives a monthly check for a fraction of your Social Security (see Chapter 5). Even without adoption, however, your dependent grandchildren (over 18 if disabled) may be entitled to benefits. The rules are complicated, so call your Social Security Office and explain your situation to them.

Adoption support payments may be available for low-income families. If the child is placed with you by the court as part of a dependency action, you will receive financial help. Special assistance programs may exist if your grandchild has a disability.

You might be able to run down other sources of financial help by contacting your local welfare office or Area Agency on Aging. Welfare and other programs may be available even if you do not have legal custody.

Check with the IRS concerning whether you can claim a child as your dependent, and look into the *Earned Income Tax Credit* (EIC), which is a special benefit for low- and moderate-income people, including those raising grandchildren even if they don't have legal custody. This program provides a cash payment even if you don't owe taxes.

*Note:* If you are raising your grandchild under a court order as a foster parent, you may be entitled to federal payments for foster care under Title *IV-E* of the Social Security Act. These payments are substantially higher than welfare payments.

## Inheritance

If you die without a will, your children, not your grandchildren, will get what you have. Even if you have adopted your grandchildren, they will split the goodies with your other children—their parents. If you don't want either to happen, you need a will and a lawyer. Since you now have adopted children who are too young to manage money, you might want to consider having a trust (see Chapter 27).

## Housing

Some "adult" communities prohibit kids. It's best to try to work things out with whoever is in charge. Realize you have some bargaining chips: it costs money to evict and the house may remain vacant; further, no one (save some autocratic Homeowners Associations we know) wants to play the part of Darth Vader and throw kids out on the street. Some state statutes prohibit discrimination against children and, even where they don't, a good lawyer might be able to convince the court to adopt a common law rule to that effect.

# b. Grandparent Visitation Rights

*Lawyers are wonderful. On a TV call-in show, a lawyer is asked, "Do grandparents have any visitation rights?"*
*"No, absolutely none. Zilch. Nada."*
*They went to station break and another lawyer told the first, "Grandparents do have visitation rights. There is a state statute."*
*After the break, the first lawyer jumped before the camera. "In case anyone misinterpreted what I said before...."(Why don't you folks like us?)*

Since the 1970s there has been a major change in grandparent visitation rights. The law previously allowed parents the absolute right to refuse visits; grandparents were at their whim. Now all 50 states allow grandparents to *petition* the court for visitation rights.

The right to petition doesn't mean you will win. Courts are reluctant to get involved in family disputes, and under the laws of most states, grandparents cannot obtain visitation rights if the nuclear family is intact—that is, if the biological parents are still together and both agree on denying visits.

The U.S. Supreme Court has even weighed in on this question. In its own inimitable way, it has confused the issue rather than clarified it. If you have a concern about visitation, you have probably heard of the case *Troxel v. Granville*, decided in 2000. Lawyers are still arguing about what it means, and state courts and legislatures continue to adjust their laws to comply with their best reading of the case. Suffice it to say that the state of the law is in flux: grandparents may have significant rights to visitation under state law, but it may be difficult to enforce those rights under Constitutional and common-law principles. Rather than starting with your legal rights, you might want to begin with practical ideas about how to cure your separation from your grandchildren.

If you are denied visitation, first try to figure out why. Maybe the parents think you are too critical or gossip too much. Perhaps there are old family issues that have not been resolved. Don't just assume that you are in the right and threaten lawsuits.

*If you were the child's parent, why would you be denying visitation? Is there anything you can do to make things right?*

Getting court-ordered visitation rights will be an uphill fight. State grandparent visitation laws differ, but usually require a showing of three things: that visitation is in the *best interests of the child;* that the family situation is *dysfunctional* in certain defined ways, such as a divorce or unreasonable refusal of visitation over several months; and that the prior relationship between the grandparent and grandchild was significant before the parents began limiting or denying visitation. Usually the refusal of visitation rights must be total, not partial. If both parents in an intact family refuse you visitation rights, it is much less likely that you would prevail.

If your grandchild is adopted by strangers, or by other family members with whom you do not get along well, what happens to your visitation rights? Courts struggle. There is a strong argument that there should be a clear break between the birth and adoptive families: grandparent visitation may undermine the authority of the adoptive parents. On the other hand, there is a strong argument that the significant relationships in a child's life should continue.

The general rule, however, favors the adoptive parents. This is clearest when the child is quite young, when neither the child nor the grandparents have formed strong emotional ties. This is less definite in the case of older children, where close ties with grandparents exist. Some courts, notably those in California and New York, have ordered grandparent visits even in the face of adoption by strangers. Given these exceptions, and a general movement away from secrecy and toward "open adoptions," if you are about to lose your grandchild in an adoption, talk with an attorney.

# c. When to Seek Legal Help

- If you suspect your grandchild is being *abused* or *neglected*, contact Child Protective Services. They will investigate and all reports are confidential.
- If your grandkids will be *staying* an extended period with you, contact a lawyer to make sure you have the proper documents to seek medical and dental treatment for them or to enroll them in school. If their stay is triggered by their parent's involvement with crime or drugs, consider adoption.
- If either of your grandchild's parents dies.

When one parent dies, the survivor automatically assumes legal and physical custody of the child, even if there has been a prior divorce which gave custody to the other parent. (This is not necessarily so in the case of an unwed father who has not been determined legally to be the father, and especially if he has not contributed support.) If the *second* parent dies, the Probate Court will probably appoint a guardian for the child (otherwise there will be no guardian). Usually, but not always, the court will follow the wishes of the second parent to die as described in his or her Will. *Encourage* your children to nominate guardians in the event of their death. This will likely avoid fights between sets of grandparents or others.

- Pending divorce of the parents.

If your child is likely to lose custody, your visitation rights may be threatened. Whether or not you can intervene at this stage will depend upon state law.

- Dysfunction in the Family.

Dysfunction comes in many forms: an arrest of a parent or child; drug abuse and alcoholism in the family; the filing of a dependency petition filed against the parents alleging neglect or abuse; or the placement of the child for adoption. To what degree you have the legal right to intervene in such situations will vary: the point is that because so much is riding on the outcome of these situations, find out.

All of these situations involve heartache, anger, and fights. Consider, every now and then, in the heat of battle, sitting in a quiet corner, whispering "Hush."

# CHAPTER 19

# FAMILY FINANCIAL DEALINGS

*Law schools use the "case method." Students learn the law by tearing apart appellate cases, "What else could the plaintiff have argued?" "Should the defendant have used collateral estoppel?" The emphasis is on winning and, after three long years, students come away with the notion that humans are only interested in winning, getting more money, and escaping all responsibility.*

This chapter is a test case. I basically advise: throw your family under the bus:

- Don't co-sign notes with your children or parents.
- Don't bail them out of jail.
- Don't loan them money.
- As for your spouse, pay the bills, but only reluctantly.

You are not legally obligated to support your kids once they turn 18 and you are not obligated to support your parents (with very few exceptions on both scores). This means, unless you have *co-signed*, the creditors of your adult children and of your parents cannot sue you for their debts. As to husbands and wives, they are *generally* responsible for supporting each other, and for paying family debts. Let's flesh out the implications of all of this.

## a. Loans, Gifts, and Bail

### Bail

Children from the best of families get arrested. The judge will set bail. If the bail is posted, your child gets out pending trial. Bailbondsmen will post the bond for you for a fee, usually 10%. If the bail is $30,000, the non-refundable fee would be $3,000. In addition, they will require that you give them security in the full amount of the bail: stocks, bonds, savings, and/or real property worth at least $30,000. If your child splits, you lose your security—your stocks, bonds, home.

This is a heartbreaking situation. It is very hard to say no to a child sitting in jail. You will hear a compelling story and heartfelt pledges of the straight and narrow. And perhaps even subtle suggestions as to why it is all your fault.

Don't! At least think long and hard before you do. Too many parents have lost their homes and savings. Too many parents have posted bail only to have their child, while on bail, commit another and more serious crime. Too many parents save their children time after time, bailing them out, repaying stolen money, making things right. The lesson their children learn is that they can get away with anything and they do, that is, until they end up in prison.

Tough-love may save you your house and your child his life.

## Loans

Lending money to relatives is generally a bad idea. You will become the creditor who is paid last, if at all. It is better to *give* the money.

Money is a funny thing—it is more than purchasing power; it's love and recognition. At work, sure we all thought we deserve more money, but what really burns us is to find out that one of your idiot co-workers makes more. (We never consider people earning less.)

Making gifts to relatives realize that you may be hurting others. *"Mom loves Sis more than me because she's always giving her money."* Best to explain *why* you are giving the money to one but not the other.

If you have made substantial gifts to one child but not to the others, at the time of your death there will be a question of whether the gifts were *advances* on that child's share of your estate, or whether they were simply *separate gifts*. Say your Will provides that your estate is to be divided equally among your three children. During your lifetime you make a $10,000 gift to one. At the time of your death, does that child get an equal share or does the $10,000 come off the top? This question *may* lead to litigation and *will* lead to hard feelings. You can avoid this by expressing your intent in your Will: "Because I have given Sis $10,000 in my lifetime, this is to be considered an advance of her share of my estate" or "I give all my estate to my three children in equal shares, without any adjustment for gifts I may have made during life." Short of, and less effective than, something in your Will, tell folks what you have in mind.

> *"I gave Sis $10,000 as an advance on her inheritance, because she is starting her own business. If you other kids do, I'll try to do the same."*

or

> *"I gave Sis $10,000 as a separate gift, not as part of her inheritance, because well, frankly, I love her more."*

# b. Responsibilities for Minors

*When lawyers think of what is necessary in life, we think of hamburgers and tennis shoes, not of poetry, love or community. That's legal education for you.*

You are responsible for supporting your minor children (usually until the age of 18), unless they have been legally emancipated. This obligation goes only to the necessaries of life, such as housing, food, health, and education. You are not obligated to buy them video games, or pay for nose rings.

If a creditor provides your minor child with a necessity, they can look to you for reimbursement. But if your kid goes out and buys a Rolex, you are *not* obligated to pay for it. Your kid is probably off the hook as well. Children under 18 generally do not have contractual capacity, and hence cannot be sued on contracts they sign—great news if your children are being threatened by CD Clubs or Book Clubs.

*"Dear Record Club: When I signed your offer, I was under 18 and hence had no contractual capacity. Please stop writing me. Thanks for sharing."*

If your minor children are living on their own and are running up bills for which you may be responsible, you may be able to file an action to have the court declare them *emancipated*. This means you will no longer be financially responsible. Of course, once they are emancipated, you no longer have the legal right to supervise them either (but it doesn't sound like they were paying much attention to you, anyway). In most states, when a minor marries he or she automatically and immediately becomes emancipated—but we think that's a lousy reason to let your children marry young.

Some states (but not many) have expanded the parents' common law obligation to support their children beyond the age of 18. A statute in California, for example, provides:

*The father and mother have an equal responsibility to maintain, to the extent of their ability, a child of whatever age who is incapacitated from earning a living and without sufficient means.*

This expresses a nice sentiment. However, there are sufficient loopholes if a creditor of your adult child presents you with a bill. First, generally the child must have become incapacitated before age 18. Second, the bill will have to be for a necessity (as your duty is only to maintain the child). Finally, your liability extends only to your ability to pay.

A common question concerns *college*. You are not responsible for paying. (Note to divorced parents: your divorce settlement may require you to do so.) Still colleges will consider family income in determining the amount of scholarship or financial aid that will be available for your child. Using complicated formulas, colleges will look at the family's income and assets and then determine how much the family can afford to pay toward the child's education. It then decides how much it costs to attend the particular college and, after deducting the amount it deems the family should pay, makes up the difference in loans and grants to the student. In theory this means that the family will spend the same amount no matter how expensive the college attended. How much the student must *borrow* is an entirely different matter.

## c. Support Obligations between Spouses

*Your spouse is home from the hospital and you receive a bill for $20,000. You don't have any joint savings or checking accounts that could pay this. But you have stock in your name that could. Should you pay the bill?*

As to daily bills, the family assets are liable for either spouse's expenses.

The issue "who is responsible for what" really only arises if one spouse has incurred large medical bills or has received public assistance. Unless you are a co-signer on the bills, we advise against paying them without first seeking legal advice:

1. If your spouse has died, the bills should be paid first from his or her estate. Only if the estate is exhausted can the creditor go after you.
2. Under the common law necessities rule, a husband would be liable for his wife's medical care and support. However, some states have thrown out this rule as it denies equal protection (treating men differently from women) while others have leveled the playing field by imposing a similar obligation on the wife. Some states have family expense statutes which make one spouse liable for the debts of the other.

Even though you might eventually be held liable for the bills, our advice remains the same—don't pay them without first seeking legal advice. Most courts, even if they impose spousal obligations, do so only to the extent that it will not leave you broke. A lawyer can probably cut a good deal for you. Further, in the face of large unpaid bills, you should discuss the possibility of bankruptcy.

If you live in one of the states that recognizes "community property" principles (Arizona, California, Idaho, Louisiana, Nevada, New Mexico, Texas,

Washington or Wisconsin), the results may be slightly different. Still, the basic concepts apply: your individual assets (those you brought into the marriage, or gifts or bequests to you alone) will not generally be reachable for even the "community" debts incurred by your spouse—like medical care, or necessities.

# d. Your Kids' Obligation to Support You

Generally, the ungrateful brats are *not* liable for any of your debts or expenses, again, unless they are co-signers. If your children are in fact supporting you, they may be entitled to claim you as a dependent on their federal tax return.

Some states attempt to impose liability on your children if you are likely to become a public charge. These laws are generally called "poor laws" or "general assistance laws." Some may even carry a criminal penalty. However, usually they are used to "attribute" some portion of your child's income to you for the purpose of determining eligibility for public assistance, or in seeking reimbursement for public benefits supplied to you.

# e. Nursing Home Expenses

We began this chapter by advising you not to bail your child out of jail. Well, we can be heartless both ways. Your children should never sign to be responsible for your nursing home expenses.

Under a 1989 Federal law, most nursing homes are prohibited from *requiring* relatives to co-sign for their charges. In some states, however, relatives can agree to pay for extra services.

Even though they cannot require co-signing for expenses, nursing homes can *request* it—and they often do request it, usually in sneaky ways that play on the family dynamics at a time of personal emergency and confusion (like when admitting a parent to a nursing home). Some may ask a son or daughter to sign as "the responsible party." This sounds like you are signing as the person to contact concerning emergencies; what it means, according to the small print, is that you are responsible for the bills.

Tell your kids not to sign. But after *you* left them sitting in jail, they probably won't anyway.

# CHAPTER 20

# Divorce and Remarriage

*Second marriages represent the triumph of hope over experience.*
—Samuel Johnson

## a. Divorce: Property, Alimony, and Health Insurance; Alternatives to Divorce

*Divorce will be a financial disaster.* Both of you will have a lower standard of living. You will likely lose half of your accumulated property and much of your income. Expenses will increase; and then there are hefty lawyers' bills, his *and* hers.

*Divorce will be an emotional disaster.* There is less opportunity for "new beginnings" (look in the mirror). Divorce doesn't make you younger.

We'll look at alternatives to divorce after we look at the financial implications of divorce: property settlements, alimony or spousal maintenance, and health insurance.

*Dividing the stuff.* State divorce laws differ as to distribution of property. Some follow the old Spanish tradition of *community property,* while most follow the English tradition of *Dower.* While there are nice theoretical distinctions between the two, as a practical matter most judges will try to split the property acquired during a long-term marriage. Let this sink in for a moment. *If you divorce now, likely you will lose half of what you accumulated over your married life.*

Half of it.

Unless there is a lot of cash lying around for buy-outs, you will have to sell the family home. That may be just as well if neither of you has enough resources to pay the mortgage and upkeep costs alone.

Assume your mortgage is paid off and your house is valued at $200,000. Dividing its value, each of you is entitled to $100,000. If you have $200,000 in savings, one of you could take your $100,000 share of those savings, and "buy out" the other's share in the house. Of course, one of you is now broke and the other homeless—but you're the ones who couldn't get along. If you don't have savings of $200,000, most likely the house will have to be *sold* and the cash divided.

*Pension plans* present unique problems of evaluation. Assume the wage earner is 55. How much is his or her pension plan worth now, given the fact that it will pay, at 65, an amount based on earnings during the last three years before age 65, earnings which won't be earned for another seven years?

We have to project what the pension would pay at 65 and then figure out how much such a plan would cost. That might be the easy calculation. Let's say we figure it out and come up with the figure of $400,000. Fine. But what's the *current* value of a benefit which will be worth $400,000 in ten years? How much would you have to invest now in order to have $400,000 in ten years? This calculation is contentious since it rests upon assumptions as to rates of interest and inflation.

Expert economists love long, leisurely discussions concerning the future worth of pensions, with color charts and computer printouts. And, if both partners have retirement plans, both must be evaluated and then compared. Expert economists, of course, bill in *current* dollars.

To solve these difficult evaluation and current value problems, some states allow the judge to simply order that the wife receive, at the time of her husband's retirement, a percentage of that retirement. Federal law allows this to be done for Military benefits as well.

Social Security solves these problems this way. After a divorce, at the age of 62, the non-wage earner can collect on her ex-husband's Social Security account if:

1. They were married at least ten years, and
2. She has not remarried. (If she remarried after the age of 60, she does not lose eligibility.)

*Note:* If you are divorcing and have been married less than ten years, it might be smart to swallow your pride and wait a while in order to create Social Security eligibility. Conversely, you might want to curb your enthusiasm and wait until you're 60 to remarry.

*Alimony.* You can't go back to Constantinople; you can't go back to alimony. As we rush toward our brave new world, we discard old sexist traditions such as "alimony." We now call it "spousal maintenance." The basic notion is to "maintain" the non-working (or less-earning) spouse at relatively the same standard of living, while she (it is almost always she) can bring her skills up to speed to allow her to make her own way at a comparable level. While *al-*

*imony* might be permanent and thus "demeaning," *spousal maintenance* is to be temporary and thus "empowering."

This philosophy makes no sense at all in the case of elderly women. Their chances of entering the labor force and earning enough money to support themselves at comparable levels is almost nil. Recognizing this, many judges are now ordering permanent spousal maintenance. In setting the amount of that maintenance, the court will consider the assets that the spouse receives at divorce, as they may produce significant amounts of income.

If your spouse is not only elderly but also spending significant amounts of money on care (medical bills, household support, nursing home payments, etc.), the amount of spousal maintenance you are required to pay may increase accordingly.

*Health Insurance.* Many married people have health insurance only under their spouse's work policy. When both work, the couple will decide whose health policy is best and go with it. Upon divorce, one will lose coverage. However, a federal law, called *COBRA*, gives ex-spouses the right to maintain that insurance for three years. They must pay the premium, thus *increasing* their expenses. If they do not become eligible for Medicare within this three-year period, they will be severely disadvantaged, as it will be difficult and expensive to obtain other insurance. These expenses should be reflected in the amount of support ordered.

*Alternatives to Divorce.* Counseling is a good place to start. Often, the problems really aren't with each other. They are with the pressures of aging and retirement. Divorce won't make you dashing, nor will it give you things to do. Divorce doesn't solve problems; counseling might.

You can try living together but separately. Separate bedrooms, with occasional angry glares over the kitchen table, solve most of the legal problems we have been discussing in this chapter. There is no need to divide property, to obtain additional health insurance, or to pay lawyers. And just maybe if you fell out of love, you might fall back in.

Note: this is not living in sin. Rather it combines the worst of both worlds.

Another alternative is a *legal separation.* It can provide for a formal settlement of economic issues, while allowing for the continuation of health and death benefits. Under a legal separation, the parties are still married.

If you don't want a divorce and your spouse does, contact a lawyer. Don't let the matter go by default. Even in no-fault divorce states, marriage dissolutions can be delayed and sometimes counseling ordered.

There are two situations where elderly divorce does make sense:

1. If one plans to get remarried; or

2. As a device to save the family assets from Medicaid nursing home expenses.

Nursing home expenses can bankrupt families. Medicaid will pay them but only after the family has "spent down" to a certain level. In addition to other exemptions, such as the family home, the law allows for the non-institutionalized spouse to keep $75,000 of other assets. Say the couple has a large estate, say $300,000 in nonexempt assets. If they divorce, the non-institutionalized spouse will be able to keep his or her share, probably $150,000, rather than only the $75,000 which would be allowed under Medicaid rules.

# b. Marriage: Prenuptials and Wills

*First, our enthusiasm: Congratulations on your marriage!*
*Second, our wisdom: Get a prenuptial and change your Will.*

A new marriage requires a new estate plan. Do you want your new spouse to inherit all of your property? Perhaps, given his or her financial situation and the length of your relationship, you want to bypass your new spouse and leave everything to your children. If you do not rewrite your Will, things will be messy when you die.

There is a special problem if both of you have children from prior marriages. You will probably want to provide for your new spouse after your death, but at the time of his or her death, you would like to see your assets revert to some or all of the children. You both agree and draft new Wills, leaving everything to one another, remainder divided among all the children. You die first. How can you be sure your new spouse will keep his or her end of the bargain? Betrayal! The stuff of Shakespearean tragedy.

> *Double, double, toil and trouble;*
> *Fire, burn; and caldron, bubble.*
> *Eye of newt, and toe of frog,*
> *Wool of bat, and tongue of dog,*
> *Tear my Will, a thousand pieces,*
> *I leave it all to my portly nieces!*

A *living trust* is a good solution. (See Chapter 28.) The assets of both spouses are placed in trust for their use during their lives. Upon the death of one, the spouses have agreed that the trust will become irrevocable and provide that income will go to maintain the survivor (with liberal principal invasion terms to cover such things as medical emergencies). At the death of the survivor, the assets can be distributed as provided by the original trust instrument; i.e., divided among the couple's children from prior marriages. This approach is an improvement over relying on fidelity continuing for years after your death, but it is not perfect. Who will be trustee of the trust, and therefore decide whether the surviving spouse really needs that cruise, or sundeck on the house, or nursing home payment? The surviving spouse? The deceased spouse's oldest son, who is both an accountant and a lawyer and has a heart of coal? And what will happen to the trust if the surviving spouse remarries, or moves out of the house (and in with the massage therapist)?

If a living trust is not for you, a lawyer can help you set up other devices to accomplish your goals. You might want to discuss signing reciprocal Wills, and maybe even agree that neither of you will change your Wills after the death of the other spouse. Lawyers love these arrangements, as they get to charge more when you sign, and much more when your heirs fight over what the agreement meant and whether the survivor breached it. More valuably (for you), a lawyer can draft a "prenup."

> *A cartoon shows two young boys standing next to a swimming hole. There is a rope tied to a tree limb that was obviously used to support a tire used as a swing over the pond. The rope is broken. The tire is floating in the water. One boy is saying: "I'll go get another tire, you go tell Tommie's mother."*

The hardest part about prenuptial agreements is broaching the subject. Blame us. Copy this chapter and leave it on the pillow, anonymously.

A "prenuptial" is simply a written agreement between the happy couple. Sometimes, in an effort to convince clients that they actually speak Latin, lawyers use the term "antenuptial"—it just means "before the marriage," not "against the marriage." It can cover such things as:

1. Who is responsible for the debts brought into the marriage?
2. In the event of divorce, what happens to the property brought into the marriage *and* to property acquired during it? What of support obligations?
3. Who is to inherit what?
4. Who takes out the garbage?

Number four is not a joke (at least not much of one). We all tend to get a tad set in our ways. Marriages require adjustments. It might be well to hammer some things out—such as vacations, hobbies, relationships with ex's, and things of that ilk. These concerns may seem petty, but they are the stuff of life.

A prenuptial (even without number four) is a good idea in and of itself. It will help you focus on issues that may otherwise be ignored, issues that can create real friction later.

However, the potential for overreaching and misunderstanding is great. *Each of you should be represented by separate lawyers.* Given the potential conflicts between you, one lawyer should not represent you both. Both lawyers should sign the agreement—don't just recite in the agreement that each person consulted with their own lawyer before signing. Recitals may not stand up in the event of a challenge.

*Full disclosure* of assets, debts, and other matters that might bear upon the agreement must be made under most states' laws governing prenuptial agreements. Otherwise, a court will most likely throw it out.

If you are currently married and don't have a prenuptial agreement, *post-nuptial* agreements are possible, as are contracts to make Wills.

Without a prenuptial agreement, your new spouse may be entitled to half the property earned during the marriage and, in some cases, some of the property brought into the marriage. More importantly for many newlywed couples at or near retirement age, the children of your new spouse may have a claim to a share of what you think of as "your" property in the event your new spouse dies before you. Support may also be ordered in the event of divorce; you can agree in advance to limit or eliminate support payments. In other words, prenuptials can hammer out the respective rights of the parties while they still agree on most things, and still have a good feeling for what is fair and reasonable.

Of course, if a lot of money is involved, expect a fight as to the validity of the prenuptial agreement. Unlike death and taxes, prenuptials ain't certain.

But planning to remarry at your age, you are obviously not averse to taking chances. Good for you. We always applaud the triumph of hope over experience. (In an over-cautious world, there would be little joy and, still worse, little need for lawyers.)

# CHAPTER 21

# AGE AND DISABILITY DISCRIMINATION

Supervisor: *Henry, don't bother signing up for training on the new computer program. Old dogs can't learn new tricks and, besides, you would just forget it, anyway.*

Boss: *Mary, we have this great new early retirement program, but you must sign up by the end of next week or face layoff.*

Recruiter: *You are just too qualified for this job.*

Boss: *Real sorry about your disability, but we have to let you go because you can no longer do the job.*

Supervisor: *Come on over and give me a big hug.*

Co-worker: *Hey babe, look at hot pictures.*

Banker: *Sorry, no credit.*

Boss: *Sorry, old goat.*

Landlord: *Sorry, no goat.*

Discrimination is triggered by the victim's age, disability, race or sex and comes in many places: work, housing, public accommodations, and at the bank. Well and good, but what's this about "no goat"? We'll see. We have two main topics:

1. A discussion of the various laws that prohibit discrimination; and
2. Tips on how to recognize discrimination.

## a. An Overview of Anti-Discrimination Law

The law is pretty good in prohibiting discrimination.

## Age and Disability Discrimination in Employment

Age discrimination, beginning at age 40 (yes, 40) is illegal. This applies in hiring, termination, and job treatment, such as promotions or job reclassifications. Similarly, you cannot be discriminated against merely because you become disabled and have a more difficult time doing the job (assuming that your employer, or prospective employer, has at least 15 employees). The employer must work with you, trying to find "reasonable accommodations" which would allow you to go on working.

## Age and Sex Discrimination in Credit

Legislation prohibits age and sex discrimination in the credit industry. Widows, who may be forced to apply for credit after the death of their husbands, should *suspect* discrimination if they are denied.

## Disability Discrimination

While *age* discrimination, at least at the federal level, is prohibited only in employment and credit, protection for the *disabled* is far more extensive. Disability discrimination is generally prohibited in the following areas:

Housing
Public accommodations
Government services
Employment

## Racial and Sexual Discrimination

These kinds of discriminations are outlawed in employment and in many other areas as well. The "hot" area is *sexual discrimination in employment*. The law recognizes two forms of sexual discrimination: direct (supervisors demanding sexual favors) and indirect (employers allowing a "hostile work environment" to exist, such as where co-workers are allowed to post explicit sexual pictures or to make crude remarks). The law also prohibits same-sex harassment (male on male or female on female).

The protective legislation we will look at had its genesis in the Civil Rights Movement. The root notion is that the law should act to protect citizens against irrational discrimination, whether based on race, national origin, religion, sex, age, or disability. There are a few other general comments we can make:

- While we focus on federal law, many states have parallel anti-discrimination laws. State laws may provide for broader judicial relief (a polite way of saying "more money").
- Most Civil Rights laws provide that, if you win your lawsuit, the defendant must pay your lawyer. Thus you *can* afford a lawyer.
- Most Civil Rights laws are enforced by governmental agencies. It is easy to report discrimination and let them investigate and take appropriate action. These agencies will contact the other side, hear their side of the story, and then try to conciliate the matter without going to court.
- In all cases of discrimination, it is important to act quickly. If you wait too long, your complaint may be barred by the Statute of Limitations. Further, much of your evidence might be lost. People move and forget.

Perhaps you are still worried about "no goat." It's a good place to start.

# b. Goat Discrimination

Discrimination against pets can be devastating. Pets provide substantial physical and mental benefits to their owners, particularly older people who live alone. Recognizing this, Congress passed a law in 1983 prohibiting owners of *federally assisted housing*, designated for the elderly or disabled, from having flat rules against pets, including cats, dogs, and fish. Thus you can keep your cat unless the landlord shows that it is a nuisance or a threat to the health or safety of others. (Lions, crocodiles, and T Rex, all have to go; old goats fall in the grey area.)

Although this law has a narrow application, if you are renting from a private landlord, you might point to it if you want to keep a pet. A creative lawyer might be able to convince a judge that it would be against public policy to allow a private landlord to evict an elderly tenant because the tenant kept a cat. A good landlord might see that the basis of the federal law makes sense, even if it doesn't really apply to his or her apartment complex.

# c. Credit Discrimination

The Equal Credit Opportunity Act prohibits creditors (stores, credit card companies, and banks) from discriminating against any applicant on the "basis of race, color, religion, national origin, sex, marital status, or age," or because the applicant is receiving public assistance.

Creditors can turn you down if you are not credit-worthy—if you have a history of late payments or if your income and assets do not justify the amount of money you wish to borrow.

Thirty days after you apply for credit, you must get a decision. If you are turned down, the creditor must tell you why. Don't be satisfied with explanations such as "Bad credit risk" or "Bad credit record." Insist on details, and if the creditor remains vague, call the local office of the Federal Trade Commission, which enforces the Equal Credit Opportunity Act. Again, widows and older persons should suspect discrimination.

# d. Housing: Disability Discrimination

In the area of housing, it is illegal to refuse to rent or sell to a person because he or she is disabled, while it is legal to discriminate on the basis of age. Federal law does not outlaw *age* discrimination (as opposed to disability discrimination) in the sale or rental of housing. (Uncle Sam, despite his appearance, is younger than you thought.) If you have been turned down because of your age, the only recourse you may have is state law; check with your State Attorney General's Office to see if your state prohibits age discrimination in housing.

On the other hand, federal law does outlaw housing discrimination against the disabled. This protection is afforded by the "*ADA*"—*Americans With Disabilities Act.*

A disabled individual is a person who has a "physical or mental impairment that substantially limits" one of the major life activities, such as walking.

A covered owner or landlord cannot *refuse to sell or rent* to an individual simply because the person is disabled, unless the handicap is such as to threaten the health and safety of others or would lead to substantial property destruction. The only housing exempted from the ADA is single dwelling residences rented or sold without a Realtor; small housing complexes of four or fewer units where the owner occupies one; and housing run by religious organizations and private clubs.

Incidentally, it is also a violation of federal law to refuse to rent or sell to a tenant because of race, color, religion, sex or national origin. Those protections are provided by the Civil Rights Act of 1964.

*An Important Note to Disabled Renters.* You have a right, at your expense, to make *reasonable modifications* (for example, put in ramps or grab bars, or lower or raise counters) to your rental to accommodate your handicap. Your landlord cannot refuse to allow you to do so, although the landlord can insist that you agree to restore the place to its original condition when you leave.

Disabled victims of housing discrimination can either file their own lawsuit or contact the federal Department of Housing and Urban Development (HUD), or a state or local housing enforcement agency. The State Attorney General's Office can point you in the right direction.

# e. Employment: Disability Discrimination

The Americans with Disabilities Act of 1990 (ADA) also protects disabled individuals in employment. The first reported case under the ADA concerning employment discrimination involved a 56-year-old executive who was discharged after being diagnosed with terminal brain cancer. He sued and won $250,000.

If a physical or mental disability prevents you from doing an acceptable job, you have no recourse against an employer. However, your employer cannot *assume* that you cannot do the job simply because you are disabled. If you become disabled, your employer must allow you to try to do your job and cannot simply assume you can't.

Further, your employer must work with you in figuring out how to change the job so you can do it. An employer must make "reasonable accommodations for known physical or mental limitations of an otherwise qualified individual." If a disability is interfering with your performance, are there things you or your employer can do to remedy the problem? Changing the height of desks, getting additional training, or taking more frequent rest breaks may help. How far employers must go in making "reasonable accommodations" is unclear. On the one hand, they must make good faith efforts and not just go through the motions; on the other hand, they need not incur unreasonable expenses.

The requirement of reasonable accommodations throws new light on an old dilemma: *If you are having a hard time doing your job because of a disability, should you tell your boss?* The fear is that, if you do tell, you will be fired. However, if the employer doesn't know of your disability, he or she is under no obligation to offer reasonable accommodation and, if you are fired for bad job performance caused by your disability, you will not be able to claim the ADA's protection.

Only small employers are exempt from the ADA: those with fewer than 15 regular workers. However even small employers may be covered by state or local statutes, and may even be motivated to do the right thing when the law has clearly defined "right thing."

Disabled individuals may also face discrimination in government programs (no programs for the deaf in school) and public accommodations and facilities (no ramps in retail stores). These aspects of the ADA are beyond our scope, but if you feel that you have suffered because of your disability at the hands of a government agency or private business, you should contact the federal Equal Employment Opportunities Commission (EEOC), which enforces the ADA, or your state's Attorney General's Office. You can also seek private counsel.

# f. Employment: Age Discrimination and an Aside on Common Law

Before we give you the details of employment law, let's take a brief look at "common law" and one of history's very first cases—*Barney Rubble v. Fred Flintstone.*

*Common law* is judge-made law. This is opposed to *statutory law,* which is made by the insurance industry. In the early days of our country, we followed the law of England (despite the fact that we didn't think much of the King). The law of England at the time was mostly judge-made. Here is an example of how the common law works:

Let's take the first employment; it probably involved Fred and Barney. Fred had hired Barney to help him fix up the cave, but, after a couple of days, fired him. Barney went to court and complained, "Fred fired me without any good reason. I was doing a real good job."

The *factual question,* to be decided by the jury if there were a trial, would be "Was Barney doing a good job?" But, before the matter could get to this point, a *legal question* would have to be answered by the judge, "Does an employer need good cause to fire someone?" If the judge held "Yes," then there would be a trial as to whether Fred had good cause; if the judge held "No," there would not be a trial because, as a matter of law, employers could fire for any reason they chose.

Some are critical of the judiciary, arguing that judges should not "make law." But note that to decide the case, the judge had to decide the question— the judge would be making law either way.

The first judge, perhaps a secret admirer of Wilma, said "Sorry. Barney, I hold that an employer can fire anyone for any reason or for no reason." Thereafter, other judges, wishing to "treat like cases alike," followed the ruling of the first judge. Over time, it became "law," the *common law.*

This is the concept of following *precedent,* also known as *stare decisis,* and it, at least in theory, creates predictability. Employers and employees will know the rules and will be able to plan their lives. Important decisions will not turn on the whim (or politics) of individual judges.

Some have argued that the doctrine of precedent cannot hold, cannot keep its promise that like cases will be treated alike. This is because judges can "*distinguish*" prior cases. Assume a judge is dealing with a case involving a ranch-hand fired from a dinosaur ranch. She can write: "The rule laid down in the case of *Fred v. Barney* only applies in cases of individuals working in caves; the case before me involves employment at a dinosaur ranch, and I will adopt a different rule to govern this kind of case."

The more flexible the law, the more judges can fine-tune it for unique situations. Maybe there are important differences between cave work and ranch work that would justify a different employment rule. However, the more flexible the law is, the less predictable it becomes. If it is flexible enough to deal with every unique situation, the law may collapse into the individual whim of the judge. To solve this timeless jurisprudential dilemma would double the price of this book.

Common law starts with the notion that an employer can fire you for any reason at all. Even if you are doing a great job, you can be fired to make room for the employer's third cousin from Toledo.

Rather than call this "The Third Cousin from Toledo" rule, lawyers labeled it the "at will" doctrine. It left employees quite vulnerable. Unless you have a contract or your employer has an employment policy to the contrary, the employer is not even obligated to tell you why you are fired. Many are told by their lawyers, swirling their mustaches, not to. "The less they know, the harder it will be for them to sue."

So where can you find protection?

If you were fired for no good cause, your only hope is to argue that your employer promised not to do so. This is a question of contract law. However, if you were fired (or demoted or passed over) because of your age, this is a question of statutory law. We'll look at both.

## Contract Rights

If you are one of those rare individuals with an employment contract, the "at will" doctrine does not apply to you. The contract has to be for a specified period of time such as a year. The contract can be oral—but then, of course, it is much more difficult to show what it provided. With a contract, an employee can be fired only according to the contract's terms, which typically require "good cause"—that may include sleeping on the job, but not making room for the boss's distant relatives.

Even if you don't have an employment contract, you may have contract rights you don't know about, and they are the first place to look if you have problems at work.

## Union Contracts and the Obligation of Unions

Labor unions enter into collective-bargaining agreements with the employer. These spell out a worker's rights concerning termination and conditions of employment. *Unions have a duty to represent you* if your job is covered by a collective bargaining agreement, *even if* you are not a member of the union and even if your shop foreman has lost a major bet with you on the Super Bowl. Further, labor unions cannot discriminate on the basis of age.

## Employee Manuals as Contracts

Some employers have an employee manual or a set of work policies which may describe the circumstances in which an employee can be fired or laid off, and what kind of notice must be given. Creative lawyers have argued that these policies in effect become part of the employment contract and hence are legally binding on the employer.

## Legislation: The Age Discrimination in Employment Act (ADEA)

If you have no recourse to contract rights, turn next to legislation. It has made major inroads into the "at will" doctrine by prohibiting discrimination based on race, sex, and age. Our concern is with *age* discrimination, so we turn to the provisions of the Age Discrimination in Employment Act (ADEA) which was passed by Congress in 1967.

A major aspect of this legislation is to outlaw mandatory retirement. The narrow exceptions deal with matters of public safety; for example, airline pilots must retire at age 60. Another exception, approved by the Justices of the U.S. Supreme Court: state law can require retirement of state court judges, but federal judges are immune.

The other major aspect of this legislation is that it protects people 40 and older from discrimination in terms of hiring, firing, promotion, and pay. This applies to both part-time and temporary workers as well. What employers cannot do is to treat people over 40 differently because they assume that, because of their age, they cannot do as good a job as younger individuals. Employers can, however, fire individuals for bad job performances, even if those poor performances are due to the aging process, and can also reduce the work force, as long as they do not single out the elderly.

This law applies to almost all employers (private and public, profit and non-profit) but only if the employer has 20 or more employees. Certain high-ranking employees aren't covered, nor are top managers.

# g. Proving Discrimination and Why Employers Discriminate

Occasionally there may be direct evidence of age discrimination. In one case, the defendant fired the plaintiff, calling him an "old goat." The old goat sued and won big bucks; with a nod to Winston Churchill, "Some goat!"

> *At the beginning of World War II, Hitler bragged that Germany was about to grab England like a chicken and break its neck. Churchill, in one of his great speeches, repeated Hitler's threat, and then paused.... "Some chicken!" he roared. Thunderous applause. After several minutes, the audience fell silent. Another pause....*
> *"Some neck!"*

Most employers are too cagey to call you an old goat. (This awkward construction in no way suggests that *I* am calling you an old goat.) Not all employers are so closed-mouth, however; in one notable case the 76-year-old employer turned down a 74-year-old applicant, saying "people our age are considered dinosaurs."

Employers are likely to claim they just love older folks but that you, alas, cannot do the job. How can you prove that they are in fact discriminating against you because of your age? To win an age discrimination suit, you don't have to prove that age was the *only* factor in an adverse employment decision, only that it was a factor. How? We recommend three basic steps:

1. Ask yourself: Does my employer have a reason to discriminate against me?
2. Demand explanations of conduct you believe might constitute discrimination.
3. Sit down and write out why you think you have been victimized.

Why do employers discriminate against older folks?

## 1. To cut insurance costs

Seniors get sick more and hence have higher bills. To avoid higher premiums, a company might refuse to hire or might fire (or force into retirement, or make life hell so that they quit) older workers. This is against the law.

Employers cannot discriminate against seniors on the basis that they trigger higher benefit-plan costs. Employers can, however, insist on spending the same amount on all employees. This may result in lesser coverage for older workers; the same premium will get more coverage for a younger worker than for an older one.

## 2. To cut payroll and to weasel out of retirement commitments

New hires are paid less than folks with experience. Some employers are tempted to cut costs by replacing more senior workers.

As to weaseling out of retirement commitments, federal law provides that, once you have worked for a company for five years, you have a vested right to be in the company's retirement plan (if they have one). This means that the employer cannot get back its contributions to your account. Be very suspicious if you are fired as you approach the five-year mark.

## 3. To let stereotypes do their thinking (it is easier that way)

Some employers simply assume that over a certain age people won't be able to do the job. *Most of us can.* Studies suggest mental function remains high well into the seventies.

Civil rights legislation protecting minorities, women, the disabled, and the elderly can be thought of as anti-stereotype legislation. Employers cannot simply assume that, for example, no elders can do a job simply because some elders cannot. Individual decisions must be made. Further, these laws force employers to think through job qualifications. Employers may simply assume that people need to have certain skills to do a certain job when they really don't. It is a violation of law to have a job requirement that is not really needed if it acts to discriminate against the elderly. For example, if a job requires no heavy lifting, employers cannot insist employees pass strength tests that would discriminate irrationally against the elderly.

After thinking about whether there was a motive to discriminate against you, the next step is to *demand an explanation.* If you weren't hired because you "aren't qualified" or are "too qualified," ask "In what respects?"

University professors, for example, are not over-qualified for repetitious, boring and mind-numbing jobs. Just look at their publications!

If you were fired because you "can no longer do the job" or "no longer get along with customers," demand specifics. Be suspicious of vague answers and the refusal to respond.

If you are going to talk your employer, take someone with you. You might need a witness later.

*Writing down why* you think you have been victimized should prove worthwhile. Writing is simply a great way to slow your mind to allow you to sort things out. Things will come to you that you would overlook if you just thought about it.

Now some tips for specific situations:

*If you weren't hired, consider:*

- Was there anything the interviewer said or asked that indicated age bias? Did the interviewer tell you the job qualifications and did you meet them? Vague qualifications coupled with "You aren't qualified" are suspicious.
- Did the interviewer tell you why you weren't being hired? If they were to "get back to you later" and later you were simply told "Nope," write a letter: "Why didn't I get the job? In what ways wasn't I qualified?" A failure to respond to this inquiry increases suspicions.
- Was the job kept open? You could have a friend call or even apply. If the employer is hiring a lot of folks, are any of them your age?

*If you think that your employer is setting you up to be fired:*

- Watch the paper trail of bad evaluations. Respond to them in writing.
- Talk with co-workers your age and see if the same thing is happening to them.
- Record the incidents that you feel are suspicious.
- Seek legal advice early on, *before* the axe falls.

# h. What to Do: File a Complaint, Soon

Typically, if someone runs you over, you can go directly to court (at least after you get out of the hospital). Not so with most civil rights legislation or with age discrimination legislation. The law requires that you first file a complaint with the governmental agency whose job it is to enforce that particular law. The idea is that the agency will investigate your complaint and try to resolve the dispute. If it cannot, and it believes you are right, it *might* go to court on your behalf. Even if the agency finds you are wrong, you still can go to court after you have given the agency time to investigate.

If your state has an age discrimination law, you must first file a complaint with the agency that enforces it. If your state does not, then you have to file with the local office of the Federal EEOC (Equal Employment Opportunity Commission). Things can get complicated and these offices will guide you through the ropes.

What you need to know now is that you need to *act quickly.* If you wait too long to file a complaint, it may be barred by the Statute of Limitations. (The length of Statutes of Limitations varies from state to state.)

Your possible remedies under federal law include payment for lost pay, reinstatement, front pay (if reinstatement isn't appropriate) and injunctive relief (a stern judicial warning not to do it again). Awards for pain and suffering are not allowed. However, if there was a *willful* violation, your recovery can be doubled. Punitive damages are not allowed under the federal law although they may be if you pursue other theories of recovery.

In 2009 the Supreme Court made it more difficult to bring an age discrimination age. It held that the plaintiff must show, by a preponderance of the evidence, that age was the "but-for" cause of the adverse employment action.

# i. A Concluding Note on Early Retirement

If an employer has a pension plan, it will provide full benefits when a worker retires, usually at the age of 65. (It cannot *require* retirement because, again, mandatory retirement is almost always illegal.) Employers can, however, offer workers the opportunity to retire early and offer such incentives as

- paying full retirement benefits now; and
- supplementing payments with additional cash ("bridge payments") to help out until the worker becomes 65 and thus eligible for Social Security and Medicare.

If offered early retirement, *you don't have to take it.* Think long and hard about retirement and the loss of income, daily direction and status it may entail. And, if you are interested, there may be room to negotiate better terms. One big item will be health insurance and who is to pay the premium.

We've covered a lot of ground in this chapter. For old goats, we're doing fine! Some chapter!

# CHAPTER 22

# IDENTITY THEFT, SCAMS, AND THE NATURE OF EVIL

*No man can play an active part in the world unless he believes that his activity is important and good. Therefore, whatever position a man may hold, he is certain to take that view of human life in general, which will make his own activity seem important and good. To maintain this idea, men instinctively mix only with those who accept their view of life and of their place in it. This surprises us when thieves boast of their adroitness, prostitutes flaunt their shame, murderers gloat over their cruelty. We are surprised, however, only because the circle, the sphere, of these men is limited, and principally because we are outside it ...*

—Tolstoy, *Resurrection*

That pretty much sums up evil.

The nature of evil, while marginally relevant to our topic, was basically a tease, one designed to assure you that the chapter might have a modicum of intellectual content. I know your intellectual interests run deeper than simply finding out how to get a free credit report.

Spend a few minutes considering the Tolstoy quote. What about the people outside your circle? What do they make of you? Is there any way to get outside of our circle to find the truth about whether our activities are important and good?

This is a fairly long and, frankly, dismal chapter. The main points:

- Never give your Social Security number, or any account information, to any *unsolicited* email, letter or phone call *even if* it seems legitimate and threatens dire results if you don't, such as cancelling your credit card or being unable to protect your account from unauthorized users.
- Learn to hang up when you get telephone calls thanking you for last year's donation.

- Realize that you will never win a lottery you never entered and that no one from a country you never heard of is willing to split $20 million (U.S.) if you help them.
- Never trust the Will Rogers looking guy who comes to your door promising a free roof or furnace inspection.
- Repeat the flimflam man's motto: "I never tricked an honest man" and freeze up if a deal is too good to be true.

If you still get cheated, *scream*. Crooks count on victims blaming themselves. "I must be getting senile. I don't want anyone to know how stupid I was. I'll just forget it." But you are *not* alone. Graduates of Harvard's Business School, by their own reckoning quite brilliant, get taken just as we people on the pavement do. The only difference, they get taken for a whole lot more. Recall Madoff.

# a. Identity Theft

Don't lose your identity! Be true to your real self. March to a different drummer. Do it your way. Don't be the man in grey flannel suit. (Oops: wrong book, wrong decade.)

Identity thieves first get personal information about you and convince others that they are you. The information is usually numbers—social security number, credit card numbers, bank numbers. With the numbers they open a credit card account in your name and run up a lot of bills (occasionally in cahoots with dishonest merchants).

You won't see the bills. Thieves have them sent to them, not to you and, unless they are *very* new to the game, they don't pay them. You learn of the bills when the Collection Agency comes calling.

Where do they get the numbers? By running off with your purse or wallet, by going through your mailbox or garbage, by invading your computer, and by working in offices that have your numbers and copying files. *Protect your numbers.*

- Never, not once, give any of your numbers to an unsolicited email, letter, or phone call. No bank, financial institution, or governmental agency, no matter how official it sounds, and no matter how urgent and dire it seems, *will ever send you an email requesting that you respond by giving them financial information.* (Crooks will.)
- Don't keep your social security card in your wallet or purse. If a routine form, say at the doctor's office, has a space for your social se-

curity number, leave it blank. (They never check; if they do, tell them you forgot it—but make that is the only lie you tell your doc.)

- When shopping on line, use a credit card, not a debit card which can be used to get at all of your account.
- Shred important documents. Buy a crisscross shredder; shredders are not only for targets of grand jury investigations and politicians.
- Keep important documents (tax records) in locked files. Identity thieves may be relatives, colleagues, visitors or, we kid you not, plumbers!
- Get a locked mailbox. (Ideally.)

How will you know that you have saved your identity? Well, do you have a flower in your hair? Are you giving peace a chance?

## Credit Reports

Check your credit report for accounts you never opened. You are entitled to one free credit report per year; if you are clever, you can get three. The *only* website authorized by the government to fill orders for your free credit report is www.annualcreditreport.com. (Despite their catchy jingles and ultra cute ads, other websites offering free credit reports *ain't*. To get your report you must sign up for other services.)

The law requires *each* of the three nationwide consumer reporting agencies to provide you with one free credit report per year. Go to www.annualcredit report.com and answer the questions, then select one of the reporting choices: Equifax; TransUnion, or Experian. They will try to head you off into buying something, like your *credit rating* or *email alerts*. Keep going, unless you are convinced to buy, and eventually you will get to your free credit report. Check for fake accounts. Four months later, repeat with a different choice.

## A Note on P1ssw1rds

I come up with killer passwords for our various internet and bank accounts, ones that no one will ever figure out and ones that I will never forgot until, it seems, the next day. If you suffer this affliction, you can use very easy passwords and simply substitute numbers for the vowels or consonants: 1a111o111.

## Protecting Credit Cards and Checks

Some thieves do it the old fashioned way and steal your credit card number or forge your checks.

*Check your credit card bills.* Under the Federal Fair Credit Billing Act, you have 60 days to report billing errors, including unauthorized charges, situations where the goods or services were not delivered or accepted, clerical errors, and failure to indicate payments made. These reports must be in writing.

*Check your bank statements.* The Uniform Commercial Code, a law in effect in a vast majority of states, provides that, if you report a forgery within 30 days after you receive your statement, the *bank will pick up the loss.* After 30 days, the bank need not pick up the loss unless you can prove that the bank was negligent. This will be an uphill fight.

*If you have a vulnerable relative being cared for by others* it might be a good idea to have their credit card bills and bank statements sent to you or your computer. Crooked caretakers have access to both credit cards and checks and, to protect their misdeeds, destroy the incoming statements.

# b. Scams

*You can fool some of the people some of the time—and that's enough to make a decent living.*

—W.C. Fields

## Phone Fraud

"Sorry, I can't talk right now, my house is on fire."

"Sorry, I can't talk right now, I'm giving a commencement speech."

These ploys, even if true, never work. Phone solicitors have heard them all before and have rehearsed responses to keep you on the line: "Have you saved the cats?" "Are you working in any Tolstoy quotes?"

Consumers are bilked $40 billion annually by phone scams. Once they get you talking, you're a goner. Hang up! Most of us are simply too nice. Sure it's impolite, something our parents told us never to do, and the caller seems nice, calls you by name and asks how you were doing, like an old lost friend. You won't hurt their feelings! You are only a name and number on a computer screen—and a target.

In a current scam the caller alerts you to the fact (which isn't) that your car warranty is about to expire and, just think, you will be facing thousands in repair bills unless.... Don't go there. The warranty they offer is likely to be so full of exceptions (such as "no prior conditions are covered") to be essentially meaningless. If you are at all tempted, get the warranty sent to you *before* buying and check out the company with the Better Business Bureau, BBB.org.

If you haven't already, get on the Do Not Call List: www.donotcall.gov.; 1-888-382-1222, TTY 1-866-290-4236.

Even if you have a do-not-call, charities can still get through, usually beginning by thanking you for the generous contribution you made last year. (I for one never realized how generous I was last year!) "I don't contribute over the phone. Send me some literature and the receipt for last year's contribution." Now they hang up.

- Never agree to make a purchase or give money on the first call. Insist on thinking it over. Resist the "Limited time" offer. Legitimate sellers will give you time to think.
- Never give your credit card number to a caller.
- Never be nice!

## Internet Scams

> *Dear American Friend. You have been referred to me by a Distinguished and Most Honorable friend. My father was the treasurer of a small African country, one that you and no one else has heard of. He was murdered by ugly rebels. Before his death he was able to deposit $25 million (U.S.) in a Swiss bank. (Had he been corrupt, it would have been much more.) Honorable American friend, a land I have always loved, I need your help in getting that money before it falls into the hands of the ugly rebels. If you help me I will give you half. Please answer this email.*

Answer it and you must send money to cover assorted costs (bribes for unruly warlords) or your bank information to facilitate the transfer. Once you are in a little, these people keep coming at you. One university professor lost tens of thousands of dollars. (We hasten to add, a Professor of English, not Law.)

Scams play on your fears.

> *Alert from Chase Bank Security. Third parties have attempted to access your account. We will have to suspend your access to your accounts, unless you send us, immediately, your Social Security number, your account and PIN numbers, your date of birth, your mother's maiden name, and your favorite flavor of ice cream.*

This is known as "*phishing.*" The bait comes in many forms: "alerts," "updates for your credit union," "unauthorized activity warnings," "immediate cancellation of your trading privileges." Their emails look quite official and some purport to be from the U.S. Government.

Scammers don't need to fool many. Charities that send out solicitation letters do very well if they get a 3% response: if you are sending zillions of emails at virtually no cost, you need very few bites.

Again, no bank, seller, financial institution, or governmental agency *will ever send you an email requesting that you respond by giving them financial information.*

Another internet fraud (don't these people ever sleep?) involves "hot stock" tips. You get an unsolicited email, touting a very low price stock which is about to "take off," "explode," "go through the roof." These schemers buy cheap stocks, send out their emails to drive the price up, and then dump their holdings, collapsing the price. (Of course, this may have been the strategy of the New York Stock Exchange.)

## You've Won!

> A hotdog stands next to his mailbox, opening a letter. "Congratulations, you are a wiener."

The chances of winning a state lottery or Powerball are the same whether you buy a ticket or not. The odds of winning the Powerball jackpot are 1 in 146.1 million which means that, if you bought 73,050,000 lottery tickets, it would be even money that you would *still* lose, and, even if you did win, good luck finding the winning ticket!

You receive a letter or email announcing that you won $2,000 in the Canadian lottery. In your excitement you skip over the fact that you didn't *enter* the Canadian lottery. No matter. All you have to do is send back $200 to process the award. The letter may even contain a very official-looking cashier's check in the amount of $2,000, but, you are instructed, to cash it you must first wire back the $200. The check is fake. Or you may be asked to send your bank account information so that your winnings can be wired directly to your account.

## Home Repair Scams

Will Rogers, or maybe someone who just looks like him, comes to your door to offer a *free* inspection of your roof or heating system. Dollars to donuts, you will *need* a new roof, or a new furnace, and, lucky for you, his company can fix the problem. (These folks will not be bonded, will not be local, and will not be any good.)

> Burly repairmen from the Holland Furnace Company would offer a free inspection, tear the furnace apart, and then give the home owner the bad news. "Yep, it's broken. We will fix it and put it back together for $800. Otherwise, we are out of here."
>
> This worked pretty well, until they tried it at the Godfather's house.

Occasionally the Universe makes us jump and cheer.

Folks may claim to be city inspectors checking for violations. *Don't let them in your house.* No government official has a right to enter your home without a *search warrant.* (That was what the American Revolution was about—that, and if we recall correctly, tea.) Take their card and phone the city to see if they are for real. If they are for real, they can come back.

## Home Mortgage Scams

These are not to be confused with *Mortgage Rescue Scams* which are discussed in Recession Blues, Chapter 23.

Here crooks offer loans which seem too good to be true, requiring only low monthly payments. *Don't bite.* Many have lost their homes, others fell into a spiral of increasing debt. Lower payments do not mean lower interest; they mean a longer time paying back the loan, a longer time your house will be at risk. If you get behind, you may be forced to refinance at still higher interest rates or risk losing your home when the lender forecloses.

Loan offers may come door-to-door, by mail or through the internet. While first mortgages, those that finance the purchase of your home, are extensively regulated, second mortgages, home improvement loans, and home equity accounts are much less regulated. This gives crooks their opening. If you have to borrow against your home, risky even in the best of times, always use reputable, established banks: folks who have been in town a long time. It is always best to have any loan or mortgage agreements reviewed by someone independent, such as an attorney.

## Obituary Scams

Reading the obituaries, cheats send fake bills to the decedent hoping the family will pay. Often they are for pornography. As we advise in our chapter on death in the family, don't pay any of the decedent's bills until the immediate crisis has passed.

## Health Care Scams

Apricot pits don't cure cancer, Compound Q doesn't cure AIDS, and Snake Oil doesn't cure much of anything. Fraudulent cures cost money, may delay an actual cure through traditional medicine, and may kill you.

No matter your ailment, from cancer to wrinkles, from alcoholism to ulcers, someone will offer you a cure. The American Medical Association advises extreme caution if the cure is claimed to be quick and easy or that it involves a "secret" formula or machine to cure disease. Some scammers even try to sell their product by claiming that the health care industry and the government are conspiring to suppress it.

Before taking any new form of medicine, at least talk to your pharmacist! *Drugs can interact in bad ways.* You can also get advice from local offices of the American Medical Association, the American Dental Association, the American Cancer Society, the Arthritis Foundation or similar organizations.

Be leery of the word "natural." Without getting into a philosophic discussion of what is natural (and the fallacy that "natural must be good"— cancer is natural), just realize that before a drug is approved by the FDA, it goes through millions of dollars worth of tests, looking for side effects and effectiveness.

"Natural remedies" generally have not been tested for either effectiveness or side effects. Personal testimonials mean little because you don't know (1) whether anything was ever wrong with the person; (2) whether what was wrong with them is wrong with you; and (3) even if they got better, why they got better; it could have been for a host of other reasons.

## Door-to-door Sales

*A high school friend sold encyclopedias door-to-door. He was a legend. The pitch was that the set was brand new and, as they were saving millions in advertising costs, it could be placed in your home for pennies a day. "That's a lie," a customer said. "I bought a set ten years ago."*

*"Well, then you must be in the market for a new set!" He closed the sale.*

Door-to-door sales are rife with fraud, false claims, and dishonest sales pitches. They usually aren't a good idea.

- Before you answered the door, you didn't even know you needed the product.
- You have little idea as to what is a fair price or as to whether competing models have better features. (*Consumer Reports* would come in handy.)
- You don't know anything about the seller or even where to find him if the product never gets there or breaks when it does.

As to the "substantial savings" you get because the seller doesn't have to maintain a retail store or engage in advertising, the commission structure on door-to-door sales offsets these amounts. Salesmen pocket a large part of the purchase price (no wonder my friend got all the girls).

Bottom line: *never*, well almost never, buy from door-to-door sellers. (Two thumbs up, however, for Girl Scout Cookies.)

If you do purchase from a door-to-door seller, you have *three days* to cancel the sale under a rule of the Federal Trade Commission. You have the right to cancel any *credit* purchase (as opposed to *cash* purchase) *for any reason you want*. This rule applies even though the goods have been delivered to you. You simply have to write the seller by midnight of the third business day after the contract was signed. The seller must give you a "notice of cancellation" to use for this purpose. (Some dishonest sellers won't give you this.)

The cooling-off period does *not* apply to cash purchases, internet sales, sales that were first discussed at the seller's place of business, telephone orders, mail orders, or emergency home repairs.

Most states have statutes which parallel the federal rule.

* * *

We could have skipped this entire chapter and simply remind you of Tarzan's remark:

*"Jane, I need a drink. It's a jungle out there."*

But what if you ignore the cardinal rule? What if you throw caution to the wind? What if you actually *trust* another human being? What if you don't get the *promised* $12.5 million (U.S.) from that far away country?

## c. Scream!

Start with the Consumer Affairs Office of your state's Attorney General's Office or that of your County Attorney's Office. If they can't help, they can point you on your way; there are a plethora of laws and agencies that might be involved: State Unfair and Deceptive Practices Laws; Section 5 of the Federal Trade Commission Act; U.S. Post Office (mail fraud); FDA (foods and drugs); Securities Exchange Commission (stock and bond frauds).

Consider a lawyer. Laws prohibiting consumer fraud may give victims not only the right to get their money back, but also to sue for money damages, punitive damages and statutory penalties. Attorney fees may be recoverable if you win. Even if you were not cheated out of a great deal of money, a lawyer might take your case if a lot of other people were also cheated by the same person or company: class actions are possible.

If the amount is small, consider filing a complaint in *Small Claims Court*. The forms are easy to fill out and you don't need a lawyer. You just go to court and tell your side of the story and the other side does likewise. Then the judge rules.

Don't worry if your beef is with a large corporation. They can be sued in Small Claims Court. Occasionally they won't show up and you will win a *default judgment*.

If you do have a hearing, on your way out, you stand before a TV camera and are asked what you think of the judge's decision. (Oops, wrong show.)

Scream!

> "*Hello. Office of Consumer Fraud. May I help you?*"
> "*Yes, I've been cheated.*"
> "*Sorry, you will have to wait. I have three Harvard MBAs on hold and, boy, did they get taken!*"

# CHAPTER 23

# RECESSION BLUES: FORECLOSES, BILL COLLECTORS, BANKRUPTCY

This chapter deals with home foreclosures (scams to avoid, steps to take), bill collectors (their barks and bites, who to pay first), getting sued, bankruptcy and dire straits.

When it looks like you will be falling behind on your bills or mortgage, borrowing more money is not the answer nor is ignoring your problems. Get debt counseling, and keep in touch with your creditors. Most importantly, don't try to make ends meet by not buying your meds!!

*Debt counseling agencies* can help you with a budget and can contact creditors. Some are free. Contact your Area Agency on Aging or your local Information and Referral.

## a. Home Foreclosures

If you are having, or will likely have, mortgage problems, go to the HUD (Housing and Urban Development) website: www.hud.gov. It will advise:

- Talk to a foreclosure avoidance counselor.
  It gives the names of local HUD approved counselors whose services are *free*.
- Talk to your lender.
  There are many options, from temporary loans to refinance or loan modification.
- Find local or state sources of help.
  Again the website will direct you.
- Contact HOPE NOW which provides counseling.

Realize that you have some cards to play. Banks are not eager to foreclose as it is costly and ends with them owning a house that most likely stands empty.

Much is in flux. For example, at this writing, it is not possible for you to go to Bankruptcy Court to have the loan modified. There are proposals in Congress to allow this.

The good news, if there is any, is that things don't happen suddenly; the sheriff will not show up one day, unannounced, to evict you. You will get plenty of notice (harassing calls and threatening letters) and the lender will have to go to court to get an eviction order.

What happens in a foreclosure is this. The lender takes your house and puts it on the market. When it sells, the proceeds are deducted from the amount you owe on the mortgage. If there is more, then you get the excess. The problem is when there is less, the problem of the *deficiency judgment.*

Say you owe $100,000 on the mortgage and your house in foreclosure sells for only $75,000. You still owe $25,000. Can the lender come after you for that amount? It depends on what the mortgage document provides (is it a recourse loan?).

To avoid this possibility, you can probably get the lender to agree to a *short sale* or a *deed-in-lieu of foreclosure.* This allows the lender to avoid going to court and gives you peace of mind: the debt is cancelled and there will be no deficiency judgment.

As a legal matter, if there is a deficiency judgment entered against you, *that* judgment can be discharged in bankruptcy.

This leads to one final point. Some high-end buyers, who are *"under water"* (owe more on their homes than they are currently worth), think that a smart move would be to simply walk away and find another house. That is not a good idea. Credit will be ruined and a deficiency judgment may come back to haunt them.

## Mortgage Rescue Scams

Crooks find out who is in trouble by checking public records. They come in many ways (mail, email, or in person), and in many disguises (claiming to be affiliated with Churches or charitable foundations). They all feel your pain and  promise rescue: they will save your house.

Some promise, for a fee, to renegotiate your loan; they have "extensive experience" and, in fact, know folks inside your bank. Once they have the fee, they are out of there. Others have more complicated and more dangerous proposals. You deed over the house to them and they will lease it back to you for a year or so and then, when you are on your feet again, they will sell it back to you. They may even offer to help you find a job or deal with other debts. Once they have the deed, however, they sell your house: you lose it and your equity.

*Never pay a fee to someone to renegotiate your loan and never sign over your house to someone else.*

If you are offered such a pitch, or have already fallen victim to one, the FBI has set up 35 offices to deal with mortgage rescue scams—contact one—or your state's Attorney General's Office.

## b. Bill Collectors: Barks and Bites

Creditor barks are worse than their bites.

- There is no imprisonment for debt—you won't go to jail.
- Social Security checks are safe (until you put them in the bank).
- You won't get thrown out in the street (only the bank which holds your mortgage or, if you rent, your landlord, can throw you out).
- Your car and most of your personal property (TV, furniture, kitchen appliances) are safe *except* from creditors with security interest in them.
- Collection agencies cannot tell your neighbors or employers that you are a "deadbeat."
- Creditors cannot sue your children (unless they co-signed).
- You are not liable for the debts of your adult children (unless you co-signed).

*Most creditors are willing to deal.* Most will give you more time and perhaps cut the bill *if* they are convinced that you are in good faith and are willing to work with them. It costs them money to sue you or turn the matter over to a collection agency. Plus you have the bankruptcy card. Thus there is room to negotiate.

Work with your creditor *before* the matter is turned over to a collection agency. When this happens, the creditor loses between 30% and 50% off the top. This means, if you pay *most* of your bill, the creditor comes out ahead by not turning it over to an agency.

*Collection Agencies.* The Federal Fair Debt Collection Practices Act protects you.

- Collection agencies *cannot* contact other people (except to learn where you are) and cannot tell them that you owe any money.
- Collection agencies *cannot* call late at night, use obscene or threatening language, or threaten to publish your name as a deadbeat.
- If you tell the agency you are not going to pay the bill or that you don't want further contact with it, it must stop contacting you, except to advise you that it is filing suit.

- If you get a lawyer, then the agency can only communicate with your lawyer.

*If you dispute the debt,* write the collection agency. It must then obtain verification of the debt and communicate that verification to you before taking further steps to collect it.

If you have been mistreated, contact a lawyer; a federal act gives you the right to sue. Or you can file a complaint with the Federal Trade Commission. Check with your local U.S. Attorney's Office.

## Avoid "Bill Payer Loans" Like the Plague

Actually plagues are very hard to avoid; otherwise they would never be plagues, only a few dead rats in the harbor. (Oops. Wrong book, wrong century, hopefully.) Bill Payer Loans seem too good to be true—pay off all of your bills at once and still have *lower* monthly payments. Where's the catch?

*Longer repayment schedules.* Most credit card bills treat the loan as a loan for 36 months: your minimum monthly payment is 1/36 of the outstanding balance. Most small loan company loans are for 72 months: your minimum payment is only 1/72 of the outstanding balance. Because the payback period is much longer, monthly payments go down *even if the interest charged is significantly higher.*

*Pre-payment penalties.* Unlike credit cards, you can't pay them off all at once to avoid further interest payments.

*Security interests.* Debts owed credit cards, doctors, and hospitals are *unsecured.* That means that if you default, these creditors will have to go to court before they can take any of your property and, even then, they will be limited in what they can take. Bill Payer Loans are generally *secured* which means that you have put at risk your home, car or furniture. Often these lenders aren't so much interested in getting your property if you default as they are in having the *threat* of taking your property to force you to pay them rather than, say, buying your meds.

## Avoid "Debt Counselors"

No doubt there are agencies that can help you but make sure they are legit. A call to your Area Council on Aging or local Legal Aid office might get you a good referral. *However* crooks have invaded the area offering remarkable results in lowering your outstanding bills. Horror stories abound; don't be one.

# c. Which Bills to Pay First

In George Orwell's parody of the Russian Revolution, *Animal Farm*, the animals rose up, took over the farm, and created Animal Paradise. Their Constitution spoke to their idealism: "All Animals are Equal."

Alas, this utopia was not to last. Soon the pigs took over and grabbed the good stuff. They were, after all, pigs. Noting the apparent contradiction between their behavior and their Constitution, the pigs realized one would have to change. They opted to amend their Constitution:

*Some Animals Are More Equal than Others.* Some creditors are more equal than others in the sense that they can hurt you worse. While paying something on all your bills, give priority to some. Priorities are based on how badly the creditor can hurt you. Of course, you should also consider paying off higher interest debts before others.

*Court Ordered and Government Creditors.* Child support and alimony are *top* priorities. If you don't pay them, *you can go to jail*; not for debt, but for contempt of court.

Debts owed to the IRS are *not* dischargeable in bankruptcy, and interest and penalties on IRS debts can be substantial. Don't ask what your government can do *for* you; ask what it can do *to* you.

*Creditors Who Can Cut Off Services.* Don't pay your car insurance, your health insurance, or your fire insurance, you lose your coverage; don't pay your electric bill, you lose your lights.

If you are renting, your landlord can *evict* you for non-payment of rent. To do so, however, the landlord must first go to court and serve you with papers. Depending on the market, your landlord may have less of a hair trigger than other creditors. If you are evicted, the landlord must find a new tenant or the place stands vacant, bringing in nothing.

*High Interest Debts.* Here we are probably talking credit cards and, Heaven Forbid, PayDay loans.

At the lowest priority are the most virtuous: hospitals, doctors, dentists, accountants and, most virtuous of all, lawyers. Before they can reach any of your property, they must go to court and get a judgment. Further they are most vulnerable to losing part of their claims in bankruptcy. While it seems like these should be your lowest priority, realize that in with some you are paying a high rate of interest and this might put them near the top.

# d. If You Get Sued: Wage and Property Attachments

If a creditor sues you, it will serve you with an official looking document known as the Complaint. Service, with rare exceptions, must be by hand; the creditor cannot simply mail you the Complaint. Usually a process server will show up at your house or your place of employment and ask you your name and then hand you the papers. It is not a great experience.

The Complaint will state why the creditor (known now as the "Plaintiff") thinks you owe it money. The Complaint will then pray for judgment and state how much it claims you owe. This will include the amount owed on the debt and, most likely, attorney fees and court costs. These can run up quickly.

It is important to read the Complaint to see if the Plaintiff got things right. Often they don't. Common consumer defenses include:

*Fraud or misrepresentation on the part of the seller.*
*Failure of consideration: what was purchased broke.*

If you get served, you gotta see a lawyer *quickly*. Legal Aid offers help to low income defendants. Most local Bar Associations have referral programs which allow you to talk to a lawyer for a minimal payment, say $25 for a 30-minute consultation.

If you and your lawyer decide to fight the Complaint, your lawyer will write an Answer which will be filed with the court. Thereafter, the lawyers will negotiate a deal. Often, even at this late stage, creditors are willing to compromise. If a deal cannot be made, the matter will be set for trial, often far in the future.

If you ignore the Complaint, hoping it will go away or waiting for a better time to deal with it, after about 30 or so days, the creditor will get a *default* judgment against you in the amount asked for. Once this happens, it can get court orders allowing it to attach your property.

Once a creditor gets a judgment against you (either by default or after a trial), it becomes a "judgment creditor" and can:

- Attach your wages—up to 25%. ("Attachment" is a Court Order directing your employer to pay up to 25% of your salary to the creditor rather than to you. It can continue until the judgment is paid in full.)
- Attach, by court order, your stocks, bonds, vacation homes, and bank accounts. Once an asset is attached, it can be sold and the proceeds applied to the judgment. Monies left over go to you.

The good news is that a judgment creditor cannot get any of your exempt assets. Exemptions are generally governed by state law, but let's take a look at the common ones

*Your Home.* Most states allow you to file a "Homestead Exemption" which will protect your home from execution. Homestead laws protect homes only of a certain value; check with your County Clerk for more information.

*Your Furnishings and Car.* Most states make most home furnishings and one car, below a certain value, exempt from execution. In addition, your tools needed for work are exempt.

*Social Security Checks.* These cannot be attached (executed upon). Bank accounts can be. So once Social Security payments are placed in bank accounts with other funds, they may lose their exempt status. *Keep them in separate accounts* or use cash.

For a lot of people, most of what they own is exempt from execution. Lawyers call this "judgment proof." If you are living on Social Security, have homesteaded your modest home, and have no stocks and bonds or large bank accounts, there is nothing your unsecured creditors can go after. If you are in this situation, consider writing your creditor: "Stop bothering me. I will pay when I can. But I am judgment-proof."

# e. Bankruptcy

Law schools offer courses in bankruptcy law; lawyers specialize in the area; there is even a special court that hears nothing but bankruptcy cases: bankruptcy is not for beginners, and is not for "Do Your Own" books.

Before 2005 bankruptcy law was pretty complicated, but not complicated enough for the credit card industry. Sure, the industry pushed its product to anyone with a mailbox. However, it became very upset when some folks acted "irresponsibly" by running up large debts on their numerous credit cards (Duh!) and then, when they were hopelessly over their heads, had the gall to seek bankruptcy protection. In 2005, Congress "reformed" the law: it is now much more difficult to seek bankruptcy shelter. (The good news is that it is even easier to get credit cards.)

But enough political commentary. Suffice it to say, going bankrupt is a perfectly respectable thing to do, that you can do so and still keep most of your belongings, and that you should go to a lawyer, not a bookstore.

# f. Dire Straits

If you are really down on your luck see the discussions of:

Medicaid (Chapter 11)
SSI (Chapter 6)
Title 8 Housing (Chapter 10)

# PART 4

# In Case "Something Happens"

## On the Pitfalls of Self-Help Books

*Yogi Berra, on the way to a friend's funeral, remarked, "If you don't go to theirs, they won't come to yours."*

This section deals with "estate planning." We begin with documents you can sign now that will allow you to appoint a trusted friend or relative to make your medical and financial decisions if you become unable to do so. We then look at ways to pass your property on: the main courses (Wills, trusts, and living trusts), and the condiments (life insurance, joint ownership, and IRA accounts). We will discuss how to avoid probate and whether you should. We will even tell you what probate *is*. We end describing estate and gift taxes.

If you don't have an estate plan, this section is a *must*. You will learn of all the marvelous things you can accomplish. Even if you have an estate plan, this section may give you some new ideas.

Our topics here are the stuff of self-help books: *Write Your Own Will, Create Your Own Trust, Commit Your Own Malpractice*. This is *not* a self-help book. Self-help books have inherent problems; we're happy to share:

*State laws differ.*
> What works famously in California may violate Oklahoma statute or Vermont common law (and folks in Oklahoma and Vermont may be thankful).

*Law changes.*
> Probate used to be horrible, something to avoid at all costs. Not so today. Estate taxes used to be a big worry. Not so much today.

*One size doesn't fit all.*
> You did it your way. Why stop now? Self-help books compress life's complexity into three or four choices.

*Self-help authors don't tell corny jokes.*

This section is *not* a lawyer substitute. But it will give you a general understanding of how the law deals with life's really tough problems: death and disability. With a basic understanding meeting with your lawyer will be all the more productive and less expensive.

# CHAPTER 24

# KEEPING CONTROL: LIVING WILLS, HEALTH CARE POWER OF ATTORNEY, JOINT ACCOUNTS, AND POWERS OF ATTORNEY

Death is scary. Disability is scary. Dementia is terrifying. Waking up in a place we do not know, surrounded by strangers busy with other things. Nancy Mairs in *Waist-High in the World* describes it as the *"manic terror that things are slipping from our grasp."* Every time we lose the keys, "Is this the beginning?"

Dementia is not a certainty but it is a possibility. Take steps now to assure that if your medical and financial decisions slip from your grasp, they will be made by people you trust in accord with your wishes. You'll need some documents:

*A Living Will.*
*A Health Care Power of Attorney* (sometimes called a *Proxy Designation*).
*A Durable Financial Power of Attorney.*
*A Living Trust* (for some, but not all).

All of these items will be included when your lawyer prepares your Estate Plan. Here we provide background information. We'll discuss Living Trusts in their own chapter as these Shmoo-like devices can accomplish wondrous things in addition to financial management in the event of disability.

## a. Medical Decisions: Living Wills, Health Care Powers of Attorney, DNRs

*Living Wills* state what kind of medical treatment you want, or don't want, if you are dying and are no longer mentally competent. These were discussed in Chapter 2 and you were advised to forego forms and write your own. Be that as it may. Your lawyer may disagree.

All elder law lawyers would agree that you need a *Health Care Power of Attorney*. They are actually more important and more effective than Living Wills which are often ignored. Basically you appoint someone to make your medical decisions *anytime* you are unable to do so, due to unconsciousness or mental incompetence. There is no need for you to be in a terminal state as there is with Living Wills.

What if you don't have a Health Care Power of Attorney? Two possibilities, neither of them good. Say you are in the hospital, unable to make or communicate your wishes, and an immediate decision must be made whether to amputate an arm. One possibility is that your family and doctor simply agree. However, if the treatment is major or if there is disagreement, then your family will have to go to court to get a formal guardianship, a time-consuming, expensive, and often heartbreaking process.

To avoid the hassle and expense of guardianships, some states have passed *Family Agency Acts* (some states refer to the family members as "surrogates"). These list those who can make medical decisions when you can't, usually your spouse first, then your adult children, and thereafter other relatives and, in some states, domestic partners.

Even if your state has a Family Agency Act, you should still have a Health Care Power of Attorney.

- You might not like the person the statute selects: families fight and spouses may be too sick or too depressed to take on this added burden.
- In some cases, the most significant person in your life may not be "officially approved." This has been painfully illustrated during the AIDS crisis where longtime companions have been refused entry into hospital rooms.
- State laws may restrict the decisions that can be made by family members, or may give them much more authority than you are comfortable conveying.
- Finally, the person designated by the Act *may not make the decisions you would want made.* Their power may come as a total surprise, at the worst possible time.

Have your lawyer draft a Health Care Power of Attorney. Give the matter some thought before you get there. *First, who do you want it to be?*

Don't necessarily appoint your spouse. He or she may be sick at the time decisions must be made or may be too depressed or confused to do so. Usually children or long-time friends are better choices. If you select one child but not another, wisdom would dictate explaining your choice to both of them. Appoint a back-up.

*Second, what powers do you want the agent to have?* Unless the document says otherwise, your agent may not have the power to move you to a nursing home or to take you from the hospital against doctors' advice. And, unless the document says otherwise, your agent may not have the power to remove you from life supports. That's where the Living Will comes in.

Before leaving the topic of health care directives, a few words on *DNR* (Do Not Resuscitate). These are serious documents. They direct hospital personnel not to do the "Stand back, Clear, Zap" routine made so popular by shows like *ER* and *House*. Depending on your age and condition, you may be asked to sign one when you enter the hospital. Sounds heartless, but it may be a very good choice. Usually emergency procedures, often quite painful, don't work, except, of course, on television where they succeed close to 90% of the time. In real life, in *your* life, less than 20% survive and, of the survivors, over 80% of them are dead within a year.

Elderly folks who do not want to be "rescued" by paramedics fill out specialized directives that they not be resuscitated in the emergency room, at home, or at the mall. State laws and procedures vary widely on DNR designations and advance directives prohibiting resuscitation; be sure you know whether your planned approach will be legal and effective.

One hears stories of EMTs saving older folks who don't want to be saved. One remarked, "That's what we are trained to do. If it is clear a loved one doesn't want interventions, just don't call us immediately."

# b. Financial Decisions: Joint Accounts, Powers of Attorney, Trusts

If you suddenly become unable to handle your own finances, who's going to pay your bills? Make your investments? Give your gifts?

If you do nothing now, your family will be forced to go to court to get formal guardianship or conservatorship of your estate. Not only is this a complicated, time-consuming and possibly expensive choice, the person appointed to make your financial decisions may not have the legal authority to do what you wish, such as give money to a favorite charity or to a grandchild who has cut his hair, removed his nose ring, and has given up his spark and gone to law school.

To keep control of your finances, you have three choices: *Joint Accounts, Powers of Attorney,* and *Trusts*. If your estate is large, clearly the way to go is to create a trust. However, as trusts are viewed primarily as a method of passing property at the time of death, we will defer our discussion of them until later in the book. Joint accounts (often touted by self-help books) and Powers of Attorney, both present legal complications and probably should be generally avoided. That said, some specifics.

## Joint Accounts

If your income consists mostly of Social Security checks, pension checks, and dividends, joint accounts are fine. It is fairly easy to set up a joint checking account (arranging to have the checks deposited directly into it). The co-owner can now simply write checks to pay your bills.

Most joint accounts also come with the right of survivorship. That means the co-owner owns the account at your death. In Chapter 26, we discuss joint ownership as a method of avoiding probate and point to better ways.

Joint accounts are easy. But life never is. The dangers of joint accounts:

1. Without putting too fine a point on it, the other person may use the money for their own expenses. (They always *intend* to put it back.)
2. Further, their creditors might come after the money. Creditors can include persons who sue for such things as automobile wrecks, as well as divorcing spouses.

A *designated signer account* avoids the problem of the other person's creditors getting the money. Trusts and powers of attorney also avoid the creditor problem.

Some use joint accounts as ways of passing money at time of death. Say you want to leave a small amount to each of your grandchildren. You can set up joint accounts with the right of survivorship. The problem is that the joint owner can take the money at any time. If you want to prevent this possibility, set up a *payable on death (POD) account*. The beneficiary you list will be able to close the account by showing the bank your death certificate, but, before that, neither he nor his creditors can reach it. A variation of this is used for brokerage accounts: these are called *transfer on death (TOD) accounts*.

If there are a lot of assets involved, setting up joint accounts and joint ownership to cover them all will prove too cumbersome. You will need to give someone a more general power over the assets. A Living Trust, discussed in Chapter 28, is one solution. Here we discuss the other—Powers of Attorney.

# Powers of Attorney

With a properly executed Power of Attorney, the person designated can manage your bank accounts, stocks, and other assets. A Power of Attorney is simply a specially prepared piece of paper that allows one person (called the agent) to act as a deputy and make legally binding decisions (buying and selling real estate, for example) for the principal (that's you).

Powers of Attorney can help in many situations; for example, you will be out of town and it is necessary for your daughter to sell your car. However, it is a *very bad idea* just to give anyone a *general* power of attorney. They can use it to get everything you own. Yes, you trust the person, a general power shows trust and love, and that it will "avoid complications down the road". But realize that closes friends may be secret gamblers, addicts, or jerks.

How can you protect yourself? Have a Special Power of Attorney which limits the power of the agent to doing certain things, such as "Sell my Ford Explorer" or "Withdraw money from Savings Account 1234 at People's Savings." You could also limit the time frame: "Good only to August 1 of this year."

If you are thinking of using a Power of Attorney to cope with your possible legal incapacity, think again. A traditional Power of Attorney is valid only as long as you are competent. To prepare for incapacity, you must create a *durable* power, one that remains effective even if you are incapacitated.

You probably don't want to give that power unless and until you are incapacitated. To accomplish this, use a *Springing Durable Power*. It "springs" to life when you become incapacitated. Your lawyer can draft triggering devices, such as certification by your attending physician. Or your lawyer can simply keep the Power and not give it to your agent unless and until you become incapacitated.

A downside to springing powers is that third parties might be more reluctant to honor them, insisting on documentation that the spring has sprung. Because of this, some lawyers recommend against using springing powers.

A lawyer can draft the needed document. Some issues to consider.

# Who do you want your agent to be?

Name a back-up. Tell that person of your decision, as well as folks who might be upset because they weren't chosen (other children, for example). You can name two people as agents. Must they agree, or can they act separately? A lawyer can draft a document that allows separate decisions for minor matters, joint decisions for major ones.

Try to avoid putting your agent in a *conflict* position. If your agent will inherit your estate, he or she will have an interest in keeping as much money in your estate as possible. If you end up in a nursing home, for example, your agent may resist spending your money for things you really want or need.

## What powers do you want your agent to have?

State law will determine the agent's powers under a general power. It is best to discuss with your lawyer what precise powers you want your agent or agents to have. Consider giving the agent the power to sign IRS and state returns; open bank accounts and safe deposit boxes, and have the safe deposit box drilled if need be; change beneficiaries of pensions and life insurance; make loans and gifts to others (this power may make you nervous, and with good reason); pay herself for work as your agent.

A few words are in order about the power to make gifts. If your estate is large, it may be appropriate for you to be making regular gifts to your children, grandchildren and other beneficiaries of your estate. In that case, it is a good idea to give your agent the power to continue (or initiate, if you know you should be making gifts but just haven't gotten around to it) your pattern of gift-giving. Conversely, if your estate is more modest, it may be appropriate to give your agent the power to make gifts to help you qualify for Medicaid or other public benefits at some future time. However, the value of this planning technique has been substantially reduced by recent changes in the law. Finally, you may just want your agent to be able to do what you might do—to help out family members who need some assistance to go to college, or buy a first house, or pay for medical emergencies.

If your agent will be making investment decisions for you, you may wish to write out general directions as to aggressiveness or security. ("Buy low, sell high" won't do.) We discuss this issue further in our chapter on Living Trusts, as the trustee will also have broad powers over your assets. There are some limits to an agent's powers. They can't divorce your spouse nor can they write—or revoke—your Will.

## c. Durable Powers of Attorney Compared to Living Trusts

Compared to a Living Trust, a Durable Power of Attorney is cheaper and quicker. There is no need, as there is in the case of a living trust, to take the necessary legal steps to transfer your assets; the Durable Power covers whatever you list.

However, a Living Trust is more certain. Whereas some banks and businesses may refuse to honor a Durable Power, most will honor the directions of the trustee of a living trust. Further, a Durable Power is not an estate planning tool: at your death, the power of attorney ends, and your property simply remains in your estate. So what happens to your stuff when you die?

Nice segue.

# CHAPTER 25

# WILLS AND ESTATE PLANNING

*Lawyers have given up on the meaning of life. Instead we focus on what to do with the decedent's stuff.*

In the last chapter we mentioned that your lawyer would include a living will and a health care power of attorney as part of your estate plan. No doubt you squirmed: "Lawyer? Estate plan? Nobody said anything about that. Isn't it enough I bought this lousy book?" A quick look at your excuses.

## a. Bad Excuses

### I don't even want to think about it.

What this gains in honesty, it loses in insight. Of course you think about death. In fact, like the rest of us, you spend great amounts of energy pretending you don't. Face facts, make plans, and move on.

### I can't do anything until I get my records in order.

Nope. You can create a trust and put "everything I own" into it or you can write a Will which provides "My three kids each get $20,000 and the remainder goes to the Denial of Death Foundation" or even "I don't care what happens as long as Uncle Joe doesn't get anything."

### I'm not sure what I want to do with my property.

Unless you start writing, you will never be sure. Writing things focuses the mind. Nothing is in stone. You can always change your Will (rather than call them "changes" or "Second Thoughts", lawyers call them "codicils"—we are, after all, a learned profession).

## I don't have time to meet with a lawyer.

Nope. You can write out your own Will. *Right now.*
But what if you stay on the couch, doing nothing, waiting for Godot?

# b. Dying without a Will: The Costs

If you die without a Will or Trust, your property will pass by intestacy. Worse things have happened. State intestacy laws represent the legislature's best guess as to how most people would want their property distributed, generally first to their spouse, then to their children, and then to more distant relatives. There are problems:

- Your property may not go to whom you would want it to. Many states provide that at the death of one spouse, only half of his or her property goes to the surviving spouse, the rest to the children. You may want all of your assets to go to your spouse, or all to go to your children. We have seen very few folks who wanted to split their estates equally between spouse and children.
- Intestacy laws treat everyone the same: children take in equal shares even though some may be younger, some may have special problems, some may have already gotten a college education or a shiny red convertible at your expense, and some may be brats.
- Under intestacy, none of your friends, distant relatives, or favorite charities receive anything.
- You won't be able to nominate guardians for your minor children. It will be up to a judge to decide, and the decision might not be the best.
- You won't be able avoid the problems of outright gifts to minor children and disabled relatives.
- If you die without an estate plan, you can't pick the person who will administer your estate. This may lead to family fights about who that person should be.
- If you have a business, it will be shipwrecked.
- All of your assets will be tied up in probate for awhile; family members who rely on them may have a rough go of it.
- Estate taxes may take a large portion of what you leave.
- You won't avoid probate.

A good estate plan can avoid all of these problems. We will show you how as we discuss the various estate planning devices in this chapter and those that follow.

# c. Holographic Wills

Holographic Wills are the first choice of nervous flyers everywhere.

> *If I die before I land,*
> *This is my stuff, I do hand:*
> ............
> ............

OK, fine. Take your best shot. But Shakespeare wasn't about to take a small plane to Duluth, on a dark and stormy night.

You must write this Will entirely in your own handwriting (no typing, no Word Perfect, and no just signing what someone else wrote for you). *Not* a substitute for a formal Will, a Holographic Will can fill the void until you get back home. Holographic wills are not valid in most states, and may face other restrictions in a few of the states where they are recognized.

There's no set form:

> *Holographic wills don't have to rhyme,*
> *Just be sure to date and sign.*

Here's an example:

> *Date....*
>
>     *I intend this to be my Will to be effective upon my death. I have no other Wills. I am of sound mind and am writing this of my own free will. Upon my death, I want the following:*
>
>     *a. That my sister, Sherina Cadnum, of Albany, California, become the guardian of my two minor children.*
>
>     *b. That $2,000 of my estate go to the Humane Society.*
>
>     *c. That my children get the rest of my estate when they turn 22 but before that time my sister will keep the money for them to pay the reasonable and necessary expenses for their care, comfort, maintenance, and support, including education.*
>
>                               *Signed....*

No witnesses or notaries are necessary (but they can help). The problem with Holographic Wills, and it is a big one, is that they are recognized only in certain states. Even where they are recognized, it is best to use them only as a stop-gap measure. Formal Wills are preferable to get things right. In fact, the only reason I included holographic wills at all is that fabulous couplet:

> *Holographic wills don't have to rhyme,*
> *Just be sure to date and sign.*

You can turn that holographic will into a perfectly valid, effective will even in states that don't recognize the genre. Just write it out, or type it, or prepare it on your word processor, sign it in front of *two witnesses* and have them sign indicating they watched you sign. That should work. Probably.

# d. Formal Wills

Next to the funny birthday cards at the drugstore, you'll find the Will forms. There will be blanks to be filled in, boxes to be checked, and language designed to impress—"per stirpes", "aforementioned clause III (b) (2)", and, of course, "being of sound mind" (the latter is known as a "Sanity Clause"). In the case of a Will contest, Sanity clauses are of doubtful efficacy, although few judges have gone as far as Chico in *Duck Soup* in totally dismissing them: "I don't believe in no Sanity Clause."

If you buy a form Will, fine. But be sure to pick up a condolence card as well.

> *Granddad wanted to leave me some money but he was too cheap to get*
> *a lawyer to do it right so all he left me was this Stupid Card!*

An estate plan won't cost you much. Lawyers don't make their money writing wills; they make their money upsetting wills. (Actually they make their money in administering estates at the time of your death.)

To speed things up, before you talk to your lawyer, give some thought to the following:

## Do you wish to give money to minors or relatives with special needs?

If you have minor children or mentally disabled relatives you probably don't want to make outright gifts to them. Trusts are the answer. They allow you to delay and condition gifts, to be paid out over a span of years. Such trusts, when properly drafted, allow the individual to continue to receive public benefits while the trust assets can be used to meet supplemental needs. See Chapter 27.

## Who do you want to administer your estate?

When your Will is probated (bills paid and gifts distributed), the person in charge is known as the executor or personal representative. You can name that person in your Will. It's important. There will be discretionary calls; pick someone your family will trust. In the case of remarriage, where two families will be involved, fights over probate can be bitter. Consider joint executors— one Hatfield, one McCoy—but if you are going to take that approach, choose the nicest of the Hatfields and the most accommodating of the McCoys. These two are going to have to work together, and if they have to go see the Judge every time they try to pay the electric bill, the cost of handling your estate will quickly become exorbitant.

## What special gifts do you want to make?

"My wedding ring to my niece, Jessica" and "$2,000 to Public Radio." What is left of your estate is the *Residual Bequest* and it is usually the largest. It can go to specific individuals or into a Trust. Bills are paid out of this Bequest— if the bills are large, the residual beneficiary might not get anything. This might mean you should cut back on your specific bequests.

Many people think they need to list all their assets and identify the recipient of each. That's fine if you really feel that way, but if not, you might try dividing at least the cash by percentages.

## What if someone dies first?

Assume you have three adult children and want to divide what you have into three equal shares. What happens if one of the three dies before you? Should the other two now divide your estate or should the children of the deceased child divide the one-third? Or should they take a share equal to your two surviving children (one fourth for each)? Your lawyer, who spent three of his or her span of years on such fascinating quandaries, can draft language to accomplish what you wish. Here's where *per stirpes* comes in.

## Do you want to keep your house in the family?

Should you give your house to the children now, or as part of your Will? This is tricky, but your lawyer can walk you through the options.

## Do you want your family business to continue?

This is extremely tricky. You may have to consult a specialist, and not just a qualified estate planner. Family business succession planning is a special skill, and the odds of success do not start out in your favor.

## Will your Will cause family friction?

Sometimes you might not wish to treat your children equally. One might have special needs or maybe you have already given one money or property. To avoid bitterness (there is nothing worse for a child than to think their parent loved a sibling more), consider putting in your Will why you are treating your children unequally.

There are certain dangers in reciting in your Will why you are doing what you are doing. While that might make it easier for your heirs to understand your choices (and hence resent them less), you make your Will more vulnerable to attack. "Dad said in the Will that he was cutting me out because I smoked dope and that's not true—or at least I never inhaled—and putting that in shows that he was incompetent at the time he signed the Will." Defamation suits can arise out of Will recitals.

Another way, probably a better way, of explaining your choices is a family meeting. Maybe he wasn't smoking dope after all and this will allow him a chance to defend himself. Another good idea: write your loved ones a letter, not part of your will, telling them why you are doing what you have done.

# e. Taking Arms Against a Sea of Troubles (Disgruntled Heirs)

It is curious that, even if you inherited everything you have from your parents, you can turn around and cut out your kids (their grandkids), leaving everything to, say, a Playboy bunny. Not so in Shakespeare's time; Falstaff's wenches were out of luck. English wealth was land and English lawyers figured out ways to keep the land in the family for generations. Each generation, actually the first-born son, would inherit only a life estate; at his death, it would automatically go to his first born and so on. The system was hard on second-born sons and on all daughters, but it did fill the ranks of the ministry and of the military, and it gave us *Pride and Prejudice*. Our view of wealth, that it is individual and not family, is not inherent in the nature of the universe.

Today the only one you can't cut out (in most states) is your current spouse who will take one-third or one-half of your property, or perhaps half of what you acquired during your marriage. You can cut out a spouse only if you have been abandoned or if the spouse signed a prenuptial giving up all claims. (Playboy bunnies: the price of inheritance is constant vigilance!)

Your Will can be contested by disgruntled heirs—individuals who would take some or all of your estate under intestacy laws—or by those who are named as beneficiaries in an earlier Will. (If you leave your money to a trust and its ultimate distribution cuts these folks out, they can contest it as well; thus accompany the trust with a Will that reflects the cautionary steps we advise here.) If your Will is thrown out, your estate will be distributed under intestacy laws or, in some circumstances, pursuant to your earlier Will.

How can you protect yourself from sore losers? (Lawyers work both sides of the street; later advice for disgruntled heirs. Chapter 38.)

Will contests are usually based on one of three theories:

- You didn't realize you were signing a Will at all—perhaps someone asked you to sign the grocery list, and then slipped the Will under your pen;
- You were subject to undue influence by one of the Big Winners; or
- You were incompetent, and therefore legally incapable of executing your Will.

Protect your Will from these attacks.

- Name all of your children (legitimate or not), and spouses (current or not), even if you don't want to leave anything to them. If you don't, the claim will be that you forgot all about them, thus indicating that you were incompetent.
- No one who will inherit should sign as a witness to your Will (that doesn't automatically invalidate the Will, but it makes the challenge easier). Better yet, don't even have the person in the room or even in the lawyer's waiting room.
- As to legal capacity, first make sure you have it. This is a good reason for not putting off doing a Will. You could be in an accident tomorrow which would leave you mentally unable to execute a Will.
- To show you had capacity, consider videotaping your signing. (One of our colleagues suggests getting Leading Citizens to be witnesses. They are found under "L" in the Yellow Pages.)
- Finally include a *No contest clause:* "If you contest this Will, you are a worse loser than I thought and now you will get nothing!" If they

are successful in contesting the Will, it, including the clause, will be thrown out. If the person gets nothing under your Will, there will be nothing to lose by the contest. Leave them *something*, enough to make them think twice about losing it if their contest fails.

Of course, most people do not need to worry about these precautions very much. If you intend to leave your entire estate to your spouse and children, they are the same folks who would receive everything if the Will was successfully challenged. So why would they challenge it? They wouldn't, and won't— and no one else has any standing to do so.

Again, family conversations can help reduce misunderstandings and hurt feelings. If your family knows why you did what you did, there will be less chance of challenge. More importantly, it will prevent family members resenting other members who seemed to get more.

Neither family conversations nor crafty lawyer drafting will prevent all Will contests. Maybe novels will. The case of *Jarndyce and Jarndyce,* in Dickens' *Bleak House,* showed the human toll of litigation. Families become obsessed and fly apart; individuals, awaiting their inheritance, are ruined. Lawyers and litigants should think past their clever quibbles, nitpicks, hurt feelings, and blood oaths; they should pause where now they rush.

# CHAPTER 26

# AVOIDING PROBATE

*In the movie Ghostbusters, Bill Murray removes ghosts from haunted houses. This brings him into close contact with them. He has one rule—"Never have romantic relations with a ghost." This works well enough until he meets a very seductive ghost. "Well, it really isn't a rule," he muses, "it's more of a guideline."*

## a. Avoiding Probate

Despite the hype of self-help books, which have turned "probate" into "plague," avoiding it shouldn't even be a guideline. The devices we describe in this chapter will help you avoid probate, but don't choose them because of that; choose them only if they make sense for you and your situation. But first, what is probate?

"Probate" comes from the Latin "to prove." (Lawyers love butchering Latin. It makes us look, well, educated.) Originally "probate" just meant the process of proving the validity of a Will. Now it means much more. It includes determining the heirs in cases where there is no Will, and paying the decedent's debts, and taking care of taxes, and much more.

If you have a Will, at the time of your death your heirs present it to the Probate Court. An executor (in many states called a Personal Representative) will be appointed (usually the person you named in your Will), who will gather your assets, pay your bills, and distribute what's left according to your Will. If you die intestate (without a Will), the same process will occur, but the executor (now often called "administrator" or, once again, Personal Representative) will be chosen by the court (don't worry about strangers—it will probably be one of your children, your spouse or another relative, and may even be the person your family all agrees upon) and your property will be distributed according to the state's intestacy law.

Why avoid probate? Until it is complete, and it can be lengthy, your heirs will be out there hanging: until the court changes title, they cannot sell or borrow on the property, stocks, or saving accounts that you are leaving to them. Your family may be short of cash.

One way to avoid the problem of short-term cash problems is to deposit sufficient cash in either a joint account (with survivorship) or in a *payable at death account.*

In any event, probate is much improved today. Most states provide for "family allowances" which allow for immediate distributions to families to meet their short-term needs. Further, many states have informal, inexpensive, and fairly quick probate processes. With smaller estates, surviving heirs simply file a document with the proper court and the clerk will walk them through the steps. No lawyers! In these states, the costs and hassles of avoiding probate can be worse than probate itself.

In some states, however, probate remains expensive and/or lengthy. New York, California, Illinois and Florida are often cited as states where probate is less attractive for one reason or another. In an effort to streamline the probate process, a national group of lawyer activists developed the Uniform Probate Code thirty years ago; it has now been adopted in almost half the states (particularly in western and midwest states). The Uniform law introduced what was then a radical new idea: let the heirs figure out what needs to be done, and keep the Probate Court out of the picture unless and until an actual conflict arises. That approach has been followed in a handful of other states which have not adopted the actual law.

Before trying to avoid it, ask your lawyer how complicated and expensive probate is in your state.

Another important principle: don't confuse *avoiding probate* with *avoiding estate taxes.* Uncle Sam wasn't born yesterday. As we will see, much of the money you get out of your estate as a method of avoiding probate may still be counted as part of your estate for tax purposes. However, as we will see in a later chapter, estate taxes are not a concern for most of us (unfortunately, you gotta be rich).

Most estate plans consist of a Will and some form of trust, often a living trust. We describe trusts in the following chapters. Here we take a quick look at some of the other devices you can use to pass on your property:

- Lifetime Gifts
- Gifts to Minors and Disabled Individuals
- Life Insurance
- Joint Ownership
- Retirement Annuities, Roth IRAs and Traditional IRAs

# b. Lifetime Gifts

Don't be too clever.

*Two friends from grade school remained close. One became rich and the other did not. The rich man, wanting to acknowledge his deep love for an old friend, decided to pay for a cruise for him and his family. His lawyer advised, "Wait until next year; it will make better sense from a tax point of view." The rich man waited; next year, his friend was dead.*

Pay attention to the tax implications, but make your decisions about gifts based on how much the recipient needs, how much the gift might help, and how much you can afford.

Gifts to children can cause resentments. Money is often confused with love. Mom must love Sis more. Let the others know why you are doing what you are doing.

*"I am giving Sis a $10,000 advance on her share of my estate."*
*"I am giving Sis $10,000 to help her start her own business."*
*"I am giving Sis $10,000 because I love her more."*

Gifts also present a tricky tax problem. In the case of *appreciated assets,* such as property and stocks, it is often best to pass them as part of your estate rather than by lifetime gifts. Why? Because if you pass them at death, the beneficiary gets a *stepped-up basis.* In the case of gifts, the beneficiary takes your basis. Say what?

*Assume you paid $100,000 for a hot new internet stock and it is now worth $200,000. If you give it to your daughter as a lifetime gift (don't sons get anything in this book?), she will keep your basis of $100,000. If she sells it for $200,000, she will have a taxable capital gain of $100,000. On the other hand, if you pass the stock to her under your Will, she will get a stepped-up basis when she takes it at your death. The stepped-up basis is the worth of the asset at the time of death, here $200,000. If she now sells it for $200,000 she will have no capital gain. (Maybe she'll take her brother to dinner.)*

Some good tax news: the gift you give to your daughter will not be taxable to her as income. Of course, you don't get any income tax deduction. There may be *gift tax* implications. If you give away more than $13,000 per person per year (double that if you and your spouse are making the gift jointly), you must file a gift tax return. However, you need not pay any gift tax until the total of all such excess gifts in your lifetime exceeds $3,500,000.

# c. Gifts to Minors and to the Mentally Disabled

Outright gifts to minors and mentally impaired adults create a host of problems. If you give stock to your 12-year-old granddaughter, it will now be in her name. Although she is the owner, she can't sell it, even to pay for emergencies (minors do not have contractual capacity). Most likely, her parents will not be able to sell the stock either. A guardian (of the estate) or conservator will have to be appointed for the child and this will require a court proceeding.

There are problems at the other end as well. When the child turns 18, the child is outright owner of the stock and she can squander it.

Many grandparents want to leave money to their grandchildren to be used for medical emergencies while they are minors and for their college education thereafter. With estate planning, this goal can easily be achieved; without planning, it cannot be.

Consider *Uniform Gifts to Minors* or *Uniform Transfers to Minors:* laws which allow you to appoint a parent or other responsible adult (of your choice) to be the child's financial guardian for the gift. One downside of this approach is that the income on the gift will be taxed at the parent's rate until the child is 14. Another is that the gift will be considered entirely available to the child when he or she gets around to applying for college financial aid and this will mean less college aid. Finally child may get the money outright at 21 and you might think this is too soon.

Special trusts are now available for educational expenses as well. The most popular (and with good reason) are known as "Section 529 plans" after the section of the Internal Revenue Code providing favorable tax treatment. Check with your bank or broker; they will happily take your money. Also look online for the leading authority on Section 529 plans, www.savingforcollege.com.

The same kinds of problems arise with gifts to mentally disabled individuals, but worse: a disabled adult (or child) may never be able to manage money. As with minors, mentally disabled adults do not have contractual capacity to manage their affairs and may squander money if they get the cash. Again, trusts are a solution.

A further note on the mentally disabled recipient. If the person is receiving some form of public assistance, money received from a gift or trust may make the person ineligible or at least reduce their benefit. Carefully drafted trusts (usually called "Special Needs Trusts") can avoid this problem. Legal help is required.

# d. Life Insurance

Beneficiaries of your life insurance policies collect upon your death by simply presenting your death certificate to the insurance company. This feature makes life insurance an attractive estate planning tool if the concern is to get some money to your heirs quickly. Probate, even in the best of cases, takes time—and proceeds from life insurance policies may come in handy.

The proceeds from your life insurance do not pass through your estate and are not subject to creditors of your estate. Life insurance can be a good method of avoiding probate. You take money from your estate *now*, using it to pay the premiums, to have it paid out on the other side, so to speak. However, because life insurance proceeds likely will be figured as part of your taxable estate, it should not be used as a device to avoid estate taxes unless special steps are taken. Sorry, you'll need the advice of a tax lawyer.

On the other hand, some advise folks to cancel their life insurance policies because their kids are most likely grown and buy long-term care insurance instead.

# e. Joint Ownership

Some tout joint ownership of property and stocks as the best way of avoiding probate. The basic idea is that when you die, the joint owner simply files the right piece of paper and the title will be rewritten in that person's name alone. No need to go to Probate Court.

But except for smaller items, such as a car and relatively small bank accounts and stock holdings, joint ownership is not a good idea.

- There are several forms of joint ownership; only some have a "right of survivorship" which vests title in one joint owner at the time the other dies. *Without* such a survivorship aspect, joint ownership does not avoid probate: at the death of one joint owner, his or her share stays in his or her estate.
- Even with survivorship, joint ownership doesn't avoid probate, it only postpones it. When the surviving owner dies, the property will be in his or her estate. Trusts can avoid this.
- Joint ownership presents problems if both owners die at the same time, and may have adverse income, gift, and estate tax consequences.

- Joint ownership means you give up control over the asset; while it is easy to add someone to a title, it is hard to get them off.

  *Many married couples hold title to their house as joint tenants with right of survivorship, and that usually (but not always) works out just fine. But assume a couple has been separated for several years, with the wife living in the house. In her Will she leaves everything to her daughter. When she dies, however, the daughter may not get the mother's interest in the house: it passes, without probate, to the surviving husband. The husband is now free to sell the house or leave it to anyone he wishes.*

- As long as property is in joint ownership, the creditors of the other person can attempt to reach it. And, of course, joint owners can always cash in and run off to Brazil.

- In some states, joint ownership won't even speed transfer of assets upon death, and some states automatically freeze these accounts until tax officials can check things out. (Banks assign employees to read the obits.)

- Joint tenancy assets are still included in your estate for purposes of calculating your estate tax, at least to the extent that you were the one who put the money into the asset.

# f. Retirement Annuities, Roth IRAs, and IRAs

Don't overlook the possibility of using your retirement nest eggs as a method of providing for your loved ones after your death. For example, if you had a pension plan and have decided to take an annuity, consider appointing a loved one as your beneficiary. Your monthly check will be reduced but, if you can afford it, your beneficiary will continue to receive a monthly check for years or for life, depending on how it is set up.

The new *Roth IRA* is definitely worth a look. A major advantage the Roth IRA has over a traditional IRA is that you need not begin drawing on it after age 70. This means the entire amount, with its earnings, will be available to your beneficiaries. It will create a lifetime stream of tax-free income for them. They will have to begin drawing on it at the time of your death.

It is possible to convert any IRA you currently have to a Roth IRA. You will have to pay any taxes due on it at the time of conversion, but this might be well worth it. You should talk to your accountant.

Finally, you can pass money to a loved one by designating him or her as your beneficiary under traditional IRAs.

# g. Living Trusts

A very popular device to avoid probate is the *living trust*. One advantage it has over the other estate planning devices (such as Wills and various forms of joint ownership), is that a living trust also solves the problem of having someone else deal with your financial affairs if you become incapable of doing so. That is, a living trust has many of the advantages of a Durable Power of Attorney which we discussed in Chapter 24.

But before we turn to living trusts (and decide, once and for all, whether to capitalize them), we will describe the most wonderful legal device of all—the Trust!

# CHAPTER 27

# TRUSTS: LEGAL SHMOOS

*Remember Li'l Abner in the "Funnies"? The Shmoos were unique beings that did just about everything—shopped, cleaned, set the table—and then cooked themselves for dinner.*

Trusts are like that. They do about everything. In basic form, trusts are quite simple. They are written agreements between the trustor and the trustee, providing that the trustee will use the money or property the trustor puts into the trust for the benefit of a third party, the beneficiary. Say what?

You (the *trustor, grantor* or *settlor*) give money or property to a *trustee* (a bank, a friend, or, as we will see, *yourself*) to be managed and used in trust for the benefit of the *beneficiary*(a minor child, a disabled relative, or, as we will see, *yourself*). The money or property is to be used as directed by the *trust instrument* ("for the college education of my grandchildren" or "for the medical care of my niece Joanna").

Trusts cannot live forever, although they can hang in there a very long time. When their time is up, the trustee distributes the remaining assets to the individuals named in the trust instrument. Thus, trusts are like Wills in this regard; they are a way of passing money and other assets after death. Many people use trusts as part of their estate plans.

## a. The Marvelous Trust

The basic virtue of trusts is that they allow you to delay and structure your gifts. You can provide money for your grandchildren's education without fear they will drink it all up, and you can provide lifetime support for a disabled nephew. Trusts are quite flexible and can be tailored almost any way you want:

*"The trustee shall accumulate interest until my grandchild enrolls in college and then the trustee will pay for tuition, room and board, and necessary books for four years of college and any graduate education thereafter. After my grandchild finishes his education, the trustee shall pay*

*him the interest on the trust until he turns 40 years old, and then the principal shall be distributed, one-half to him and one-half to the Denial of Death Foundation."*

You can create trusts during your life (called *inter vivos trusts*) or you can create them as part of your Will (*testamentary trusts*). Or you can create one now, but fund it with a nominal amount (say, $10 or, in some states, nothing at all), and then have other assets pour over into it from your estate at the time of your death (let's call these *standby trusts*).

Why can't you keep your property in trust forever? English nobles tried.

*My beloved country estate, Blackacre, I leave in trust for my first-born son, for his use during his lifetime, and thereafter for the use of his first-born son and thereafter for the use of his first-born son, etc., etc., etc.*

English judges, who gave us much of our common law, were not fools. If these trusts stood up, neither they (nor *their* first-born sons) were likely to get very much of anything. (It was, by the way, *always* the first-born *son*.) So these judges, clever old codgers that they were, came up with the *Rule Against Perpetuities*. It is so complicated that it drives law students batty. The California Supreme Court went so far as to hold that lawyers don't even have to understand it. (I kid you not!)

Basically, the Rule means that at some point you will have to let your incompetent heirs finally get their grubby hands on the property. Trusts can last only for *a life in being plus 21 years*, which is much easier to say than figure out. Before you go trying to figure it out, you should know that several state legislatures have been tinkering with it for decades. Unsuccessfully. Now no one understands which rule lawyers don't have to understand.

If you are considering using a trust, the first thing to do is to ask your lawyer to explain the Rule Against Perpetuities. It's like hitting a home run your first time at bat; it will signal that you are not to be trifled with. You won't gather useful information this way, but it's fun to see members of the learned profession squirm.

# b. Trusts for the Disabled

If you want to provide for a relative who is mentally disabled, you can create a trust for their benefit, to pay out income during the course of their life, with the ability of the trustee to invade the principal for emergencies. One problem to avoid: the income may make the individual ineligible for welfare assistance. Your lawyer can draft around this problem by creating what is known as a "Special Needs Trust." With such a trust, the beneficiary can receive some benefits (travel, for example, or entertainment, education, extra therapy, furniture, paid companionship, or almost anything but cash, food or shelter) without any effect on welfare services. In some cases it might even be both possible and advisable for the Special Needs Trust to provide food and shelter. This rapidly developing area of the law really calls for involvement of a lawyer with expertise in the field.

# c. Revocable or Irrevocable?

If you create a trust during your lifetime, the basic choice is whether you want to make it revocable or irrevocable. A revocable trust allows you to change your mind and tell the trustee to return your property. Times change and you may need your property back to make ends meet. Or you may change your mind as to whom you want to get your property. (You move to Los Angeles and now, rather than give anything to the Denial of Death Foundation, you want to give everything to the Denial of Goodtaste Foundation.)

One *disadvantage* of revocable trusts is that the law treats the money in them as yours; just as you can get your money back, so, too, your creditors. The other is that the transfer of assets to a revocable living trust is not a "transfer" for tax purposes. Income it earns is reported on *your* individual tax return. A transfer to an irrevocable trust is a taxable event since you are forever giving the stuff away. It may be subject to the Gift Tax.

The pros and cons of the *irrevocable* trust are the mirror image of those of the revocable. You can't change your mind but it usually (not always—and that can actually be a good thing) pays its own taxes. Further gifts to them may help reduce estate taxes.

The most common use of irrevocable trusts: to own life insurance policies on the life of the person who established the trust. This technique helps get the life insurance out of the insured's estate for tax purposes, without giving the policy outright to the kids (maybe they can't be relied on to keep the insurance current). The second most common irrevocable trust: the Special Needs Trust described above. Most, but not all, of the other trusts we deal with are revocable.

# d. Administering the Trust

English novels teach us that trustees tend to be conservative (at least when they're not falling in love with their shy, beautiful ward, who is, in turn, madly in love with a poor but struggling—and destined for greatness—doctor).

Trustees are in something of a bind. They have obligations both to the current beneficiary and to those who will take the remainder of the trust when it ends. The law calls these folks the "remainder men"—better than "left-over men." If the trustee is too free and easy giving the current beneficiary money, or invests the trust's assets only for the benefit of the income recipient, he may be sued by the remainder men. Help him out.

> *I intend that the provisions of this trust be liberally construed and that the term "education" include trade and art schools, educational travel and all necessary expenses related thereto, including the purchase of a car.*
>
> * * *
>
> *I intend reasonable medical care to include the costs of non-traditional pain relief, such as hypnotism, bio-feedback, and massage, and I authorize medical treatment at home even if it costs more than institutional care.*
>
> * * *
>
> *In making discretionary distributions and investments, the trustee is to consider first the interests of the income beneficiary; the trustee has express authority to distribute trust principal even to the exhaustion of the trust estate if she, in her sole discretion, deems it appropriate to do so.*

# e. Powers of the Trustee

What your trustee can and cannot do with your money will be a matter of state law. Best to have your lawyer draft what you want.

No power to buy speculative stocks, or options? No power to buy "sin" stocks?
Authority to invade principal to handle emergencies?
Power to make gifts?
Power to settle claims?
Power to hire accountants and others to help administer the trust?

# f. Choosing the Trustee

Banks and other financial concerns will not get involved unless the trust is large, in the range of $150,000 to $500,000.

For smaller trusts, relatives are often used. First you should check with them to make sure they are agreeable. Should they receive a fee for their services? Honesty is important—a trustee can run off with the money. Also consider the trustee's:

* Relation to the beneficiaries;
* Financial skills and stability;
* Age in relation to beneficiaries;
* Geographical proximity.

Co-trustees are possible, perhaps a bank for wisdom and a relative for compassion.

In one case a dying woman named her manicurist as the trustee. She really liked and trusted her. Unfortunately, she didn't know finances, lost the entire million dollars, and got sued by the beneficiary who got nothing. You can read this story broadly, competence trumps well-meaning and agreeable; or narrowly, don't appoint your manicurist.

Always name an alternative or successor trustee, just in case.

# g. Funding the Trust

You can *create* a trust and fund it later. If the trust is irrevocable, you might want to hold back assets to cover emergencies. and *fund* a trust at the same time. For maximum flexibility, you can make the trust revocable or make it a testamentary trust, one funded at the time of your death.

There is one form of trust that is very popular, the so-called *Living Trust.* It deserves its own chapter and its own *Movie Moment.*

# CHAPTER 28

# LIVING TRUSTS

*In the movie comedy Raising Arizona, a baby is kidnaped and the father is approached by one mean-looking bounty-hunter who offers to find the baby for him.*
*"Why should I hire you?" the father asks. "The police are working on it."*
*"If you want to find your baby, ask me. If you want to find Dunkin Donuts, ask the police."*

Funny story. But can I make it fit? Sure.

*"If you want a Living Trust, ask a lawyer. If you want a free donut, go to a Living Trust Seminar."*

Today's hot item is the Living Trust, sold by traveling salesman at free breakfasts, lunches, dinners, and seminars. The price ranges from $900 to $1,500 but that comes last. First, all the marvelous things these shmoos can do:

- They'll be there if you become incapable of managing your finances, thus replacing the need for a durable power of attorney;
- They'll distribute your property when you die, thus replacing the need for a Will;
- They'll allow you to avoid probate and defer, and perhaps reduce or eliminate, estate taxes;
- They'll allow you to manage your own money as you are today and to easily change your mind about the whole thing without messy "codicils."

"Wow. All that, and free donuts too. Where do we sign up?"
"Sign here. That will be $1,200."
Save your money. Nine out of ten people who purchase living trusts *don't need them.* There are many other devices to accomplish the same goals. If you are considering one, see a lawyer who knows the law in your state, who knows current tax law, and who knows other devices that may suit your needs more

closely. There is more to it than signing the papers. You must transfer your property to your trust and legal advice will be needed as to how. (On the way to the lawyer's, buy your own donut.)

# a. A Living Trust — Parsed

The Living Trust of Teddy and Larry Durbin

> *The assets of this trust shall be used for the benefit of Teddy and Larry Durbin, husband and wife, and shall be administered by them. In the event that they become incapable of administering this trust, it shall be administered by their son, Matthew, or, if he cannot, by the First National Bank. At the death of either Teddy or Larry, this Trust shall become irrevocable. Thereafter, the assets of the trust will be used for the benefit of the survivor. At the death of the survivor, the assets remaining in the trust shall be distributed in equal parts to the then surviving children of Teddy and Larry (or, for example, "shall be held in trust for the then surviving children, with the income to be distributed to them yearly, with the remaining assets distributed to them when the youngest turns 25").*

With a few more bells and whistles, that's about it! That's it? $1,200? Sure, they were *glazed* donuts, but still!

To make matters a tad worse, in all likelihood *you'll still need a Will.* Before getting to that, what have you accomplished? Let's, as we do in law school, parse the language.

> *for the benefit of Teddy and Larry Durbin, husband and wife, and shall be administered by them.*

You continue to manage your financial affairs as before, but now must sign as "trustee."

> *At the death of either Teddy or Larry, this Trust shall become irrevocable.*

This is a fancy way of saying *until* the death of either of them, the trust is revocable. This means a couple of things. First, you can change your mind and take everything out of the trust. Second, it means that the trust is not a separate tax entity. Income it earns will go on your individual return. Once a trust becomes irrevocable, then it becomes a separate tax entity, will have to get its own tax number, and will have to pay its own taxes. Third, when the trust becomes irrevocable, the surviving spouse *cannot* change who gets the remainder when the trust ends.

*At the death of the survivor, the assets remaining in the trust shall be distributed in equal parts to the then surviving children of Teddy and Larry.*

Here the Living Trust is acting like a Will. Fair enough, but don't skim. The major thing law students learn (hopefully) is how to read closely. The assets go to the "then surviving children." Pause and consider the implications of that.

Assume the Durbins have two kids. One has children but dies before Larry and Teddy. As the trust is written, the decedent's children get nothing. Assume one of the Durbins dies and then both of their children predecease the surviving parent. Then the assets in the trust will be distributed as if the surviving spouse died without a Will, meaning that the relatives of the *survivor,* but not those of the first spouse, get it all.

With careful drafting, these problems can be solved. However the drafting needs be done by a lawyer, someone trained to see and resolve these problems. Not a salesman.

*The assets shall be held in trust for the then surviving children, with the income to be distributed to them yearly, with the remaining assets distributed to them when the youngest turns 25.*

The trust continues but defers distribution until the kids grow up (again, hopefully). This solves the problem of early distribution noted previously in the discussion of Uniform Gifts to Minors.

*In the event that Teddy and Larry become incapable of administering this trust, it shall be administered by their son, Matthew or, if he cannot, by the First National Bank.*

Here the Living Trust is acting like a Durable Power of Attorney. Note that there is a potential conflict of interest in having Matthew act as guardian. As he will share in what is left in the trust, he may be tempted to skimp.

A further advantage of a Living Trust is that the assets do not go through probate. As a practical matter this means that the survivor has immediate access to them. If they were in a Will and had to go through Probate, as we mentioned earlier, the survivor might have to wait until that process ran its course.

Why is it, after all of that, that you will still need a Will?

Probably not everything you own will be in the trust. Most people move their major assets into the trust (stock accounts and real property). It is too much of a hassle to change your checking account, re-register your car, that sort of thing. You'll need a Will to dispose of your incidental stuff. If you wish, that Will can provide that everything you have pour over into the Trust. (This is known by the more literate of the legal tribe as a "pour-over" trust.)

Finally, you will need a Will if you are cutting your kids out of the final distribution. A trust can be attacked by disgruntled heirs, saying that you forgot them, saying that you were incompetent when you signed the documents (sugar high?) or that you were under the evil influence of the Denial of Death Foundation. In our chapter on Wills, we suggested ways to defeat these folks and, if we recall correctly, made some poignant literary references. Contesting a trust is much like contesting a Will, with this difference: a Will has to be submitted to the Probate Court, and all the potentially disgruntled heirs given notice of their opportunity to make a fuss. A Trust, on the other hand, ordinarily does not see the inside of a Probate Court, and the disgruntled heirs have to initiate the legal proceedings.

Two final matters in praise of Living Trusts, and then a Cautionary Note.

# b. Property in Other States; Blended Families

Living trusts handle quite nicely two problems that Wills struggle with: the problem of real property in different states, and the problem of "blended families."

If you have real property (land or houses) in other states, it may be necessary for your heirs to open probate proceedings in each of those states. Courts in California, for example, have no jurisdiction over land in Colorado (otherwise California would have stolen all the water). However, if your trust owns the property, the trustee can simply sign the deed and give the property to your heirs.

Remember the problem of "blended families"? Both the husband and wife have children from prior marriages. They agree that all they have should go to the surviving spouse who will then, in turn, split the reminder among all of the children. They execute Wills to that effect. One spouse dies—who can possibly forget the Shakespearean betrayal?

> Double, double, toil and trouble;
> Fire, burn; and caldron, bubble.
> Eye of newt, and toe of frog,
> Wool of bat, and tongue of dog,
> Tear my Will, a thousand pieces,
> I leave it all to my portly nieces!

A living trust solves this problem. When the first spouse dies it becomes irrevocable and hence cannot be changed. Et tu, Living Trust?

# c. A Caution: Praising Formality

Compared to Wills, Living Trusts are quite informal. There is no need, for example, for the ponderous language:

*Being of sound mind, this is my Last Will and Testament.*

These are serious matters. What you decide will affect your life, your spouse's, and your family's. Ponderous language, indeed pomposity, reminds us of the momentous and complicated decisions we are making.

Alas, you face yet another of life's difficult choices: your family's security and happiness down the road, or a sugar donut, *now*!

# CHAPTER 29

# ESTATE AND GIFT TAXES

*Two things are certain in life: death and taxes. Republicans are working on the latter, advocating repeal of the estate tax. Politicians never get their priorities right.*

There is a lot of confusion about estate and gift taxes. Fortunately, or perhaps make that unfortunately, most of us don't have to worry: you gotta be rich.

Unless your net worth puts you in the top 1% or so of all citizens, you simply don't have to worry about estate. For those of you who do need to worry, *worry*. Tax rates are near 50%.

A good lawyer can work miracles.

How rich? When you die your estate (all your property, savings and the amount you pass through life insurance), must be more than $3,500,000. The "more" amount is subject to estate taxes.

Congress rewrote the estate and gift tax rules a few years ago, and the tinkering continues. At the moment, only estates larger than $3,500,000 face any estate tax liability at all, though the limit is scheduled to drop back to $1,000,000 in 2011 unless Congress takes some further steps. (No one believes that the estate tax will return to the lower figure.)

You can leave three and a half million to anyone and your estate will incur no estate taxes.

What about *gift* tax?

1. The donee, the person getting the gift, need not pay any taxes on it. However, if the gift is appreciated property (real estate or stocks) then when the donee sells it, the may be taxes due.

2. As to the donor, there are no tax consequences for gifts to qualified charities or to your spouse (assuming, of course, that they are different).

You can also give up to $13,000 per year to your each of your kids or to any person on you like. Couples can give up to $26,000 per year to any individual. You can make as many such gifts as you like (and some might even be appreciated).

If you plan to make larger gifts or gifts of property, best to run the matter by your accountant. For most of us, there will be no tax consequences even then. Unless you have made gifts in excess of one million dollars, probably there is no *current* tax on the gifts you make; it comes into play at your death. The way it works is that the amount you give away will be added to your gross estate. Say your gross estate is $4,000,000 and you have given away $1,000,000 before your death. For tax purposes, your taxable estate is now $5,000,000

# PART 5

# Disability in the Family

## Confronting the Manic Terror

When you notice a loved one slipping, they notice, too.

*"What I wanted was to maintain a sense of control. Even more than the dread of becoming a burden, helplessness triggers in us a manic terror that things are slipping from our grasp ..."*

So Nancy Mairs writes of her slide into the physical disability of multiple sclerosis. Her inspiring book is *Waist-High in the World*.

Severe disability will put heavy strains on you and your family. We'll look at how to cope with physical disability (making a home senior-friendly, home care versus nursing home care), and how to cope with mental disability (short term solutions and legal guardianships). As you will be making decisions for others, what does the law say on how you should go about it?

It's easy to get caught up in all these details. Step back and come to grips with how it is for your parent, for your spouse. Your number one job is not helping them find hearing aids or even a good nursing home; your number one job is to be with them facing the "manic terror" as things slip from their grasp.

For a tangle of reasons we are reluctant to sit with someone suffering and honestly confront their future and, indeed, ours. Like J. Alfred Prufrock, we "come and go, talking of Michelangelo."

"You're looking good."

"Are the nurses treating you right?"

"How about them Bulls?"

Who are we kidding? Our lives are changing and current events are not our most pressing problem.

"Dad, I know things are rough on you now. Don't worry about being a burden—not only am I happy to shoulder it, I insist on the privilege. We'll get by. And I'll be here to help you keep on top of things. What's your biggest fear?"

Now, the safe stuff.

197

# CHAPTER 30

# THE SLINGS AND ARROWS OF OUTRAGEOUS FORTUNE

Yep, they're coming.

Some were described in Chapter 3, Growing Older. Here we look at depression, memory loss, hearing loss, and financial confusion. While taking arms against them may not end them, there are things we can do that will help. The next chapter deals with severe mental incapacity and the last two of this section deal with home care and nursing homes.

Let's begin with a typical problem.

> *Your loved one is becoming more difficult. They seem to have lost interest in living and are becoming more forgetful and less helpful in caring for themselves. And they are getting grouchy. What should you do?*

First, what *not* to do. Don't assume that this is an inevitable part of aging and that nothing can be done. Conversely, don't assume that the behavior is within the person's control and that shouting at them will improve things. Sitting by doing nothing, or making things worse by losing your temper, are preludes to elder abuse and lousy lives for everyone involved.

*Most conditions can be improved, or at least accommodated.*

The easiest conditions to correct are those caused by bad meds or hearing loss. More difficult are those caused by depression and dementia. Finally, we will look at the situation where the person only needs help in paying their bills.

## a. Check for Bad Meds

Improper medications can lead to depression, physical ailments, and memory loss. *One in five* seniors is taking either the wrong dosage or the wrong drugs. Dosages that were fine before may become toxic as one ages. Drugs from different doctors, for different conditions, may interact badly. Don't assume that each doctor knows what the others have prescribed, and while pharmacists are good and getting better at catching drug interactions, don't assume that all the problems have been noted.

Additionally, many medications the elderly take can make depression worse. They can include steroids, anti-cancer drugs, tranquilizers, anti-anxiety drugs, and drugs for Parkinson's, high blood pressure, heart disease, rheumatoid arthritis, and pain.

If your loved one starts to sink, check the meds *first*. Take all the prescription bottles to the pharmacist. As a general matter, this should be a yearly routine.

> *A hospice nurse was asked, "Do people ever get better and leave?" "More often than you think. We take them off most of their medications and they no longer look like they are dying."*

# b. Hearing Loss

We should have stayed with Sinatra. And Doris Day.

Is your irritable, listless loved one going deaf but too vain to admit it? Some signs: complaints that you mumble; that voices get lost in background noise; turning up the TV; blasting talk radio as teens blast hip-hop. (Their turn will come.)

Presbycusis (age-related hearing loss), can be devastating. It isolates and distracts from family and social life. And once one gets used to partial deafness, it may be harder to correct later.

Don't blithely accept your father's repeated assurances that he hears well enough. Refusal to acknowledge hearing limitations is commonplace, and also unhelpful. Insist on a hearing test and point out (loudly?) that there have been vast improvements in hearing aids—they are no longer bulky and ugly and they no longer distort sound. Some are even digital and more snappy than teens' iPods.

Hearing Aids can be expensive. The average cost is around $2,000 but some go over $5,000. They are not covered by Medicare or by most insurance policies. In selecting a Medicare HMO, coverage in this area may be important. You can get information on state and federal financial help from the Better Hearing Institute (1-800-Ear-Well). Hear Now (1-800-648-HEAR or 303-695-7797 hearing impaired).

Selecting who to buy from is as important as what model you buy. New digital models can be individually adjusted to match the individual's extent of hearing loss and the cause of hearing loss. *One size does not fit all*; as individual adjustment makes all the difference, avoid web or over-the-counter purchases. Seek a qualified audiologist. For the guidelines concerning purchase, visit betterhearinginstitute.org.

# c. Depression

Depression, when it doesn't lead to suicide, destroys life's pleasures, both for the victims and their families. About one in seven over 65 suffers depression and, of that number, 70% to 90% go untreated. This is tragic: more than *80% of elders will respond well or completely to treatment.*

Why this dismal record? Symptoms are often overlooked. Many elders, and their families, *expect* them to be depressed, what with deaths of friends, or unsatisfying retirement, or moves to a new home. *Depression is not a disease of circumstance; it is a disease of chemicals.* While depressing events can trigger episodes of depression, if they do not lift within, say, six months, you are dealing with brain chemistry gone amuck. And some depression happens without being triggered by external events.

*Depression may be masked.* The person may not feel sad and the usual signs of depression—sadness, poor appetite, bad sleep, and quitting activities once enjoyed—may not be present. Instead the depression may present itself as memory problems, irritability, anxiety, loss of energy, and vague aches and pains.

*Treatment is often resisted.* First, there is the stigma of depression; and second, not only electric shock, but many of the other treatments suffer from bad raps. But side effects have been greatly reduced. There are many new drugs. A patient will be put on one and, if that doesn't work, after 6 to 12 weeks, another is tried.

> *Anti-depressant drugs were first discovered when doctors giving medication for TB noticed that their patients were happier than they should be.*

Ken Kesey's book, and Jack Nicholson's movie, *One Flew Over the Cuckoo's Nest,* gave electric shock something of a bad name. But, like many of the victims of the 60s (soldiers, cops, Sinatra), it is making something of a comeback. It is used as a last-ditch treatment for severe depression. The treatment itself has undergone dramatic changes, resulting in dramatic reductions in harmful side effects.

Women are much more likely to become depressed and a vitamin B12 deficiency has been linked to it.

Two bottom-line points:

1. Depression is an illness of the mind, caused by chemical imbalances; it is not a moral failure nor a self-willed choice. Like any other disease, it should be treated.
2. Treatment is promising, not only to improve mood and enjoyment of life, but also to reduce physical infirmities, prolong life, and occasionally reduce the symptoms of dementia.

Alcoholism is a frequent flyer with depression. Look for hidden bottles; remember vodka is "breathless."

# d. Memory Loss and Alzheimer's

Memory loss is *not* the same thing as dementia and does *not* necessarily lead to it. Although dementia usually entails memory loss, it is much more. It is the inability to think things through, the inability to recognize options and choices, and the inability to make sound decisions—what the psychologists sometimes call "executive function."

All of us will lose some memory. The first to go is short-term memory, "What did you have for breakfast yesterday?" Names fade quickly; they are arbitrary—our dentist could have been named Sally instead of Carol. We may forget her name but not that she is a dentist, and certainly not those long, pointed, curled, threatening silver things she handles so deftly.

Memory loss is irksome and frightening: is this the first sign? Reassure the elders in your life that memory loss does *not* inevitably lead to dementia or senility. It does *not* necessarily get worse. Few become senile. Being fearful is a good sign. Geriatric physicians will ask patients, "Are you worried about memory loss?" and if the answer is, "yes," they are relieved. The answer that troubles them is, "No, my memory is fine."

I don't want to make light of dementia. The National Institute on Aging estimates that 5% of those 65 to 74 suffer from dementia of the Alzheimer's type, and the percentage grows quickly after that, reaching 50% for folks over 85.

## Executive function

If you are concerned about a relative, you might want to test their "executive function" by asking questions like, "If you wanted to take a trip to Europe, how would you go about it?" If the answer touches upon travel agents and airline tickets, fine. Be concerned with "I don't know" or "I would ask my daughter to take care of things." Consider a medical checkup.

If a relative is suffering from any form of dementia, you will need a lot of emotional support and a lot of physical help. Sources of help can be found at Area Council and on the Web. Buy a copy of "The 36-Hour Day" by Nancy L. Mace and Dr. Peter V. Rabins—it contains invaluable advice, information and comfort for anyone with a family member suffering from dementia. Then buy another copy for each of your siblings, adult children and friends from church.

## Wandering off

One constant fear is that the person may wander off. When this happens and police must be called, tell them that the person has dementia. Otherwise they will not give the matter the attention that it demands.

There is a *"Safe Return Program"* that can help. For a one-time $40 registration fee, a bracelet and clothing tags will be provided. The items have a toll free number on them: if someone finds the person, they call the number and the operator will then contact the caregiver listed in the database. This service is 24 hours a day. For more information, call the Alzheimer's Association at 1-800-272-3900 (hearing impaired 312-335-8882).

Many fear that Alzheimer's is genetic. Autopsies disclose that close to half of those who were thought to have Alzheimer's actually did not. This is one good reason for an autopsy.

# e. Paying the Bills: Social Security Checks and Durable Powers of Attorney

One task is helping your relative with their finances. Don't be tempted by your little voice that whispers, "The money will soon be mine; buy that new car." It's theft.

Paying the bills with the person's checks can be a problem. You can get the social security checks. VA checks, and pension checks, issued in your name as a *representative payee.* No court involvement is required, and the level of accounting and oversight is manageable. Contact social security, the VA, or pension fund.

Another possibility is a *convenience signer account* (really just the bank's version of a power of attorney) offered by many banks. This will allow you to sign the person's checks. They are better than joint accounts because the convenience signer does not have an ownership interest in the account; their cred-

itors cannot get the cash. On the other hand, at time of death, the convenience signer cannot simply take what's left in the account. In other words, it
cannot be used to pass money at the time of death.

If the financial situation is more complicated—because of ownership of
cars, houses, stocks, real property—then you should consider joint ownership or, more generally, a *Durable Financial Power of Attorney*. These choices
are described in Chapter 24. If the disabled person becomes unable to make
medical decisions, a *Durable Health Care Power of Attorney* will be required.
(See Chapter 24.) These documents *must* be signed while the person is still
competent. Once a loved one starts to slip, feel time's winged chariot hurrying near. If the needed documents are not signed, then you will have to seek
something more formal. Which leads nicely into a discussion of Guardianships. Turn the page.

# f. Rehospitalization

When an elderly relative returns home from the hospital, follow-up is
critical. A recent study disclosed an alarming rate of readmission of
Medicare patients, frequently with medical problems other than those that
led to the original hospitalization. One of the main problems is lack of com-
munication between the hospital docs and those is charge of the follow-up,
be they family, nurses, or other doctors. Be aware of this problem and insist on understanding what needs to be done to prevent relapse. Often this
will involve several medications and several doctors. Expert advice is available. Most hospitals have social workers who can make recommendations.
Professional Geriatric Care Managers can also be of help. These folks are
usually nurses or social workers who can coordinate medical care and generally keep track of things. Call their Association at 520-881-8008 or look
online at www.findacaremanager.org.

Again, be aware of the problem and realize that you may not have the
knowledge or energy to solve it by yourself.

# CHAPTER 31

# MENTAL INCAPACITY AND FORMAL GUARDIANSHIPS

*The only purpose for which power can be rightfully exercised over any member of a civilized community, against his will, is to prevent harm to others. His own good, either physical or moral, is not sufficient warrant.*

—John Stuart Mill, *On Liberty*

Sometimes it is necessary to seek a guardianship or conservatorship for a relative. It is, and should be, a painful experience. These legal arrangements allow power to be exercised over the person against his will, not to prevent harm to others, but for his own good, both physical and moral.

The right to make our own decisions, even foolish ones, defines adulthood. It is premised, however, on our capacity to make responsible decisions. Obviously, we need not actually *make* responsible decisions. Making bad decisions is part of adulthood, too. (Alas.)

## a. What Is Legal Capacity?

Legal capacity involves the ability to recognize alternatives, to weigh pros and cons, and to project into the future. We don't, for example, give much credence (nor did John Stuart Mill) to a five-year-old's adamant:

> "I'm running away and I'm taking Puppy with me, and this time I'm really serious!"

Grown-ups make decisions for children because children do not have the mental capacity to always know their best interests, or those of their puppies.

To check on someone's capacity is to engage them in a conversation concerning recognition of alternatives, judging pros and cons, and projecting into the future.

> "What else might you do other than running away?"

205

"What's going to happen when you get there?"

"Why is running away better than, say, locking yourself in the bathroom and screaming?"

Some use the "planning a trip" question. "Mom, if you were going to take a trip back to your hometown, how would you go about it?" "I'd ask you" is not a passing-grade answer.

Most of the elderly, even old age (defined as "older than us"), retain mental ability. Mental functions do not necessarily diminish. But some elderly do lose legal capacity. Accidents, strokes, disease, and acute depression happen. Then someone must step in.

# b. Formal Interventions: Guardianships and Conservatorships

There are essentially three kinds of guardianships:

*Guardians of the Estate.* These may be known as Conservators and provide for *management* of the ward's finances.

*Guardians of the Person.* Provide management of living arrangements and medical decisions.

*Plenary Guardians.* These have both powers and are appropriate only if the individual is incapacitated in both areas.

Various states call these guardianships by various names. The essential point here is that *mental capacity is not an all or nothing thing.* A person can lack the ability to understand and manage his finances but be perfectly competent to decide where to live and what medical treatment to have. Even these categories, financial/personal, are too board and some courts will narrow a guardianship still further, say over the person's stocks and bonds but not his day-to-day finances.

Most guardianships are sought at the insistence of third parties:

1. Financial institutions may require appointment of a guardian or conservator to allow access to funds;
2. Hospitals may require appointment of a guardian for certain medical treatments; and
3. Nursing homes may require guardianship for admittance (under the laws of some states, formal guardianship is required).

Routine formal guardianships are quick and relatively inexpensive. A short court hearing will be held and usually the *ward* (the disabled person) will not be present. The person seeking the guardianship, his lawyer, and the lawyer for the ward (usually court appointed) will meet in an informal hearing to see if all is in order.

Contested guardianships are more like trials. When are guardianships contested?

1. When relatives seek to prevent an individual from squandering his money, and the individual wants to go on doing it. (You say "Vegas Fling," I say "It's my money!")
2. When relatives squabble as to who should be in charge of the ward's affairs.
   Note: Even after a guardianship has been granted, another relative or friend can petition the court to remove that guardian if the guardian is cheating the ward, or otherwise not doing a good job.
3. When there is a family fight over discontinuing life-sustaining treatment in the face of terminal illness. (Living Wills help, Chapter 2).

*What Will Happen in Court?* State laws govern guardianships and they vary a great deal. Here we will give an overview.

The Probate Court where the disabled person resides or is located usually has jurisdiction to grant a guardianship or conservatorship. A petition may be filed by almost anyone, including neighbors. In almost all cases, a lawyer will be needed by the petitioner and thus the costs may be substantial (in the neighborhood of $500 to $3,000). In many states (but not all), a separate lawyer for the ward and/or a court investigator will also be appointed, incurring an additional cost. *Pre-disability planning* (Durable Powers of Attorney) saves these costs. (Chapter 24.) If physicians testify, or if the matter is contested, the bills could be much higher. These charges will usually be paid by the ward's estate. All interested parties must be notified of the hearing, which they can attend.

What is required in the petition will vary by state. It will include allegations of why the guardianship is needed and often what plan the proposed guardian has for the ward. A listing of the ward's income, expenses, and assets may also be required. Some states require that the petitioner also explain why there is no less restrictive alternative to guardianship.

*The legal concept of* least restrictive alternative *is that, when the law is forced to interfere with a citizen's rights, it must accomplish its goal in the most narrow and unobtrusive possible way. For example, in the area of Free Speech, assume the mayor is concerned that a protest parade will disrupt traffic. He cannot simply bar the parade, but he can insist that*

*it take a certain route. In the context of guardianships, there may be al-*
*ternative steps that can be taken to protect the elderly person short of*
*guardianship: trusts, durable powers of attorney, or simply sitting down*
*and getting the person's consent to what you recommend.*

The court hearing comes quickly, usually in a few weeks (and emergency situations can make the system respond even more quickly). The proposed ward usually will not be present unless the matter is contested, though he or she has the right to attend. Some judges will even go to the person's home to conduct the hearing.

The individual has a right to an attorney (to resist the guardianship or to object to a particular person as guardian) and, in some states, if the individual has not selected a lawyer, one will be appointed. In some states, before the hearing, the court will appoint a Court Visitor (sometimes called an Investigator).

*A Court Visitor, someone with a background in social work or medicine,*
*may visit the ward before the hearing to make recommendations. Court*
*Visitors may also visit the ward thereafter to see how things are going.*

At the hearing, the judge (in some states, the jury, if requested by the ward) first decides whether the individual is incompetent or not. If the person is found competent, everyone goes home to the puppy. If the decision goes against the individual, two questions remain: what kind of guardian should be appointed (financial or personals), and who should be the guardian?

Who should be the guardian? Usually it will be the petitioner, who is often a family member or close friend. However:

- In the case of large or complicated financial estates, it might be a bank or trust company.
- If no family member can or wishes to serve, the guardian can be a social service agency or other institution which will charge a fee. Public Guardians are available in some states for individuals who cannot afford a fee or have no one else who is willing and qualified to act for them. If relatives are bitterly divided, a Public *Guardian may be appointed as the default choice.
- Private fiduciaries are also available in most communities. For information, you can contact the National Guardianship Association, 526 Brittany Drive, State College, PA 16803 (814-238-3126 or www.guaardianship.org) or the National Association of Professional Geriatric Care Managers, 1604 N. Country Club, Tucson, AZ 85716 (520-881-8008 or www.caremanager.org).

Typically, family members serve without charge. Expenses (lawyers, accountants, travel) can be charged against the ward's estate. Institutional guardians charge for their services, usually on an hourly-fee basis or for a percentage of the estate assets.

# c. Disabled Parents in Distant Cities

If your parents live far away, you won't be there if they become disabled. Urge them to have Durable Financial Powers of Attorney and Durable Health Care Powers of Attorney. These will authorize old friends to act in the case of their disability. As to a personal guardian, one option might be a local social service agency or a private care manager. See above. If your parent lives out of state and you wish to be appointed guardian, you will have to go to that state to do so. Further, some states, but not most, require that the guardian reside in the same state as the ward.

# d. Individuals Who Are a Danger to Themselves or Others

Guardianships are for mental incapacity, not for insanity. If an elder, or anyone for that matter, is suffering from mental illness that makes the person dangerous to themselves or others, then civil commitment should be considered. States have procedures that can be used to commit dangerously mentally ill people to state or local hospitals for treatment of their condition. Some states, but not all, allow for civil commitment of individuals who are in need of treatment—such as individuals who refuse to take needed medical treatment.

For further information about such care, contact a local mental health screening agency, which you can locate by calling a nearby hospital or law enforcement agency.

# CHAPTER 32

# DECIDING FOR OTHERS

*You've called the hospital. Your mother has been in a bad auto accident and is unconscious. Her chances aren't great but the doctors tell you that they would be much improved if they amputated her arm. If you were the patient, you would have the amputation. You also believe that amputation would be in your mom's best interests—much better to live. However, you recall her telling you that she would rather be dead than to lose an arm. What do you decide?*

You may be called upon to make decisions for others, informally (as someone helping with their finances), or, sometimes, formally (as a court-appointed guardian). The law gives some guidance.

## a. What the Law Directs

Our grisly and no doubt unrealistic hypothetical (please, no nitpicking doctors writing in; some of these folks are worse than lawyers), illustrates three decision-making approaches:

1. Do what you would do if you were the one;
2. Do what is in the "best interests" of the other person;
3. Do what they would do for themselves. This is known as *substituted judgment.*

State laws that address this issue, in the context of guardianships, are fairly uniform in rejecting the first approach. The reason for this is simple: we want to preserve as much of the disabled individual's autonomy as possible. Just because someone cannot make their own decision doesn't mean we should ignore their personhood. As a surrogate decision-maker, the cardinal principal is that you are deciding for the other person, not for yourself.

The choice is between "best interests" and "substituted judgment," and state laws vary on the proper standard to follow. Academic journals that spill a lot of ink on such issues usually favor "substituted judgment," as it best protects individual autonomy. Being the captain of one's own ship means the right to make your own decisions, even if they are not in your "best interests."

However, on the street, things get muddier. Seldom does the real world present sharp distinctions between "best interests" and "substituted judgment" and, when it does, it probably doesn't matter too much because clever boys and girls can manipulate them.

- As to *substituted judgment*: "Sure, Mom said she would rather die than have an amputation, but she said that when she wasn't actually facing the decision. Who knows what she would say now?"
- As to *best interests*: "Sure, it seems like increasing the chances of recovery are in her best interests, but knowing how she feels about amputation, maybe not."

If you are making decisions for others, just remember to do your best in figuring out what they would decide, not what you would decide in a similar situation. Even that ain't easy.

# b. Combating Self-Interest

*Your uncle is making a fool of himself, chasing windmills, running through his money, and causing his family great embarrassment. You can do nothing or you can have him locked up on his estate, where he will be out of physical danger, have all the comforts of home, and live the life of all good uncles, quietly protecting your inheritance. What do you decide?*

Who's the uncle?

Don Quixote, Fighter of Dragons, Dreamer of Impossible Dreams, Reacher of Unreachable Stars. If you are like his niece, you lock him up, while in song assuring the audience, and yourself:

*In my body, it's well known*
*There is not one selfish bone …*
*I'm only thinking and worrying about him.*

Usually, it's money.

Say you are managing your parents' finances. As you or your children will inherit, you will want the estate to be as large as possible. This perfectly normal desire may distort your investment and health care decisions.

You will be tempted to invest in growth stocks rather than in stocks paying the highest income, when higher income may be in the best interests of your parents. You will be tempted to skimp on nursing home amenities that would improve your parents' lives.

Of course, things are never simple. Your parents have an interest not only in their own well being but also that of their family. It might very well be that they would choose to have their money go to the college education of their grand-children (or a vacation for you) rather than a plasma TV set at the nursing home.

There are no easy answers. Perhaps the most important way to cope with the problem of self-interest is to admit that you have it. Repeat:

> *In my body, it's well known,*
> *There is one selfish bone,*
> *At least!*

Knowing temptation is the first step in resisting it. But then?

Philosophers have offered other solutions. Kant recommended that we uni-versalize our decision as a way of factoring out our own interests. "How would you have all nieces decide the issue? Do I think all uncles should be locked up?"

Note that the judicial doctrine of precedent operates in much the same way as does Kant's approach. As a judge's decision will become precedent and thus followed by future judges, the judge must think in terms of choosing the best rule of law for all similarly situated persons, not just the parties before him. It forces the judge to universalize.

Others recommend that when you are faced with a difficult decision, think of a wise person you know and ask, "How would he or she decide?" At first blush, that struck us as not very helpful but, having tried it, there is more there than you might think. Of course, we can always cheat by picking some-one we think will come out where we want to: "How would Bernie Madoff come out on this one?"

Conversations can be more helpful than philosophy.

> *"If you move into a nursing home, should I go first class or keep an eye on the grandchildren's college education?"*

One more quote, this one from someone you've never heard of, a legal his-torian by the name of A.V. Dicey.

> *A man's interest far oftener distorts his judgment than it corrupts his heart.*

This is the crux of the matter. Sure, Quixote's niece knew what she was up to, knew she was acting selfishly, knew her heart was corrupt. When we are in such situations, more often it is our judgment that is distorted, and we re-ally believe that we are acting in our relatives' best interests and doing what they would do themselves.

# c. Court-Appointed Guardians: Powers and Duties

No more quotes. Dry stuff. State laws vary as to the specific powers and obligations of guardians, those individuals appointed by a court to make personal decisions for their ward. If you are appointed guardian, the judge will review your responsibilities and powers. Here's a likely list.

- You have the powers and responsibilities of a parent of a minor except that you do not have a support obligation. You are responsible for seeing that the ward's personal needs, such as food, clothing, and shelter are met. But you do not have to pay for these things from your own pocket. You do not need to live with the ward.
- You are responsible for the ward's medical decisions, often even over his or her protest. Generally, you have the power to place the ward in a nursing home but not, without court approval, a mental health institution.
- You must take reasonable steps to protect the ward's personal effects.
- *Never, ever, not once, co-mingle funds.* It is simply too easy to forget that you put some of the ward's money in your checking account. People go to prison for things like this. Always have separate accounts.
- You are entitled to be paid a reasonable fee if the court approves.
- You cannot simply walk away from your responsibilities. You must go back to court to be relieved of them.
- You will be given an official court document to show to banks, doctors, and others.
- You will probably be asked to report back to the court yearly or even more frequently.
- *Never, ever, not once, co-mingle funds.* It is worth repeating.

*Keep records.* Even if you are not court-appointed, records are a very good idea. Indicate what you spent, why, and, hopefully, the ward's involvement in the decision.

> *After extended discussions with Uncle Quixote, in the presence of good friend Sancho, we used $4,000 to visit the windmill region of Spain. He <u>did</u> reach the Unreachable Star and I will never again sit on the sidelines, smug in my cynicism.*

# CHAPTER 33

# HOME CARE

*"In the unlikely event we lose cabin pressure...."*

If you're a nervous flyer, you froze, only to hear the cheerful flight attendant warble something about oxygen masks dropping on your head, and then advising, as the plane careens downward (will flip over?), that you should put on your mask first (are they serious?) and then put one on your screaming child. (Thankfully there is reassuring news: the seats can be used as floatation devices, even on flights across Arizona.)

Flight attendants are right. As a caregiver, take care of yourself *first*; otherwise you won't do a good job caring for others.

In almost one in four homes, someone is caring for an older relative or friend. This is a sharp increase, over threefold in only ten years. People are living longer; those over 85 are members of the fastest-growing age group in the country. Hospitals, to cut costs in the face of government limitations, now release people much sooner. Medicare is effectively saving money by throwing the expense to families.

A typical caregiver for a senior spends 18 hours a week providing care: doctor visits, managing finances, and providing hands-on help. Two-thirds of the caregivers also work outside the home and, of these, more than half have to make workplace adjustments: coming in late, going part-time, giving up promotions.

Think what things would be like *without* Social Security.

## a. Oxygen Masks for Caregivers

Caring for others is hard work. Expect resentment. Expect exhaustion. And expect guilt.

*"I'm not doing enough. My dad did so much for me. And I just want to go the movies."*

Support groups help you deal with the emotional side of care giving. Many are formed around specific illnesses such as cancer, diabetes, heart disease, arthritis, or Alzheimer's.

*Time out* is your oxygen mask.

- Adult Day Care programs are available.
- *Respite care* is available to give you a break. Some is offered in the home; some as temporary stays in a nursing home. Insurance and Medicare may cover the costs.
- If you work, your employer might be agreeable to flex time. Many corporations now have eldercare programs to help employees find resources they need.
- Under the Family and Medical Leave Act, companies with more than 50 employees must allow *unpaid* leave to care for sick family members.
- You can hire part-time or full-time help. Be cautious. Be sure that the person is qualified and be sure, as sure as you can, that the person is honest. Theft is a worry; so too, abuse.
- Local programs offer things like Meals on Wheels and transport for doctor visits. Your Area Agency on Aging is a good place to start. Or call Eldercare Locator Service, 1-800-677-1116.

There are many fine books on caring for the elderly. For example Joy Loverde's *The Complete Eldercare Planner.*

# b. Making Your House Safe and Elder Friendly

*Seniors fall.* Are your rugs secure? Does the shower have slip-proof mats? Are there grab bars? Are the tables that they will use solid so they won't flip? Do your kids leave their toys on the floor? *Seniors lose night vision.* Are there enough night lights to get them from bed to bath? *Seniors lose strength.* Do the chairs have arms that they can use getting up? Are there grab bars near the toilet and bath? *Seniors have slower reaction times.* Is the hot water heater set so that it will not produce scalding water? *Seniors have emergencies.* Do you have smoke detectors? Do you change the batteries? Are phones accessible? Cordless phones are best.

Some of the costs associated with home care might be picked up by Medicare, Medicaid, or long-term care insurance. For example, Medicare Part A, with a 20% co-payment, will cover the cost of "durable medical equipment" such as wheelchairs, hospital beds, traction equipment, walkers, and similar devices. Medicare Part B will cover emergency ambulance services. Many of the costs of hospice care (care given to the terminally ill) will be picked up by Medicare. Finally, caring for a parent may allow you to claim an additional income tax exemption.

It may be necessary to make structural changes to your house (wheelchair ramps, widened hallways, modified bathroom facilities). If you are renting, your landlord *must* allow you to make these changes as long as you agree to take them out when you leave.

An occupational therapist can be quite helpful in making specific suggestions. For example, if the elder is a gardener but has knee or hip problems, raised plant beds can work wonders. Someone with bad arthritis will find level handles more friendly than door knobs.

## c. Get Your Siblings on Board

It is very hard to truly appreciate the monetary cost and heartache of caring for elders. All too frequently siblings who are not the caregivers accuse the caregiver of wasting money, of taking advantage, and, when the Will is eventually read, of using undue influence. Sit everyone down as soon as you can to discuss this problem.

"Okay, you take Dad."

At the end of the day (more honestly, at the end of the chapter), there may come a time when home care is simply too demanding: on you, on your job, on your family. Time to consider a nursing home. You may be pleasantly surprised.

# CHAPTER 34

# NURSING HOMES, GERIATRIC CARE MANAGERS

"Nursing home."

What image comes to mind?

Probably a negative one, old folks slumped in wheelchairs staring at TV static, images from movies or long-ago visits to a grandparent, all we remember is beds, wheelchairs, smells, and the joyous sense of rebirth when we got outside.

Old images die hard. It is clearly possible to live with dignity, with meaning, and with humor in a nursing home. There are new friends to be made, new hobbies to be tried, and new books to be read.

In many ways a good nursing home care is better than home care. While residents lose privacy and sense of home, nursing homes provide better medical treatment with nurses, certified nursing assistants and sometimes physicians, on staff. Most provide extensive activities, such as exercise programs, craft classes, and field trips.

And there is a lot to be said for hanging out with folks your own age. You can talk about Ed Sullivan, Howdy Doody, and the Honeymooners. There is no need to pretend you know who Twisted Sister is (or are). And you can shuffle along at your own damned pace.

The decision to place a loved one in a nursing home is similar to the dilemma raised by child care some years earlier: no matter how loving and energetic you are, hired folks offer expertise, activities, and friends.

Many fear dying in a nursing home. It's always possible to return home at the time of one's last illness and receive hospice care.

You have three kinds of concerns: cost, selection, and actual services. As to cost, nursing homes are quite expensive and very little of the cost will be covered by Medicare. Chapter 12 deals with this problem and discusses long-term care insurance and Medicaid.

Children are generally *not* financially obligated to pay for their parents *unless* they agree to. When signing the initial paperwork, nursing home officials will likely ask you to sign up—refuse, even though it might put you in a "bad light." (Better in a bad light than in a poor house!)

Some states have laws requiring families (usually meaning adult children) to contribute to the care of an adult relative unable to pay for his or her own care. Those laws are generally unenforceable, both because of practical considerations and also because of federal limitations imposed by the Medicaid and Medicare programs. Times change, and with tremendous budgetary pressure placed on the states by the cost of long-term care programs, the rules may change, too.

# a. The Need for Planning: Geriatric Care Managers

Far too often, individuals are put in nursing homes on a more on an emergency basis—usually when they are released from the hospital after a fall, a major accident, or a heart attack or stroke. Such decisions, pressured as they are, may not the best. If an elderly relative is living on their own, or in your home, it is not too early to at least begin thinking about nursing homes.

There is a new niche profession: *Geriatric Care Managers*. These folks can help you begin thinking about choices that may have to be made down the road. They usually have training in gerontology, social work, nursing, or counseling and should have extensive knowledge about the costs, quality, and availability of services in your community. They provide a bundle of services, from financial and physical assessments to recommendations of living arrangements. If you and your parents live far apart, a geriatric care manager can also help you make long-distance arrangements, and can be your surrogate eyes and ears to monitor future care.

When a elderly relative comes home from the hospitalization is a critical time, otherwise they may relapse. A professional care manager can help you coordinate the follow-up treatments.

The field is unregulated but there is a National Association of Professional Geriatric Care Managers. In making your selection, ask about training, scope of services, and letters of recommendation. For help locating a member, call the Association at 520-881-8008 or look online at www.findacaremanager.org.

If you decide to go it alone, a network can help you decide if a nursing home is necessary and, if so, which one. It might include friends and relatives, doctors and health care professionals, clergy and social workers.

One task is to decide what level of care is needed.

*Hospice care:* This is end-of-life care, often at home, usually (but not always) paid by Medicare.

*Skilled-nursing home care:* This usually follows hospitalization and is designed for the short term; it is expected that the patient will return home. Some of the costs are picked up by Medicare—but only if the patient is deemed to have *rehabilitative potential.* Once the professionals determine that continued therapy (physical, occupational and speech) will not help the patient improve, Medicare benefits will usually end—and therapy will likely end at the same time.

*Custodial care:* This is long-term. It is expected that the patient will *not* return home *unless* it is to die at home. The costs of custodial care are not covered by Medicare.

There are a host of alternatives to nursing homes, depending on the level of disability, including subsidized senior housing, Board and Care Homes, and Continuing Care Retirement Communities (CCRCs). For a discussion of these options, see Chapter 10.

# b. Selecting a Nursing Home

Some nursing homes are great; others, both figuratively and literally, stink. How to find a good one? Talk to knowledgeable folks, then visit at least two homes, and, always remember, "It's the location, location, location!"

*Long-Term Care Ombudsman.* There are over 500 local long-term care ombudsman programs. Ombudsmen visit nursing homes, take complaints, and advocate for residents. They are a great source of information and advice. Although they cannot recommend particular homes, they can answer questions concerning:

- survey results
- number of complaints
- results of their investigations

Other good sources of information about nursing homes include:

- hospital discharge planners and social workers
- doctors and clergy
- volunteers who help the elderly
- the National Citizen's Coalition for Nursing Home Reform (www.nccnhr.org), which has published a good guide called "Nursing Homes: Getting Good Care There" (now in its Second Edition)

- Medicare itself, which by federal law must maintain a database of nursing homes and their past performance. You can locate local nursing homes and read about their history of inspections and incidents at www.medicare.gov/NHCompare/. The Medicare site includes an excellent checklist for comparing nursing homes.

Visit *at least two (to allow for comparison) and visit each several times, at different times of day. Things you might want to look at:*

*Staff.* Does it seem adequate to give individual attention or does it seem overworked? How does the staff treat the residents?

*Mealtimes.* Do residents socialize? Residents needing help should be integrated with other residents rather than eating alone.

*Resident rooms.* Personalized or institutionalized?

*Residents.* Reasonably well groomed, clean, and dressed?

*Restraints and bedsores.* Too many residents physically or medically restrained and too many bedsores spell trouble.

*Activities.* Take a look at the schedule of activities and show up to observe some. Speaking of activities, does the home have policies concerning resident sex?

*Location.* The more the family can visit, the better. Not only are the visits good in and of themselves, but nurses will pay more attention to residents who do not appear to be abandoned. If you have questions concerning a family member's care, you have the right to inspect medical charts. The nursing home has 24 hours to make them available.

# c. Patients' Rights

The federal Nursing Home Reform Act (NHRA) applies to any home that has Medicare or Medicaid patients (a majority of such homes). The NHRA requires that a patient Bill of Rights be given to residents and their families. The most important, the right:

- to an individualized treatment plan;
- to see all of one's clinical and other records;
- to complain and be free from reprisal;
- to send and receive uncensored mail and to make private calls;
- to refuse treatment; and
- *not* to be physically or chemically restrained except to prevent physical harm, and then only upon instruction of a doctor.

We cannot stress the importance of the right not to be restrained except under very limited circumstances. In some nursing homes, patients are routinely tied to their chairs. By their arms. Considerable medical evidence indicates that this actually *increases* the incidence of injuries, as patients struggle against restraints, get caught in the restraining devices, or are simply left inadequately attended to once the staff perceives that the danger of injury is reduced. If you need ammunition in dealing with a facility, look at the website of "Untie the Elderly," a project of the Kendal Corporation, a faith-based organization active in the Northeast, at www.ute.kendal.org

# d. Abuse

The best way to prevent abuse is always to suspect it and to visit often. As to the signs of abuse and what to do about it, see Chapter 14. To minimize abuse and neglect, and to help improve the quality of care, adopt the "cookies and thorns" approach. Bring cookies to the facility's staff, and think of your job as being a constant thorn in the facility's side.

# PART 6

# DEATH IN THE FAMILY

## Introduction

Probably best *not* to put off this part until you actually need it. You will wrestle with the dilemma of learning, or ignoring, a terminal prognosis, learn of the wonderful world of hospice, ponder the curious yet empowering notion of "dying well," and be reminded of the critical need for human touch. That's Chapter 35. The next chapter deals with "pulling plugs," the debate over physician-assisted suicide, and the law surrounding cases like that of Terri Schiavo.

Chapter 37, Death in the Family, has one important insight: that there is no proper way to grieve, that there are no stages of mourning, and that there is no goal to mourning. Other than that the chapter deals with all of the running around one must do in terms of funeral arrangements and bill paying. The last chapter gives you the nuts and bolts of probate.

# CHAPTER 35

# HOSPICE, DYING WELL, AND BEING THERE

*Art Buchwald, newspaperman, decided enough is enough. He stopped kidney dialysis. He gave a last interview, to Tom Brokaw. "Art, what do you think you will you miss the most?"*
*"Global warming."*

There will be sadness and grief—we are dealing with terminal illness. But, as we are also dealing with people, expect humor and moments of grand transcendence. We'll discuss the wonderful promise of hospice care, the curious notion of dying well, and the importance of being bedside. First we look at a terrible day that may be in your future. Your spouse has given the doctor permission to discuss her medical condition with you. (Federal law, HIPAA, requires that permissions be given.)

The doctor tells you:

*"Your spouse has pancreatic cancer and has only a short time to live. She seems to be in denial. Should we tell her?"*

## a. Disclosing a Terminal Prognosis

Talk *now*, so that you will know what to do *then*.

*"Dear, let me ask you something. If you had inoperable cancer and only a short time to live, would you want to know?"*

Expect something flip.

*"You decide. I'm too busy with these tomatoes."*

Press!

*"That's not fair. I want to know what you want me to do."*
*"O.K., then tell me. Now I've got to get back to these tomatoes."*

*"Why would you want to know?"*

You want a discussion, not an answer. Discussion forces us to think long and hard, about death, about life. We may learn things about ourselves we didn't even know. But what if, when and if the time comes, you still don't know your spouse's desires?

Most people assume that disclosure of terminal diagnosis is generally a very good idea. However, to force this knowledge on someone who doesn't want to know is as bad as keeping quiet when the person would want to know.

The question is whether your spouse would want to know. Your emotions may distort your decision. You *may not* tell because you don't want to face the truth. Telling seems to make it more real. Telling will trigger an emotional crisis, a crisis you may not be prepared for. Or you *may* tell simply because you are too uncomfortable keeping the secret.

Try to put aside your fears. *Would my loved one want to know?* There are good reasons *not* to tell.

*Doctors have been wrong before.* A Native American at a Death and Dying Conference explained that, when an individual is hospitalized, family and friends get together and decide upon a spokesperson to deal with the doctors.

"If I have to give you a terminal prognosis," a doctor from the audience asked him, "would you want me to tell your spokesperson or would you want me to talk to you?"

"Well, if you *could* tell me I was dying, you would be God. I would love to talk to you."

*Hearing the prognosis, your spouse may give up all hope.* In Oscar Wilde's *The Importance of Being Earnest*, the funniest play ever written, the main character makes up the existence of cousin Earnest. When he grows weary of the city, he visits Earnest. This works fine, but around the second act, Earnest becomes inconvenient. The solution: Earnest's death is announced, his death coming shortly after his doctor had given him only "a short time to live." Another character, hearing this, is quite impressed and remarks:

"He seems to have had great confidence in the opinion of his physician."

Usually, however, the doctors have it right, and hope does not turn enough diseases around. There are good reasons to tell:

- *Your loved one will probably find out accidentally, from a nurse or hospital technician.*
- *Your loved one probably already suspects the diagnosis, and fears bringing it up out of a desire not to burden you.*

- *If you believe that it is possible to die well keeping the matter secret denies your spouse (and your family) the wonderful care of Hospice.*

# b. "Would it surprise you if this patient died within the next 12 months?"

Doctors often avoid the topic of death. If you have a loved one in the hospital with a serious condition, or if you have an elderly relative with chronic illness, you will need to ask. If death would not be a surprise in the coming year, it is time to give serious thought to palliative care and to hospice.

# c. Hospice Care

*What people fear most about death is not the pain; not even what comes next. People fear dying alone.*

Death in the hospital can be lonesome. And gruesome. The *Journal of the American Medical Association* studied five major hospitals and reports:

*50% of terminal patients experienced moderate to severe pain, half the time.*
*38% spent 10 or more days in a coma.*
*31% spent all or most of their family's savings during their final illness.*

Hospice care is a wonderful and loving alternative: Death comes, not with strangers, in a busy and noisy hospital, but with family and friends, at home, in a home-like setting in a hospital, or in a free-standing hospice center.

Hospice has been an amazing success. It wasn't there for our grandparents. It was started in 1967 in England and first came to the U.S. in 1974. There are now over 3,300 hospice programs in the U.S. and about one-third of us die in hospice. (The next great death and dying movement, gaining strength today, deals with improving pain management for terminal patients, putting controlling pain right up there with controlling disease and putting aside old fears about "creating addicts.")

In the early days of the hospice movement, disease fighting medications (as opposed to pain and comfort meds) were *not* given. Recently there has been a movement, known as "open access," which allows the hospice patient to continue some disease-fighting treatment.

Hospice care is provided by a team, likely a doctor, a physical therapist, a nurse, a counselor, and a spiritual advisor. The goals of hospice are to eliminate pain (they assert that they can be almost 100% effective) and to educate the patient and the family about the dying process so that it can be as humane as possible.

Care is essentially *free*. Congress, realizing that 25% of all Medicare funds are spent on treatments in the last year of life, and realizing hospice is less expensive than intensive care, added hospice to the list of benefits. Medicare pays for doctors, drugs, medical appliances (beds), social workers, home nurse visits, home health workers, short-term nursing, and short-term hospital stays. Hospice care does not end with the death of the patient; bereavement counselors, if requested, follow up with the family for a year.

Given all of this, why is it that only a forth of us die in hospice?

First, denial that death is coming, denial not only by the patient and the family but by the doctors as well. Again, you must push the prognosis: to be eligible for hospice, a physician must attest that death is likely within six months.

Second, hospice is thought of as a place to die; going into the program is like giving up. But many walk out of hospice. It seems that when all of the drugs the patient is taking to cure the disease are stopped, leaving only those to help with the pain, many patients get better. The combination of powerful drugs can lead to deathlike symptoms.

But hospice is not a place to die nor a program about death; it is a place to be comforted and a program about life. The sad truth is that not only do too few use it but those that do do so much too late, within the last few weeks of death. How long could they have had that comfort? *Six months!*

To learn more about hospice, go to www.law.arizona.edu/hospice.

# d. "Dying Well"

*"I want to die like my grandfather did, in his sleep. Not screaming like his passengers in the back seat."*

If we only hope for a death that doesn't involve a lot of pain, we are selling ourselves short; we are selling our families short. Hospice talks of dying as a growth experience.

*"How can dying be a growth experience? At the end, we're dead."*

We think instrumentally. Nothing is good in its own right; it is only good to the extent it becomes an instrument to be used to achieve yet other goals.

We study, not because learning is challenging and fun, we study to get a better job; we exercise, not because it's great to feel exhausted, but because it will extend our lives and improve our looks. We read books, not to enjoy ourselves, but to improve ourselves (and perhaps lord it over our illiterate friends).

Dying well is our recognition of the riches we have, not of things we can buy; it is our recognition of who we are, not of who we can become.

The actor Anthony Perkins, dying of AIDS, said:

> There are many who believe that this disease is God's vengeance, but I believe it was sent to teach people how to love and understand and have compassion for each other. I have learned more about love, selflessness and human understanding from people I have met in this great adventure in the world of AIDS than I ever did in the cut-throat, competitive world in which I spent my life.

In Robert Bolt's play, *A Man for All Seasons*, Sir Thomas More resists King Henry VIII's pressure to approve his most recent marriage despite the fact that it was bigamous according to More's religion. Henry brings more and more pressure until it is clear that More's life is endangered unless he approves the marriage. More's friend, the Duke of Norfolk, urges More to give in and thereby save his life.

> *More: I will not give in because I oppose it—I do—not my pride, not my spleen, nor any other of my appetites but **I** do—**I**.*(More goes up to Norfolk and feels him up and down like an animal). *Is there no single sinew in the midst of this that serves no appetite of Norfolk's but is Norfolk?*

Dying well involves shutting down the roles and fears and hopes we have lived—there are no more plans, no more failures, no more successes, no more appetites. Once again we are our essential selves—we are that single sinew that is Norfolk.

Of course, there will be pain. Viktor Frankl, who survived the Nazi Death Camps, wrote that people can survive pain, but they cannot survive the loss of meaning. What meaning, what purpose can there be, lying in bed, drifting in and out of consciousness, with only days to live?

*You can give your family and friends the opportunity to care for you.* They can express love and pay something back for all you have done for them. Caring for others is deeply human.

*You can tell your stories.* Children and grandchildren love to hear of times when everyone dressed up funny.

*You can drift towards greater understanding and peace.*

# e. Being There

Thus far we have been looking at this from the patient's point of view. What about yours?

One important gift you can give is to help the patient think about the future rather than focusing on morbid thoughts.

"Given your condition, what might you hope for as you see your life ahead?"

"What else would you like to do before you die?"

The patient may become excited and engaged thinking of a granddaughter's graduation or even in planning their own funeral. The trick is not to rage against the dying of the light but to celebrate the remaining light.

Dying patients crave human contact, physical contact. Read Albom, *tuesdays with Morrie,* and Tolstoy's *Death of Ivan Ilyich.* Get over your squeamishness: a caress, a kiss, simply holding wizened hands. Touch and hearing go last: hold hands, whisper memories, offer encouragement and love, and, to break the emotional intensity of those moments, tell a joke or offer an Art Buchwald moment:

> *Voltaire, on his death bed, was urged by a priest to denounce Satan. He refused, with, "This is not the time to be making enemies."*

Still, being bedside, won't be a hallmark moment. You will chastise yourself for negative thoughts. You will feel the urge to escape—it is instinctive to flee sickness and death. Your thoughts will turn from the profundity of the moment to how the death will affect you and, suddenly realizing that this seems to be your concern, you will condemn yourself as self-centered. Finally, there may be resentment, resentment stemming from being abandoned or from prior wrongs.

Don't be hard on yourself. None of us is as loving, as caring, as we would hope to be. We're human: it is not our fleeting thoughts that matter; what matters, being bedside.

# CHAPTER 36

# ENDING LIFE: PULLING PLUGS, EUTHANASIA, AND SUICIDE

## a. Ending Medical Treatment

*A patient, having had a massive stroke at the age of 80, lies unconscious in intensive care, hooked to feeding and hydration tubes and maintained by a breathing machine. There has been no improvement for the last five days. Heavily medicated with morphine, there are no signs of pain. Attending physicians say that in all likelihood the patient will never regain consciousness and most assuredly will have permanent and extensive brain damage. The doctors ask the patient's adult child what to do.*

Who is the patient?

Maybe your *mom*.

Wouldn't it be nice if she hadn't abandoned you to make that horrendous decision without telling you what she would want you to do?

Maybe it's *you*.

Wouldn't it be nice if you hadn't thrown that heavy burden on your child, forcing a decision that will likely haunt forever? Shouldn't you have helped?

Do Living Wills and Durable Health Care Powers of Attorney solve the problem? They help. But, in addition to these, have a conversation with your mom, or with your child, about the issue. In the last chapter of this book, some ideas as to how to get the conversation going and what things to discuss.

More reading might help as well: *Hard Choices for Loving People* by Hank Dunn, a former nursing home and hospital chaplain. You can read it online at www.hardchoices.com. It explains how people actually die, how end-of-life decisions get made, and what your legal, moral and ethical obligations are when you find yourself in this position.

## But what if no instructions were given? Terri Schiavo

If there is a family fight over what to do, or if doctors refuse to terminate treatment, you may end up in court. State law varies and is changing.

In 1990, the United States Supreme Court backhandedly confirmed the right of a competent patient to order the removal of life-sustaining systems. It also discussed some of the rules concerning the *incompetent* patient. A guardian can order the removal of life-sustaining treatment but, before this can be done, a state can insist that the guardian *prove* that the patient, before becoming incompetent, expressed a desire that this be done. The state can require that this showing be made by *clear and convincing evidence.* But your state probably does not have such a high requirement—unless you live in Missouri, Massachusetts or New York. Your state probably allows guardians to make the decision based on the notion of "substituted judgment"—the idea that a guardian should try to do what his or her ward would do if competent.

Terri Schiavo's case set off a national debate over death and dying issues. She had collapsed fifteen years earlier and had been kept alive on feeding tubes. Physicians testified that she would never awake from her "persistent vegetative state"— an eerie condition similar to a coma, but characterized by periods of wakefulness with open eyes and apparent response to sounds and other stimuli. Her husband wanted the feeding tubes removed; her parents did not. After extensive hearings in Florida, where the judge decided that she had expressed her preference that the tubes should be removed in such a circumstance, and after hearings in the Florida Supreme Court, in Federal Court, in the United States Supreme Court, and in Congress, the tubes were removed. She died on March 31, 2005 at age 41.

Terri Schiavo did not have a living will. Had she, this case would have been much less contentious and heart-breaking. Living wills might not end the matter, but they help. So get on it—Terri collapsed young, at age 27.

## Feeding and hydration tubes

In the absence of artificially-supplied food and fluids, a patient who cannot accept food by mouth will usually die of dehydration, not starving, and within (in most cases) about ten days to two weeks. Efforts will (and should) be made to relieve dry mouth and thirst. You reasonably wonder: is this a particularly painful way to go? A study in 1994 indicated that only 13% of those who died this way experienced discomfort. Still, some did and there may be more recent studies. Your doctor should know. Of course, the pain of this kind of death must be balanced against the pain the patient is currently experiencing.

*It is far easier to keep feeding and hydration tubes out than it is to get them out.* This is true as a practical matter, even though most state laws insist that there is no difference between the decision to withhold and the decision to withdraw. If a loved one is in a nursing home and the staff recommends such tubes, think long and hard before authorizing them. They have a financial interest in keeping the patient alive, no matter how dismal the prospects and no matter how painful the condition. Once the tubes are in, it may take a court order—or at least an extraordinary amount of effort and angst—to get them out.

# b. Euthanasia and Oregon's Death with Dignity Law

*In 1998 an Oregon woman, dying of breast cancer, became the first person to use Oregon's Death with Dignity Law. She died peacefully in her sleep, at home, surrounded by her family. Her physician had given her medication; five minutes later she was asleep, thirty minutes later, dead.*

Euthanasia involves taking *active* steps to *cause* death. It is *not* the same as removing life-sustaining help, and it is *not* the same as either suicide or assisting another to commit suicide.

This distinction, between action and inaction, between misfeasance and nonfeasance, is as old as our common law. Shakespeare skewered it. In *Hamlet,* Ophelia is to be given a Christian burial, one denied to suicides. "How can this be, unless she drowned herself in her own defense?" asked one character. The grave digger explained:

> *"Here lies the water; good: here stands the man; good: if the man go to the water, and drown himself, it is, will he, nill he, he goes—mark you that; but if the water come to him and drown him, he drowns not himself."*

Euthanasia is murder. Helping another to commit suicide, while not murder, is criminal in almost every state and every circumstance. It is not a defense that the victim wanted to die, asked for the help, was in great pain, or would have died anyway—or that the act was motivated by love and compassion. The primary exception in this country to the ban on assisting suicide, and it is a narrow one, is Oregon's Death with Dignity Law. It allows doctors to prescribe, but not to administer, drugs that kill. The patient must self-administer the lethal drugs.

Several states have considered or are considering statutes like the one in Oregon. Only the state of Washington has thus far. Before looking at the policy arguments, let's take a brief look at what Oregon requires. Two physicians have to certify that the patient (1) has, to a reasonable medical certainty, no more than six months to live, (2) is competent, (3) has been informed of alternatives to suicide (hospice, pain control), and (4) is making a voluntary choice in requesting the lethal prescription. If the patient is depressed or suffering mental illness, no prescription will be written. Nor will one be written until at least fifteen days after the initial request, and only then if the patient repeats the request. If all of these steps are properly taken, the physicians will not be civilly or criminally liable for writing the prescription and, if the patient takes the medications, it will not be deemed a suicide for life insurance purposes.

Since Oregon passed its law, not many have used it to end their lives, under 100. Most were cancer victims in their 70s. We're not sure what it means, but two-thirds have graduated from, or at least attended, college.

At one point the federal government, in a move to kill the program, threatened doctors writing these prescriptions with sanctions under federal drug laws. The Supreme Court later ruled that this was an abuse of federal authority.

Is assisted suicide a good idea?

There are very strong and convincing arguments on both sides. In support, there is the notion that freedom and, indeed, being human, entails the right to captain one's own destiny. Why shouldn't you have the right to end your own life, and to seek medical help if necessary? Why shouldn't you be allowed to avoid the great pain and expense generally associated with final illness?

There is another less obvious argument in favor of allowing for physician-assisted suicide: it may actually *reduce* suicide. Many elderly, suffering from chronic illness, fear that it will eventually lead to unbearable suffering and that, when it does come, they will no longer have the ability to end it themselves. In panic, they take their own lives. The mere promise that, if that time arrives, there will be someone there for them could stay their hand and immediately relieve their consuming fear. Once again they would be in control of their future. At peace, and finding that in fact their lives never do become unbearable, most would not commit suicide. Most people who have "saved up pills, just in case," never use them.

But there are strong philosophic and religious concerns against condoning any form of suicide. No one should play God; the guiding principle of medicine is "first, do no harm," and legalized suicide, even if not widespread, will lead to a general cheapening of human life. There are practical concerns as well: if assisted suicide is available, how can relatives be prevented from dumping expensive or inconvenient relatives? From trying to accelerate their inheritance?

There is also the real concern of the slippery slope. Although most proposals to legalize assisted suicide, like the one in Oregon, are restricted to consenting adults who have a terminal illness (one which is likely to lead to death within six months), the fear is that these limits cannot hold. Why deny a consenting adult medical help in ending a life made unbearable by severe chronic fatal illness, such as Lou Gehrig's Disease, simply because that disease has not yet progressed to the "terminal stage". Although it will surely lead to death, it will not do so within the next six months. There is also the fear that condoning suicide will slowly but surely lead to involuntary euthanasia. Once the law seems to acknowledge that some lives aren't worth living, the next step may be to put severely retarded or disabled individuals "out of their misery." Fanciful? One hears arguments that the elderly have a "duty" to step aside, and a group of severely disabled individuals, fiercely opposed to physician-assisted suicide, calls itself "Not Dead Yet." We, as a society, have too much history with eugenics and social engineering to be trusted with this tool, or so the argument goes.

## c. Double Effect Pain Medication

Pain relief, which has the *unintended* result of causing death, is neither suicide nor euthanasia. For example, physicians will prescribe morphine for certain painful cancers; as the pain increases, so, too, the dosages. Increased dosages increase suppression of breathing and heart rate, and may eventually lead to death. This is known as a treatment's "double effect." It is interesting to note that the Catholic Church, a vocal opponent of suicide (and, of course, euthanasia), does not condemn the practice.

For a very interesting book on the history of the physician-assisted suicide debate, see Sue Woodman's fine book, *Last Rights: The Struggle over the Right to Die.*

## d. Suicide

Of course, there is always suicide. There are even books; there are even advocates. Perhaps, in some circumstances, it makes sense. But consider:

- Depression can be treated and is often transitory. "This too shall pass."
- Almost all pain can be alleviated by proper medication. The reason that many die painful deaths is not the inability of medicine to control pain, but the lack of training of most doctors in dealing with

terminal illness and their reluctance to prescribe high enough dosages. Hospice, and the relatively modern pain management movement, promise adequate painkiller dosages and hence a relatively pain-free death.

- Suicide of a loved one is one of the hardest deaths to get over—guilt abounds ("Was this my fault?"). The message you send to relatives and family is of darkest human despair: "Some lives aren't worth living."

Finally, let's talk brass tacks. If your choice is to jump or to crash your car, you may go out as a murderer. If you choose a gun, it's messy. Who will find your bloody body? Who will be cursed forever by the image?

If you are feeling suicidal, talk to family, friends and spiritual advisers. If you don't, you do them a double wrong: your death and your cruel denial of their opportunity to reach out to comfort you.

# CHAPTER 37

# DEATH IN THE FAMILY

When loved ones die we are shocked to find, insulted to find, hurt to find, that the world goes on as it did yesterday: dogs bark, baseball is played, folks go to the movies. The world should stop. In *Funeral Blues,* W. H. Auden captures our feelings:

*Pour away the ocean and sweep up the wood;*
*For nothing now can ever come to any good.*

Thankfully, there will be a lot of distracting details, a lot of running around to do, a lot of business to attend to. Burial decisions, short-term financial arrangements, insurance and Social Security survivor benefits, probate. These will get you through the first several months. Perhaps, after that, things again can come to good. Not like before, but still, to good.

## a. The Myths of Mourning

On T.V. talk shows, we hear that mourning is a process, with marked stages and with final goals. Don't buy it. Mourning is different for all of us.

It is not a process you "work through" to get to some point where it is over, allowing you to "get on with your life." If there is a goal to mourning, it is not to get over the death. It is to *relocate* the loved one — to create a different kind of relationship with the person:

"*So that's what the President said. I wish I could call Dad and get his reaction. What would it be?*"

Mourning is not a momentary interruption in life. It continues for the rest of your life. You won't be "OK" for a long time and memories will always rush back, unexpected.

*The past is not dead. In fact, it's not even past.*
— William Faulkner

Depression and great distress are not inevitable. Some grieve before the death and experience the actual death with relief. Expect complicated feelings—despair mixed with relief; dark, intense moments mixed with daily chores and gossip. Life is always in the *present* tense. You must figure out what to do tomorrow morning. Don't feel guilty if you find yourself distracted by plans for dinner. There are no rules, no stages, no end points. Just be with friends, neighbors, and relatives. Talk. Cry. Tell jokes.

> *An elderly couple sits on the couch. The wife says, "If I die first, you should remarry. If you die first, I'll get a dog."*

Now, the distracting details.

# b. The First Few Days: Funeral Homes and Burial

Funeral homes can be called at any hour. They will know what to do. In addition to funeral arrangements, they will take care of official notifications and will arrange for several copies of the official death certificate that you may need in notifying insurance companies, Social Security, retirement plans, and the like.

Often the individual, by Will or otherwise, has indicated a preference between cremation and burial and what kind of service they wish. If not, these decisions fall to the family.

Cremation is less expensive. There will be local regulations as to where ashes can be scattered. Permanent urns are also available. Some are quite beautiful and moving, either in their simplicity or in their religious and spiritual themes. Others are more fanciful, such as the ones adorned with statuettes of golfers.

> *Query: In Heaven, do you always shoot a hole in one? Or is that in Hell?*

Funerals are expensive. Several years ago Jessica Mitford exposed funeral fraud in her book, *The American Way of Death*. Funeral directors were portrayed as scum, sucking the blood of grieving families, selling them expensive coffins to "show their love for the dearly departed."

Things have improved, and dramatically, but still be wary. Funeral fraud continues in many areas. In 1984 the Federal Trade Commission promulgated the Funeral Industry Practices trade regulation rules. Funeral directors must disclose the cost of all goods and services, even over the phone, and provide a written list when you inquire in person. You have the right to purchase separate funeral products and need not buy entire packages.

The average cost of a funeral, incidentally, is about $6,500, according to the National Funeral Directors Association. That does not include the cost of a burial plot or other cemetery expenses.

> *A woman's husband left $30,000 to be used for an elaborate funeral. After everything is over, she tells her closest friend that "there is absolutely nothing left from the $30,000."*
> *"How can that be?"*
> *"Well, the funeral cost was $6,500. I made a donation to the church— that was $500, and I spent another $500 for the wake, food and drinks. The rest went for the memorial stone."*
> *"$22,500 for the memorial stone? Wow, how big is it?"*
> *"Four and a half carats."*

A little over one-quarter of Americans choose cremation. Consumer frauds to watch for:

a. Quoting one price on the phone and switching to a higher one in person.
b. Misrepresenting that state law requires embalming (embalming may be required if the cremation is not undertaken relatively soon after death, but there is no blanket requirement for embalming).
c. Misrepresenting that state law requires caskets for cremation or outer burial containers for burial (most crematories require some type of rigid container, but not necessarily a traditional casket).

You will be distraught. There will be strong psychological pressures to overspend. You don't want to appear "cheap;" you don't want relatives thinking you're broke. It is a bad idea to agree to a price on your first visit to the funeral home. Ask yourself:

> *How much education would that amount buy for the kids?*
> *How much medical care for Uncle Tom?*
> *How much vacation for me?*

Look, you *deserve* a vacation!

Don't assume that funeral directors are your enemy; they can provide a great deal of emotional support and practical advice, and they have a vested interest in being helpful. They want your repeat business, and if you think they did a good job you should talk to them about making your own arrangements in advance after you get through this crisis.

## Autopsies

An autopsy is simply a post-death surgery designed to determine the cause of death and the presence of diseases and abnormalities. Although gruesome to envision, an autopsy might be quite helpful to the surviving family. For example, genetic diseases unknown to the family might be revealed so that family members can take steps to avoid them. Conversely, it might be discovered that Granddad wasn't suffering from the genetic disease his family feared. For example, it is believed that Alzheimer's disease has a genetic component; family members have great anxiety as to their own futures. Autopsies reveal, however, that only about 50% of individuals believed to have that disease actually had it.

A family can request that an autopsy be performed and can insist that it be a limited one, such as a brain autopsy looking for Alzheimer's or a heart autopsy looking for heart disease. If an autopsy is done, don't expect immediate answers. What with microscopic examinations of tissue, results typically take 30 days or longer.

The good news is that most hospitals throw in the autopsy for free. Even with fierce competition for patients, hospitals seldom advertise this feature:

*"After your stay, enjoy a free autopsy."*

Hospitals rely on autopsies to assure that doctors are diagnosing and treating disease correctly. Pathologists use autopsies to better understand the causes and treatment of human diseases. That we live as healthy as we do today is in large part due to the autopsies of yesterday. In this light, agreeing to an autopsy can be viewed as a contribution to your grandchildren.

Under certain circumstances, the law requires that an autopsy be performed: if the cause of death is suspicious or unknown, and perhaps, depending on state law, if the individual died within a year of surgery or died without a physician present to certify the cause of death. The decision about a required autopsy is usually made by the local Office of the Medical Examiner; if you feel strongly about not wanting an autopsy for your loved one, or want to limit any autopsy, you can talk to the Medical Examiner or staff and explain your position.

## Organ Donation

Even if the decedent (by Will, donation card, or driver-license designation) indicated a desire to donate, often doctors and hospitals may still seek the family's agreement even though their agreement may not be legally required. Organ donation networks are eager not to look ghoulish, or to take organs over family members' objections. That has a significance for your own decision: if you really want to be an organ donor, best to explain that to your family.

If the decedent left no instructions, the family can authorize an anatomical donation. State law lists, in priority order, who can make that decision: usually the surviving spouse, adult children, either parent, adult sibling, grandparent (in some states) and the person's guardian, in that order with some state variation. Some families have religious and similar objections to donations. However, some object in the mistaken belief that they would delay the funeral, or increase the cost. They generally don't do either.

## Notifications

Family and friends should know as soon as possible. Phone trees work well. Obituaries in local papers can be arranged by the funeral home at a modest cost.

# c. The First Few Weeks

## Immediate Cash Needs and the Safety Deposit Box Ploy

Hopefully sufficient funds were kept in joint savings and checking accounts. The joint tenant can withdraw money. Similarly there should be no problem if the assets were in a Living Trust. Even if the decedent was the managing trustee, the trust will continue with notification to the back-up trustee.

Some advise keeping large amounts of cash in joint safety deposit boxes, the idea being that upon the death of one, the other can easily get to the cash and that the cash will not show up as part of the estate, thus cutting taxes. This isn't good advice. First, as to easy access, joint checking and savings accounts achieve the same goal. Second, as to avoiding taxes, it is against the law. And banks read the obituaries. In some states they may seal joint safety deposit boxes, which can only then be opened in the presence of a state official (this state practice, once universal, is now much less common).

If the family's assets were kept in the decedent's name alone, there may be trouble reaching them. The quickest way is to immediately open a Probate Proceeding (we will tell you how momentarily) and have yourself appointed executor, administrator, or personal representative (depending on your state). You will be issued papers by the Court which will allow you to access the decedent's accounts. Most states provide for a family allowance—an amount of money payable to support spouses and dependent minor children—during probate. It allows the family to draw needed money before and during the probate process, which can be lengthy.

Don't assume, however, that a probate will be required. You may be surprised to find that most, or even all, assets have co-owners' names on them, or name beneficiaries to receive them upon the owner's death. And even if that turns out not to be true, most states provide a mechanism for collection of smaller estates (with quite a bit of variation in what makes an estate "small") without full-blown probate proceedings. Most of those statutes, however, require that you wait some period of time—typically a month or two—and provide a death certificate, so they do not offer much help when immediate cash is needed.

## Bills: Don't Pay Them!

Let things sort themselves out before you start paying any of the decedent's bills, such as hospital bills, doctors' bills, and nursing home bills. Why should you wait? If the estate is to be probated, the estate will pay the bills; if there is a Living Trust, the trustee will.

In any event, you may not be legally obligated to pay them. As a general rule, only the person (or his or her estate) who received the service is liable to pay the bill. Generally, family members (children and spouses) are not required to pay the bills out of their own pockets. This may be different in the community property states (Arizona, California, Idaho, Louisiana, Nevada, New Mexico, Texas, Washington and Wisconsin); rather than try to figure out the answer yourself, delay payment and consult a lawyer.

Some of the bills sent to a decedent after his death may even be bogus. Scam artists take advantage of a family's distress.

If creditors are getting pushy, send them a letter explaining that the individual has died and that you will need time to sort out his affairs.

On the other hand, continue to pay ongoing bills, such as rent, utilities, and, yes, the lawyer's fees for probate. If these bills are not paid, the services will stop. You may have to obligate yourself to payment of some other bills, like funeral expenses, even if the decedent's assets turn out to be insufficient.

## The Search for Documents and Notifying Insurance and Social Security

Search papers and safety deposit boxes for Wills, insurance policies, and other important papers. If the decedent was working at the time, the employer should be asked if the company maintained life insurance on its employees. Many do.

If you are the co-owner of any of the decedent's property, such as vehicles and real property (land and buildings), you should contact the appropriate governmental agency (Department of Motor Vehicles, County Recorder's Office) as to how to have the title reissued in your name only.

To collect on life insurance policies, it's best to call the agent or company and see what procedure to follow.

Contact Social Security. Social Security acts as kind of a life insurance policy. The following people may be entitled to benefits:

> *Dependent children* (including adoptive children, stepchildren, and in some cases grandchildren) may be entitled to monthly payments. The children must be under 18 or, if older, disabled or still in school. These benefits are available even if the decedent had not worked very long. The decedent had to be only currently insured: had six quarters of coverage in the last 13 preceding death (or was receiving disability benefits at the time of death). If there is such a child, then the decedent's spouse is also entitled to benefits even if he or she has not reached the age of 60.
>
> *Dependent parents* in some cases.
>
> *Surviving spouse* if
>
> a. the decedent was fully insured (had 40 or more quarters into the program) and
> b. the survivor is 60 or older (or 50 if disabled) and
> c. the marriage lasted more than nine months.

Note: If you were both drawing Social Security at the time of your spouse's death, contact Social Security because it is likely that you may draw more in survivor benefits than you draw on your own account or as the spouse of an insured member.

If the couple was not married, the survivor may still get benefits if they had, or adopted, a child together.

Bottom line: If the decedent was working or had worked in jobs covered by Social Security (most jobs), call Social Security for current information on possible benefits.

There is also a small Social Security death benefit which will help with funeral expenses. It is only paid to surviving spouses in limited circumstances, and it is less than $300, but every little bit helps. You will find that the best resource for understanding the Social Security death benefit will be the funeral director.

To begin a chapter with the moving words of W. H. Auden and to end it discussing a small death benefit seems to sin against art. But maybe, when all is said and done, life is not grand moments, but rather tiny details, those coming at us every moment.

*I heard a Fly buzz—when I died—*
*The Stillness in the Room*
*Was like the Stillness in the Air—*
*Between the Heaves of a Storm—*
*The Eyes around—had wrung them dry—*
*And Breaths were gathering firm*
*For that last Onset—when the King*
*Be witnessed—in the Room—*
*I willed my Keepsakes—Signed away*
*What portions of me be*
*Assignable—and then it was*
*There interposed a Fly—*
*With Blue—uncertain stumbling Buzz—*
*Between the light—and me—*
*And then the Windows failed—and then*
*I could not see to see—*

—Emily Dickinson (1830–1886)

# CHAPTER 38

# PROBATE

*Bleak House,* Dickens' great novel, gave probate a bad name. The probate of a huge estate lasted for generations. The estate went broke. The family went broke. The lawyers got rich.

*Bleak House* sent law school applications soaring.

There are four reasons you might want to read this chapter:

- A family member has died and you need to know if the estate should be probated. That's Section a.
- You have been cut out of someone's Will (or got less than what you think you should). That's Section b.
- You are a family member and need support money, now. That's Section c.
- You are probating an estate and need to know what to expect. That's Section d.

Unlike other chapters of this book, this one contains very little knowledge that one needs in advance, except perhaps to give you a sense of what "probate" really is and how important it may be for you to arrange to avoid it in your estate planning. If you want, you can skip the entire chapter until the need arises.

## a. Is Probate Needed?

Often it isn't. If the person who died didn't have a Will, didn't have much property, and wasn't the only legal guardian of a minor child, probate probably won't be needed. The family can simply divide the personal property— furniture, heirlooms, jewelry, computers, pets, and so forth. Personal property is defined as all that stuff we own that does not have a "title" (an official piece of paper indicating who owns something).

But what of cars, houses, land, stock, bonds, and bank accounts? These items do have "title" and before the family can get ownership of them, the title must be rewritten to show the new owner.

Often these items do not present much of a problem, either. If the title shows a co-owner, indicating the right of survivorship, it is easy for the co-owner to get the title reissued. They simply show the death certificate to the appropriate official, and a new title showing them as sole owner will be issued. With cars, the appropriate official is usually the DMV (your state's name for the agency may be different), and it may not even be necessary to show DMV a death certificate, since any one of the individuals listed with an "or" can later sell the vehicle. With land and houses, file a death certificate with the County Recorder or Clerk. For stocks, bonds, brokerage and bank accounts, simply present a death certificate at the appropriate office and fill out the forms provided; the same simple process will usually allow you to collect life insurance proceeds, IRA and other retirement accounts.

What if the title is only in the name of the person who died? Well, then probate may be needed to get a court order changing ownership. However, if not much property is involved, almost all states allow for quick and inexpensive— often free—probate substitutes. Usually it involves simply filling out a form (you can probably get one from the local Bar Association, or your local Area Agency on Aging, or even at the Probate Court) and attaching a death certificate. Big time probate, *Bleak House* Probate, is usually reserved for the rich.

If probate is required, you will probably want to hire a lawyer. People can and do file and handle probates without legal help, but it is complicated and quirky enough, and your duties are difficult enough to learn about and perform, that you will probably be better served by having counsel. At the very least, interview two or three lawyers, so that you can figure out what probate proceedings look like in your state and what the lawyers think they can do to help you with the process.

# b. Are You Disgruntled?

A disgruntled heir is someone who would get more under the law of intestacy than he or she would get under the Will (or Trust), or someone who would have gotten more under the Will but the lawyer who drafted the Will messed up.

Let's first look at the second situation. Say that Granddad meant to leave you a lot of money but you never got it because the lawyer drafting his Will did so negligently. In some states you can sue the lawyer as a "third party beneficiary" of the contract between your granddad and his lawyer. Complicated stuff; see a lawyer.

The typical disgruntled heir goes after the Will (or Trust) and tries to get it thrown out so that the estate passes by intestacy. In addition to the Jarndyce children (see the multiple *Bleak House* references above if you've forgotten the memorable Jarndyce clan), this raucous group includes:

## Surviving Spouses

If you are a surviving spouse and are not getting at least a third of the estate (half, in some jurisdictions), contact a lawyer. Sometimes "Dearly Beloved" tries to give away your stuff.

## Forgotten Children

If you are a child of the decedent (natural, adopted or illegitimate) and are not named in the Will, then you may have a claim. The argument will be that the person who died did not mean to cut you out, only forgot you. "As to my son Samson, who insisted on never cutting his hair, I give nothing" at least makes clear Manoah (Samson's father) remembered he had a son. If you were expressly cut out of the Will in this fashion, then your only claim may be that the decedent was of unsound mind or under the undue influence (arm-twisting) of someone. Delilah?

## Children Born, and Spouses Married, After the Will Was Written

The claim is that the decedent didn't mean to cut them out. State law may take care of that claim, providing in many cases that such "pretermitted" heirs take a share equal to that they would have received if no Will had been written.

## Children of Prior Marriages

Say your mother remarried and, when she died, she left everything to her new husband. This is common. However, when he dies, he leaves everything to his kids and nothing to you. See a lawyer, but don't get your hopes too high. Some couples upon remarriage agree to leave everything to the survivor with a promise that, when the survivor dies, the estate will be split between their respective children. Tempted by dark forces, the surviving spouse may renege and leave everything to his or her own children. We saw in Chapter 28 that a Living Trust can address this problem.

There is not, however, any presumption that you are entitled to receive property that once belonged to your parent after the death of your step-parent. In order to make this claim, you will need to show some agreement, and usually it will need to be more than just your parent's Will listing you as an heir if the step-parent is deceased.

## Heirs Who Suspect Lack of Capacity

"Being of sound mind" is the stock opening. (We prefer "It is the best of times, planning for the worst of times.") Despite what the stock opening says, if the testator lost legal capacity before signing the Will (or trust), it is invalid and the estate passes under the intestacy law of your state. That may not help you very much—if your rich uncle Thurston's Will is invalid, you probably won't get anything anyway. Those worthless loser cousins of yours (Thurston's kids) or, worse yet, Lovey, his new wife, will inherit Thurston's millions.

## Heirs Who Suspect Undue Influence

Large gifts to nurses, neighbors, and TV evangelists are suspect. Was the person in a position to assert control over the testator by threats or by withholding care?

## Heirs Who Suspect Murder

A murderer cannot inherit from the victim, even if named in the Will ("Someday, son, all of this will be yours."). There is a legal maxim—"You cannot profit from your own wrong." Given the nature of the world, however, this maxim is more inspirational than descriptive.

However, if Sis can prove Bro did in dear old Dad, he can't get a nickel. There's more for Sis. There is always someone willing to profit from wrong.

If you suspect both undue influence and murder, you've got yourself a novel. Throw in a few good trial scenes and a little sex, and you won't need to inherit.

No matter your complaint, if you are a disgruntled heir, seek legal advice early. Once the probate process begins, you will be facing very tight time lines—typically a matter of weeks, not months and certainly not years. And despite all the ways we have described here to challenge the validity of a Will or trust, you should know that Will contests are actually quite rare—and successful Will contests far rarer.

# c. Family Allowances

Most states have legislation which allows surviving spouses and minor or disabled children to draw living expenses from an estate while it is being probated. These laws also set aside for the surviving spouse certain property (usually the family house and its furnishings). These set-asides come off the top of the estate; that is, they must be satisfied before there are other distributions, even distributions pursuant to a valid Will.

# d. The Probate Process

The steps are typically something like this:

- Establishing the existence of a valid Will. (If the Will isn't valid, or there is no Will, the estate passes according to intestacy laws. Chapter 25).
- Appointing the executor/administrator/personal representative.
- Gathering and protecting assets.
- Settling with creditors and paying taxes (income and estate).
- Wrapping up: distribution and accounting.

Let's go through each step.

*Establishing the Will.* Any interested party, usually the spouse or an adult child, can petition the Probate Court to take jurisdiction over a decedent's estate. In smaller estates, a relative can do this simply by going to the courthouse and filling out the correct papers. In larger estates, a lawyer should be retained. In any event, this should be done quickly, as someone must be authorized to take possession of the individual's assets.

At the first hearing, there will be two orders of business: first establishing whether the decedent had a valid Will, and second, appointing a personal representative to take charge. In some states and circumstances, "hearing" may be a misnomer, since the entire thing may be done at the walk-up counter of the probate court without any fanfare or preliminaries.

To be valid, a Will must comport with the technicalities laid down by state legislatures in terms of witnesses and notaries (Holographic Wills, those written out by hand, need not meet these requirements in states recognizing them. See Chapter 25). Even if a Will is found, there may be codicils (documents that modify the original Will) and new Wills (which have the effect of voiding all or part of prior Wills). Both codicils and new Wills must comport with the technical requirements of a Will.

*Naming a Personal Representative.* The personal representative (in some states and in Bleak House called the executor or administrator) is the person or institution that takes charge of the estate and moves it though probate.

Usually the decedent has named a personal representative (and a backup) in his Will. If not, the court will appoint the personal representative. Usually it will be the person who filed the probate petition. Other relatives can, and should, intervene at this stage if they object to that person. State laws establish priorities as to who is appointed.

Usually the personal representative will have to post a bond so that, if he or she splits with the goodies, the heirs will be protected. Bonds cost money and that money will come from the estate. Traditionally people waive the bond if they nominate a family member or close friend.

*Finding and Protecting Assets.* The personal representative must search the decedent's papers, read the decedent's mail, and generally snoop around to find out what the decedent owned and owed. The personal representative will have access to safety deposit boxes and has the legal right to get information from stock brokers, bankers, and lawyers concerning the decedent's affairs. It is here you will learn that mild Aunt Mildred was, in fact, a CIA agent credited with, among other things, the fall of the Berlin Wall.

The personal representative must maintain the assets. This may involve such things as winding down the decedent's business and selling perishable assets. An inventory of assets must be prepared and filed with the court. Where appropriate, insure the assets; otherwise you might be liable for losses.

*Notifying and Paying Creditors.* The decedent's bills must be paid but not just yet. First discover the creditors, find out how much is owed and categorize the claimants. The personal representative notifies the known creditors and advises them to submit their claims. Usually ads must be placed in local newspapers advising unknown creditors to file their claims. If creditors do not present their claims on time, their debts are barred. However, if the personal representative knows about some and fails to list them, those creditors will not be barred.

The personal rep should not pay any bills until satisfied that they are legal. If the decedent had a good defense against a debt, the personal rep should decline to pay it, forcing the creditor to file some sort of lawsuit (it may be in Probate Court, or in some states it may not have to be). Further, if there is any question about the estate's solvency, the personal rep should not pay any bills before they all come in. Why?

Because, like Orwell's Pigs, some debts are more equal than others. Who gets to go to the trough first? State statutes list priorities, usually along these lines:

1. Expenses of administering estate (lawyers wrote the rules, and the rules say they get paid first)
2. Funeral and burial expenses (a reasonable amount)
3. The expenses of last sickness (reasonable and necessary)
4. Family allowances
5. Debts and taxes given preference by federal and state laws
6. Judgments rendered against the decedent in his lifetime in order of date
7. All other claims

If a personal representative pays lower priority pigs, leaving higher ones unfed, the personal representative may have to personally make up the difference.

*Paying taxes.* The personal rep will prepare and file the last state and federal income tax returns of the decedent as well as paying any federal and state estate taxes owed on earnings of the estate.

*Wrapping Up.* Locating assets and paying the bills should take at least four months (creditors are usually given at least this amount of time to make their claims). Probate often runs much longer, but finally there comes a day to distribute the goodies.

After distribution, the personal representative may have to file a Final Accounting with the Court, and must give an accounting to the heirs. Again, the disgruntled can object.

How to distribute the property? If there is no Will, this will be done according to the intestacy laws (but you know that already). If there is a Will, well, then, you need to know just a little more. There are three kinds of bequests:

*Specific bequests* (objects): To my only daughter, my 1956 Studebaker Golden Hawk.

*General bequests* (money): To my only son, $75,000.

*Residuary bequest* (remainder): To my then living grandchildren, divided equally, the remainder of my estate.

Well and good. But what happens if there is not enough in the estate to make good on all the bequests? Say the Studebaker was sold prior to Dad's death, or that Dad gave it to the Studebaker Hawks Club? Does the daughter get nothing? What if there is a Studebaker but no $75,000? Does the son get nothing?

This gets complicated and you'll need legal advice. Even if you end up getting nothing, worse things can happen. Read *Bleak House*.

# PART 7

# HELP!

# CHAPTER 39

# THOUGHTS ON DOCS (AND LAWYERS)

*A cartoon shows two judges putting on their robes. "Around the house, I'm a total idiot but, put this on, I'm it!"*

What kind of person do you want to help you? While competence is a must (and something not necessarily assured by the diploma on the wall), there are other things to consider.

Lawyers, doctors and other professions are impressive people. They are smart, well-educated, and have killer vocabularies. (When they stop talking "professional jargon," they talk "graduate school.") Often we are too intimidated to force them to focus on our concerns and to answer our questions. Don't be. Remember this. Their job is to serve *you*, to help you through difficult times. You are the boss of them!

If that's a tad hard to swallow simply remember this. While in the office they may be "it," around the house or trying to do the things you do so well, they are probably total idiots!

There is an old saying:

*"A wise man has an old lawyer and a young doctor."*

The idea seems to be that while the law doesn't change much (thankfully for those of us who write about it), there are always new medicines and new procedures; the young doctor will be (forgive me) cutting edge.

Of course all of this is foolish. Doctors, like lawyers, are required to keep current with developments in their fields through continuing education courses. In addition there are specialized journals and conferences.

In addition to knowledge, experience counts. The doctor who has done twenty procedures will no doubt do them better than a novice. Doctors are trained to treat given diseases a given way, called allogisms. Mostly this works just fine but occasionally a detour may be called for and it is the experienced physician who will have the wisdom to take it.

Several years ago researchers asked, "What makes for the best doctors?"Was it where they went to medical school? Was it a matter of grades, the "best" medical students becoming the best doctors?

First, who were the best? Surveying community doctors in the community, they came up with a list; then they went to work: what do the best doctors have in common? Not their medical school; not their academic performance —these correlations were extremely weak. It develops the "best" docs are those who read the most medical journals, those who were most interested in their calling.

Comparable studies of lawyers would probably have similar results. There are great lawyers, OK lawyers, and lousy lawyers. Fellow lawyers know who are the best and, when talking about them, no one mentions where they went to school or their class standing. What they talk about is their devotion to their profession.

Malcolm Gladwell, the author of *The Tipping Point* and *blink,* put it this way. Talent is not smarts or even education, it is the love of what one does, it is *"the desire to practice."*

You don't find competence on the diploma on the wall. No doubt some of the "best" docs and lawyers in your community went to schools you never heard of. You are not looking for prior accomplishments but for someone who is intellectually excited by their profession. Admittedly this will be a hard thing to evaluate but you may get a good impression by the person's enthusiasm and interest in your situation. While it may be awkward to ask your doc, "How many medical journals do you read?" you may work in, "Is there any new thinking about this condition—or treatment?"

What do you want from your doctor? There is the metaphor of *"care versus cure."* In the early days, docs could *cure* little so they stressed *care,* being bedside, explaining what was happening, answering questions and occasionally holding hands. Remember *home visits with the little black bags?* Now that medicine can cure a great deal more, less attention is given to bedside: the ten minute office visit following an hour or so reading battered magazines in a crowded waiting room.

Cure, however, is often expensive, painful, problematic, not to mention with long-lasting side effects. Maybe, at our age, we have a condition that, while we aren't happy with it, we can live with it. We're looking for some information and encouragement: Will the condition get worse? Given it, how can we improve our lives? In short, cure may be too painful, too problematic and too expensive; what we want is the old-fashioned virtue of *care.*

What we want is someone listens to our concerns and helps us sort though the tangle of data, emotion, and fear raised by serious illness. It takes more than ten minutes. We don't want someone hell-bent on forcing the routine cure, be it an operation or, in the case of law, perhaps a Living Trust replete with Latin phrases. In Nursing School there is a marvelous saying: "We treat people, not diseases."

Finally, ageism. It's endemic. Some doctors and lawyers are uncomfortable around older folks, often dismissing our concerns as simple signs of aging. You can get a sense of whether they are dealing with you or with some stereotype they have of aging.

If you are uncomfortable with your doctor or lawyer, get a new one. *You can always change your doctor or lawyer.* (Sometimes you may have paid your lawyer in advance; you still have a right to discharge that attorney and receive back what you have paid less the amount the lawyer has earned before discharge.)

# CHAPTER 40

# OFFICE VISITS AND QUESTIONS TO HELP YOUR DOCTOR

Your lawyer and your doctor are there to serve *you*; you are not their to fill up their afternoon nor their pocketbook. Don't be aggressive, but be more than "Next!" Be candid, insist on understanding the jargon, and prepare. Should you take Aunt Jane with you? Are there questions you can ask that will help your doctor get it right?

## a. Being Candid, Even if it Makes You Look Foolish

*Getting on a plane, we want to ask what to do if it crashes. We don't. We would rather be dead than look foolish.*

—Shelley Berman

The same thing can happen in your lawyer's or doctor's office. You might not fess up that you take scores and scores of over-the-counter medications or fear you have a sexually transmitted disease. (The Arizona retirement community, "Sun City," is known by residents as "Sin City".) You might overlook symptoms, such as weight loss (which is always serious), believing that it is simply part of growing old.

Why lie to your lawyer? To look good. But no matter how good your position is, no matter how much in the right you are, there will be weaknesses; your lawyer must know both the good and the bad. "If my client committed treason, I would like to know about it *before* the trial." In the case of abuse, both victims and abusers should seek help. A lawyer can be a good place to start. Under the *attorney/client privilege* every thing you *tell* your lawyer, and everything the attorney *learns* investigating your case, is confidential and *cannot* be disclosed without your permission: not to opposing lawyers, not to judges, and not to police.

There are two exceptions. First, what you tell your attorney in front of other people, say the attorney's staff, is *not* protected, thus it is best if no one else is in the room. Second, if you tell your attorney you *will* commit a crime or a fraud, the attorney can and probably will disclose that to proper officials. To be concrete: if you tell your lawyer "I need help because I have been abusing my parents," that is protected. However if you add "And I'm going home to beat them again" your lawyer will likely pick up the phone.

# b. Understanding Jargon

*"Now, what I want you to do, right away, and this is important, is to qubt twri pzcv jmottm plbtk!*

Far too many of us meekly smile, say thanks, and leave. We're not going to make trouble, appear stupid and confirm that we are "losing it." Studies have confirmed that many patients and clients leave without understanding the advice or, even worse, getting it wrong. (Studies have also confirmed that the sun sets in the West.)

Our advice: *You should repeat the advice!*

*Repeat the advice!*

Repeating the advice does three things. It assures that you got it right, it will help you remember it, and, it will often fill in gaps in the advice: "Should I take those two pills together?"

# c. Being Heard

*A criminal defendant is complaining to the judge. "I want a new lawyer. This one never pays any attention to me."*

*"What about that?" the judge asks the lawyer.*

*"Sorry, Your Honor. I wasn't paying attention."*

Professionals aren't good listeners. They think that their role is to ask questions while our role is to answer them. They are the experts, after all. One study indicated that doctors interrupt their patients in the first 18 seconds of the visit.

It may be awkward but a "hold your horses" moment might be necessary. Professionals, like the rest of us, jump to conclusions and, unless they are forced to hear more, may be off solving a problem you don't have but one they think you do. What you have to say is critical. One doctor sums it up this way:

"If you listen to your patient, he is telling you the diagnosis." So talk, get your story out, even if you must interrupt.

# d. Taking Aunt Jane

With doctors this is complicated. Most do not like having others in the room, unless the patient has a difficult time communicating. This makes good sense *during* the examination but, when it comes to the discussion of diagnosis and treatment, it may be quite helpful to have Aunt Jane. As a lot of information is headed your way you'll need help and, if necessary, an advocate, pushing the doc for further information or perhaps more pain medications.

If things are complicated, consider hiring a "Patient's Advocate." Usually a nurse or a person who has health care experience, these folks can provide many services, from accompanying one to the office visit, to recommending physicians and hospitals, to researching specific illnesses. These services, not covered by insurance or Medicare, can be pricey, in the range of $100 per hour. However, the services may be priceless. Ask around.

As to lawyers, someone in the room *breaks* the attorney client privilege but that is seldom an issue, except on TV. An issue arises, however, when an adult child brings an aged parent to write a Will or transfer property. To make sure that the child is not overreaching, the lawyer will insist of interviewing the parent alone. (Don't be offended—it is simply required.)

# e. Preparing

For the doctor, a list of medications and, if you have more than one or two concerns, a list of them. Alas, as we age, both lists will grow. If you have several concerns, *prioritize!* On the doctor's form there is a space of "CC"—Chief Compliant. As for your questions, write them out and take the list with you.

How about doing your own research on the internet? Responsible sites, such as *webmd* or those devoted to specific illnesses, can be quite helpful. They can help you sharpen your questions and make the most of your doctor's advice.

*However,* beware television ads suggesting ills you did not know you had and hoping that you go to your doctor shouting bloody murder unless you get what they are advertising. (We're all susceptible to suggestions—medical students are often convinced they have *every* disease they study.) The drugs they push may not be right for you and, almost for sure, more expensive than those that are just as effective. Leave diagnosis to your doctor rather, not to good-looking models who, while they are not actual patients, play them on TV. Just an idea.

As for your lawyer, preparation might well include skimming the table of contents of this book. It is truly amazing all the things a good lawyer can do for you. If you are thinking of setting up an estate plan it will save you time (and hence money) if you read our chapters on those topics—you will hit the road running. One final point: you don't need "all your papers" before you write a Will or create a Trust—so that is no longer a good excuse.

# f. Asking Questions That Help Your Doctor

It's flu season. You wake up with the classic signs: fever, cough, aches and pains. What do you conclude?

Flu.

You're not alone. Probably your doctor would too. "A lot of that going around." Both of you might be *wrong*.

In a terrific book, *How Doctors Think*, Dr. Groopman warns that doctors often misdiagnose, perhaps 1 out of 10 times. Like the rest of us, they jump to conclusions. To make sure they haven't, Dr. Groopman recommends we ask three questions:

1. *What else could it be?*
   ("Well now that you mention it, it could be....")
2. *Is there anything in the exam or tests that doesn't fit?*
   ("Well, now that you mention it, your fever isn't typical.")
3. *Is it possible I have more than one problem?*
   ("Well, now that you mention it, sometimes folks get the flu because they are already sick with....")

A good friend, Dr. Jack Boyer, suggests a fourth question:

4. *Have you considered whether I want to get the treatment or not?*

Finally there will come a time for the agonizing question.

5. *Would it surprise you if this patient (my mother, me) died within the next twelve months?*

If the answer is no, time to do some serious thinking about hospice and end-of-life. Don't expect your doctors to volunteer dismal information. In *A Death Foretold*, Dr. Christakis tells us that doctors shy away from terminal prognosis. Why? There are many reasons. For one, it tends to undercut their sense of professional competence, their belief that they can cure most anything. Further many doctors are as uncomfortable with the idea of death as are the rest of us. And they fear making self-fulfilling prophecies.

The result of patient and physician denial? According to Dr. Christakis:

> *"The great majority of Americans die in institutions rather than at home as many would prefer; most die in pain while in the care of health providers; many die alone; and many have deaths that are financially devastating for their families."*

If your physician isn't talking about death, don't assume all is rosy. You may need to force the issue and ask tough questions. While nothing is certain doctors can give time frames. In fact, to be eligible for essentially free hospice care, a doctor must certify that death can be expected within six months.

# CHAPTER 41

# FINDING AND DEALING
# WITH LAWYERS

*A noted cancer researcher once remarked that, if you know the basic
principles, the details can take care of themselves.*

If you've been paying attention reading this book, you know the basic principles. As for the details, you'll need a lawyer.

They're less expensive and more helpful than they look. A basic Will Pack-
age (including a simple Will, a Living Will, and a Durable Power of Attorney)
prepared by a lawyer to reflect your individual needs should cost around $500.

Bad idea to use self-help books and store-bought forms. A lawyer-drafted-
document will conform to recent changes in the law and will reflect your individual wishes. Not only do you get a better document; you get peace of mind
and someone to call if you have questions.

## a. How to Find the Right Lawyer

Asking friends and neighbors is a good place to start. Maybe the folks at your
Area Council of Aging have some recommendations. Most local Bar Associations have Referral Programs. Call in and you will be referred to a lawyer who
specializes in the area of your concern. There is a set fee for the initial interview,
usually under $50. Afterwards you can hire the lawyer or continue your search.

Another good place to start your search is by contacting the National Academy of Elder Law Attorneys (www.naela.org). These lawyers specialize in elder
law matters.

Picking the right lawyer is important. In all likelihood, it will be a long-
term relationship. It is probably a good idea to *interview at least two*. We see
by contrasts. Interviewing a second lawyer will tell you a lot about what you
liked and didn't like about the first. While there are objective ways to evaluate lawyers (experience, fees) probably the most important things are subjec-

tive and intangible. Will you be able to openly discuss difficult and personal matters with this lawyer? Will you like working with this person?

# b. Some Ways to Save Money

It is important to have a clear understanding as to what services your lawyer is to perform for you and at what cost. This should be reflected in a *written retainer agreement*. In writing. As to cost, will there be a flat fee or a billable hour rate? The retainer should include:

1. Fees and billing periods.
2. Scope of representation (what the lawyer will do and will *not do*).

The last point is important. Have a clear understanding as to tasks the lawyer is not agreeing to do. Many disputes arise in this area, (Lawyers neglecting to return phone calls is the most frequent source of conflict.)

In defense of my brethren, a fee of $200 an hour is, well, shocking. But that's not take-home. It is costly to run a law office: support staff (receptionists, secretaries, paralegals), rent, supplies, equipment (computers, libraries, continuing education), phones, malpractice insurance, and a whole lot more. All told, overhead can come to 75% to 80%, which takes a big bite out of the $200.

To make your visits more productive, and probably less expensive, read the chapters in this book concerning your problem, be it as a grandparent, as someone suspecting elder abuse, or as someone wishing to provide for a mentally disabled relative.

Many law firms use *paralegals* who are trained in various legal areas. Don't discourage their use—they are cheaper than lawyers and their work is supervised and reviewed by lawyers.

Finally, when it comes to saving money, don't be a pest. While you have a right to be kept up to date with the progress of your matter, frequent calls add to the bill and can be quite irritating.

# c. If Things Go Badly

In most states you have an absolute right to fire your lawyer, at *any* time, for *any* reason. If you do, you must pay for work they have already put in, but they must *return* any unearned portion of your retainer. They must give you or your new lawyer all of your papers.

However, before dropping the Big One, talk to the lawyer. As the chain-gang guard said in *Cool Hand Luke,* "What we have here is a failure to communicate." The lawyer or the lawyer's staff may not be aware of your unhappiness.

*Complain to the Bar Association.* Lawyers are licensed by their states to practice law, and every state has some sort of disciplinary procedure regarding lawyers. If you think that something the lawyer has done is unethical or illegal, you should notify the bar association in your state and give them full details. Complaints include your lawyer ignoring your case, giving you incorrect information, taking actions without your consent, missing a deadline, failing to disclose a possible or actual conflict of interest involving your case and, of course, running off with your money.

Note: Many state bar associations have funds to compensate victims of lawyer fraud.

If you have a *fee dispute* with your lawyer, most Bar Associations have arbitration procedures.

*Consider a Lawsuit.* If you have been damaged financially or your position compromised because of the lawyer's action or failure to act, you may have a malpractice claim against the lawyer. This will require another lawyer's examinations of all of the facts, but it may be well worth your while to consider such action.

Most legal malpractice claims involve lawyers who have drafted documents that failed their purpose, such as Wills that were later thrown out, or have failed to file a claim within the State of Limitations.

When all is said and done what you really want from your lawyer is commitment and interest. You do not want to be seen as "just another estate client" or "just another divorce problem." I close with two of my favorite quotes, ones I impress upon law students. The first I have used somewhere else in this book (who knows?) and it is a motto of nurses:

*Remember, we are treating a patient, not a disease.*

The other comes from the British novelist C.K. Chesterton.

*The horrible thing about all legal officials, even the best, about all judges, magistrates, barristers, detectives, policemen, is not that they are wicked (some of them are good), not that they are stupid (several of them are quite intelligent), it is simply that they have got used to it.*

# CHAPTER 42

# Help Your Family: Talk!

*When I was an undergraduate, the Anthro 101 prof told of an interesting tribe—one of the few things I remember of Anthro 101 or, for that matter, of my undergraduate days. The tribe made important decisions differently than you and I. First, they would meet formally and, after a careful review of pros and cons, decide. Nothing surprising there. The next night, they would garner festive clothes and break out brew and music. In the wee hours, they would revisit their decision. If it still made sense, fine. But if it couldn't survive the bright and flashing insights of drunken analysis, they scrapped it and, the following morning, began anew.*

Time to talk to your family about possible disability and death.

"What? I'm still young! At least not old! Talk to my family about my death? I'd rather have a root canal."

Our tribe equates *significant* and *meaningful* with *sober and somber*. No wonder we don't relish the prospect. But it doesn't have to be that way. Once the conversation begins, it can be joyous. At some point your family will begin to worry about you, about your health, about your possible death, and what will become of them. Talking will be a relief, not a root canal.

Starting is troublesome. "Tonight, after dinner, let's go into the living room to talk about my death." A tad much. A better line, "I want to tell you about my living will. Unless you understand my wishes, you will face impossible decisions." Or you might want to sneak up on things, starting with your retirement plans, moving to who gets the grandfather clock, and then to possible disability and where you want to live.

No matter your approach, at first, the conversation may be awkward. And there's good TV tonight and probably next week would be better anyway. Why now?

# a. Why?

## You owe it to your family.

It will be a gift as important as anything you leave them in your Will. Death and disability will cause great emotional strain. Difficult decisions, in unfamiliar areas, are coming. Without knowing your wishes, your family will struggle and, often, disagree. Family feuds in these times can split families forever. Lawyers specializing in this area will tell you that the family fights are less about money than about who gets the Grandfather clock and whether Sis spent too much money caring for Dad.

## You owe it to yourself.

You can fill out as many documents as you want but, when it comes to your last illness, doctors will likely do what your loved ones say. The likely choice: continue aggressive yet futile life-sustaining treatment, increasing your suffering and decreasing your estate. That is, unless you have talked with them and made your wishes known.

## You owe it to your family and to yourself.

Once you get beyond the initial discomfort, the conversation can be fun. It can lead to fond remembrances:

> *"Do you remember the trip to the farm? When Dad fell off the horse?"*
> *"What about prom night when I lost the keys?"*

And it may give folks space to say those embarrassing things that they want to say but never get around to saying.

> *"I never told Mom I loved her."*
> *"I always regret not telling Dad how much he meant to me."*

Wise folks have told us, *"The denial of death is the denial of life."* We can understand this intellectually but emotionally, well, that's another matter. We all need to push ourselves; sometimes root canals are necessary. By staying in denial, by not talking about death, families remain isolated, not saying the things that need to be said, not celebrating the events that need to be celebrated.

"Okay. I'll talk to my family. You got a checklist?"

# b. Some Things to Talk About

## Final illness

Hopefully you have written your *Living Will* as urged way back in Chapter 2. It's not too late. In any event, the model there covers some topics you should share with your loved ones:

- Kinds of treatment you want and don't want.
- Funeral arrangements. If you don't cover this, dollars to donuts, your family will spend too much on them.

## Possible disability

Who is to say "Mom, it's time to stop driving?" "Dad, I don't think you should go on living alone?"

If someone becomes senile or too ill to act, who should manage the financial affairs? Who should make health care and living decisions? Durable Powers of Attorney can address these questions. (Chapter 24). If you have executed them, why did you pick who you did as agent? Do you have special instructions for them?

## Living arrangements

What of nursing homes? Should top dollar be spent for care or should money be saved for the grandchildren or for charities?

Where do you want to stay and who will care for you? If Sis is to care for you, make sure that her siblings understand that it is a difficult and costly job. Brothers returning from Gotham may think she was wasteful.

## Property distribution

Well, who *does* get the clock? The fancy china? Lists are more reliable than memories.

Is there anything in your Will or Trust that needs explaining?

*How come Sis is getting the house? How come Brother is getting more cash? Why is Cousin Mary appointed Executor? Why is Uncle Bob defamed?*

This is especially important with *blended families* (remarriage with children from previous marriages). Suspicion between stepchildren is likely. Sit everyone down and explain who is to get what and why. Best to have everyone there at the same time to avoid "Well, that's not what they told me!"

Many folks open joint bank accounts with children or grandchildren, either as a method of passing on the money at their death or allowing it to be used for them if they become incapacitated. To avoid misunderstandings, other family members should know of these arrangements.

## Retirement plans

This might be a good time to share your thoughts and get suggestions. "Dad, you can never be a clown!"

Should you discuss your finances? If you are well off, this will mean your family can stop worrying. However, if you are too well off, as Dickens showed us in *Bleak House*, lives can be wasted in anticipation of the large inheritance.

## Where's your stuff?

Does a lawyer have your Will on file? Where do you keep your financial records?

Of course you can't cover all of these topics and that doesn't matter. What matters is that you begin the talk. It can be in spurts, in living rooms or on trips to the store. But won't it be nice if you and your loved ones feel comfortable talking about the elephant in the room?

* * *

So ends our book. Our conversation. How to end it? What to say? Perhaps a nod to happy Saturday afternoons, sitting with friends, watching cartoons:

*And That's All, Folks!*

But, writing a book, one has a generalized notion of one's readers and, after several chapters, one begins to feel great affection for them. Indeed, we have been through a lot together, some boring, some fascinating, some good, some sad. We all deserve something more than a fond remembrance of Bugs Bunny. We need someone to remind us of our common humanity and of our common gumption; we need a poet.

Dylan Thomas, in *Fern Hill*, laments lost childhood.

> *Time held me green and dying,*
> *Though I sang in my chains like the sea.*

No matter what the future brings, no matter how confining the chains, let's keep singing, you and I.

# ACKNOWLEDGMENTS

Every acknowledgment prominently lists the support of family, without which no significant project can be accomplished. Clichés are often also truisms. In addition to family, our colleagues, partners, students and co-workers all have contributed to this work in large and small ways.

We would particularly like to thank, for their contributions to this volume, Barbara Sattler, Maureen Garmon, Kinsey Humphrey, Sherina and Michael Cadnum, Judith Parker, Carol Ward, and Drs. Jack Boyer, Marvin Slepian, and Robert Shannon. We are thankful to Steve O'Keefe of Patron Saint Productions, whose candid advice greatly improved the book (we hope). Thanks also to Keith Sipe, Linda Lacy, Kelly Miller, and Martha Hopper of Carolina Academic Press for their help along the way.

Some of the material is this book was presented in *Alive and Kicking: Legal Advice for Boomers.* Prior to that, Professor Hegland wrote *Fifty and Beyond: The Law You and Your Parents Need to Know* with Allan Bogutz. He thanks Allan for all of his insights.

The very idea of aging vibrantly was planted at an early age by grandparents, and later expanded by parents and in-laws; thousands of students, clients and friends continue to demonstrate the concept on a daily basis. We owe all of them—family, friends, colleagues, students, clients,—a tremendous debt. We hope we can repay them by passing on their wisdom and insights to you.

# ABOUT THE AUTHORS

Professor Kenney Hegland has spent his career teaching law students how to use the law to solve problems. In addition to teaching at the University of Arizona, he has taught at UCLA, Harvard, and at the University of San Diego's London Program. He graduated from Stanford, attended law school at UC Berkeley, and has an advanced law degree from Harvard. Early in his career he worked with the legendary Civil Rights lawyer, C.B. King (in Albany, Georgia) and with Cesar Chavez and the United Farm Workers Union (in Delano, California). Two of his books, *Introduction to the Study and Practice of Law* and *Trial and Clinical Skills*, are widely used in the nation's law schools. Committed to helping the public understand the law, he has written and produced eight videos about law for high school students. These films are currently distributed by the Discovery Channel.

Attorney Robert Fleming has spent decades practicing elder law in Tucson, Arizona and has become one of the nation's leaders in that field. His particular emphasis is on planning for individuals with disabilities and other special needs. His professional background includes serving as the Public Fiduciary in Tucson and as Tucson City Magistrate. In addition to maintaining an active law practice, he writes and lectures extensively on elder law issues. His book, *The Elder Law Answer Book*, is one of the principal treatises on elder law used by lawyers. He maintains his law firm's website (www.elder-law.com) as a ten-year labor of love. In his spare time he is a martial artist, pilot, and scuba diver.

# INDEX